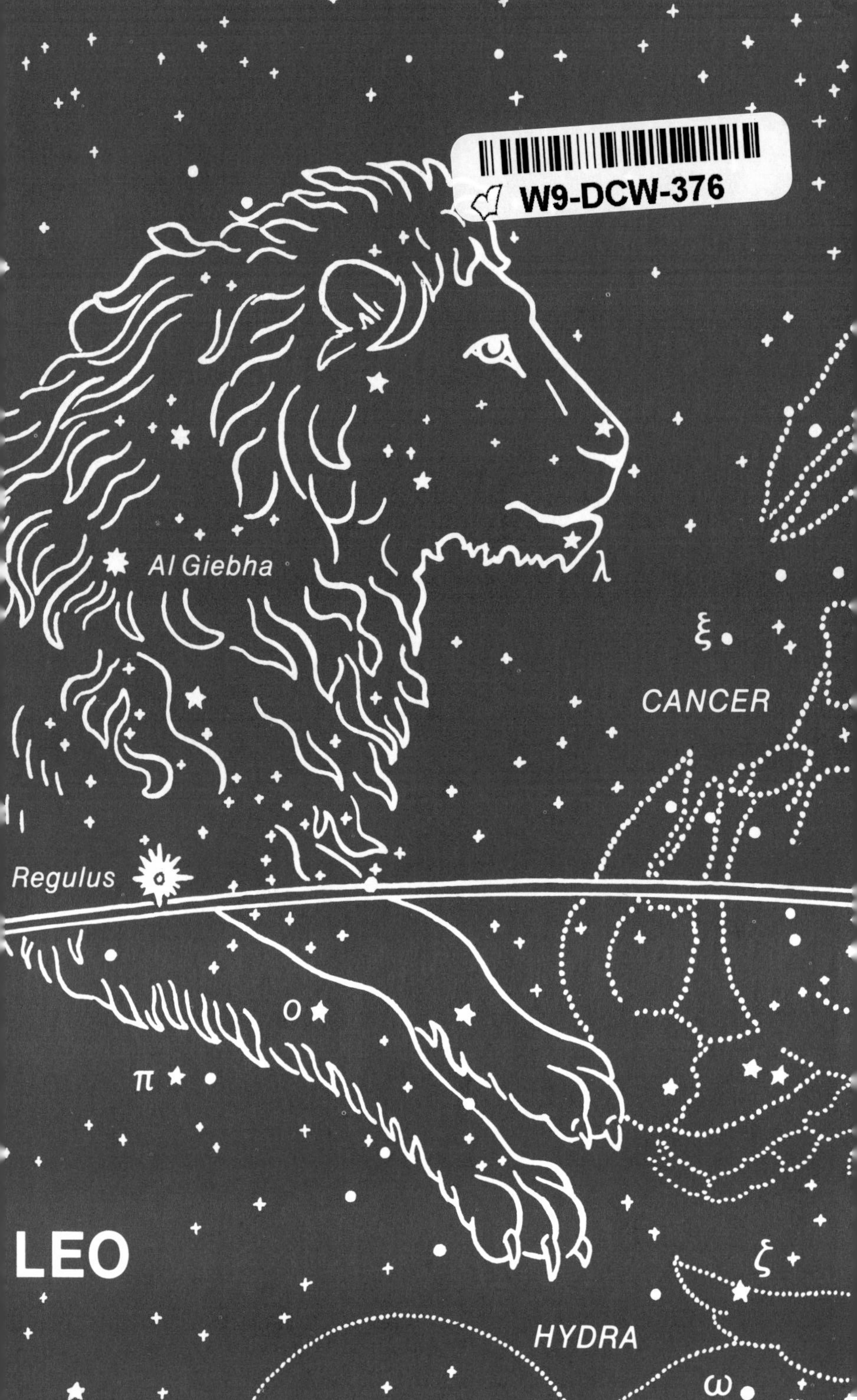

W9-DCW-376
Al Giebha
λ
ξ
CANCER
Regulus
o
π
LEO
ζ
HYDRA
ω

JESUS CHRIST
OUR PROMISED SEED

Other books by Victor Paul Wierwille

Receiving the Holy Spirit Today
Are the Dead Alive Now?
Power for Abundant Living
The Bible Tells Me So
The New, Dynamic Church
The Word's Way
God's Magnified Word
Jesus Christ Is Not God
Jesus Christ Our Passover

JESUS CHRIST OUR PROMISED SEED

VICTOR PAUL WIERWILLE

American Christian Press
The Way International
New Knoxville, Ohio 45871

The scripture used throughout this book is quoted from the King James Version unless otherwise noted. All explanatory insertions by the author within a scripture verse are enclosed in brackets. All Greek, Hebrew, and Aramaic words are italicized and transliterated into English.

International Standard Book Number 0-910068-42-9
Library of Congress Catalog Card Number 82-72672
American Christian Press
The Way International
New Knoxville, Ohio 45871

Printed in the United States of America

To my beloved grandchildren
with thanksgiving and prayer for your lives.
May each of you do your utmost for His highest.

CONTENTS

ILLUSTRATIONS

CONSTELLATION PLATES

PREFACE

One of the most celebrated of holidays around the world is Christmas. Its popularity is growing even in traditionally non-Christian countries. Merchants capitalize on its lucrative tradition of gift giving. In my own family we have always given gifts at Christmastime and gathered the family around the Christmas tree. Warm memories of love and giving arise when I think of our traditional family Christmas celebrations.

Yet tradition rather than truth is the basis for celebrating the birth of Christ on December 25. Tradition has brought us a stationary, dazzling star over Bethlehem being pursued by three wise men on the night Christ was born in a manger surrounded by shepherds and animals. Tradition has brought us Santa Claus sliding down the chimney to deliver gifts to all good girls and boys. Christmas is and always has been an incongruous blend of tradition, imagination, and a little truth.

Like everyone else, I was taught as a youngster that there were three wise men who came to see Jesus at his birth, yet nowhere in the Bible can you find the number three designated. I was taught that the sheep were grazing in the fields on the night of December 24. Yet all the books I have read on Eastern customs, plus visits to the Bethlehem area, have verified that sheep are not put out in the pastures past October because it is simply too cold. I also wondered why King Herod would have all male children two years old and under killed if Jesus Christ were just a newborn babe.

As I was growing up in the church, no one ever taught me that there could be some direct relationship between the astronomical signs in the sky and the birth of God's only begotten Son. Yet God put the stars in their courses and set them for signs and seasons (Genesis 1:14). Surely it is not inconceivable that the Lord God Almighty, the Creator of the heavens and earth, would in His infinite knowledge, wisdom, and ability coordinate the movements of the stars and planets so that they with celestial grandeur could announce the birth of His only begotten Son, the Messiah.

So how did the birthday of our savior become associated with December 25? When was the savior really born? By carefully tracking the details in the Word of God, in history, and in the field of astronomy, we can certify the time of his birth to within an hour and a half: the year, the date, and the hour. December 25, 1 A.D. is far off the mark.

In order to discover the truths regarding this subject, we must be willing to lay aside tradition, and honestly approach the subject with rational objectivity, as any honest scientist approaches an experiment. We must allow the Scriptures, the Word of God, to speak for themselves. We must also know and understand figures of speech, Eastern customs, and the study of ancient Biblical manuscripts. Sometimes it is interesting to note that our minds have interpreted God's Word from presumptions that we ourselves are not even aware we are making. When we question these presumptions, we immediately see that our mental pictures do not accurately reflect what is stated in the written Word. We must permit the Scriptures to interpret themselves and block out private assumptions and interpretations from our research study.

In Biblical research we study the Scriptures with the understanding and believing that they are God-inspired and, therefore, perfect and without contradiction when the original revelation is accurately known. Biblical research recognizes that no record in one Biblical account may contradict a passage in another record on an identical subject. As products of God's inspiration, all records will complement or supplement, and enhance each other as they enable us to see an overall view of the birth of our Lord Jesus Christ.

Secular sources of information from the fields of science, history, and ancient literature should also be utilized as tools of study when they shed light on the testimony of Scripture. However, such information or sources dare never be permitted to have more credibility than the Word of God itself. At best, secular sources will simply corroborate and give illuminating detail to truths already revealed in Scripture. All these above-mentioned methods have been employed in this work.

* * *

The coming of the Christ was by no means an unanticipated event. Indeed, the story of the coming redeemer was written in the stars when the heavens were originally put in order by God. The first part of this study examines the Biblical information regarding "his star" which was seen by the wise men. The Biblical record is enhanced and substantiated by astronomical and historical records which further underscore the magnitude of God's power and love in planning for our redemption. Once "his star" has been identified, the documentation of the very day and the time of day when the Christ was born can be pinpointed.

Whereas the first section of the book is scientific in nature, it is written with the non-scientist in mind. All of us can appreciate the greatness of God's revealed Word as He placed it with such precision in the stars.

Since all preceding history was leading up to and preparing the way for the coming of the Messiah, it is appropriate that the second part of our study should begin with the Old Testament prophecies of the promised Messiah and with the reasons why this Messiah's coming was so significant to the men of antiquity. After this, we will study the record of Jesus Christ's genealogy, his relationship to the House of David, and his divine conception.

In order to understand the context of the times in which the Messiah was born, we will examine records concerning his spiritually powerful predecessor, John the Baptist. John was a prophet sent by God over four hundred years after the Prophet Malachi. John called Israel back to God's Word and thereby prepared the way for God to reveal the ministry of Jesus Christ. With a knowledge of John and his divine mission, we can move in chronological order through the events leading to the birth of man's long-awaited promised seed. We will observe many wonderful truths concerning the parents of both John and Jesus. The ardent commitment of Zacharias and Elisabeth, and Joseph and Mary were vital in making possible both the lives and ministries of John the Baptist and Jesus the Christ.

Throughout this book the perceptive reader will be awed by the accuracy of the Word of God and the magnificence of what God wrought in bringing into the world the redeemer. His part in God's plan was so vital that he was ever foreknown and foretold, but he was not God the Father. The redeemer's actual existence began with his conception and birth to a woman named Mary about two thousand years ago. Born of divine conception into a world that was bent on killing him from his birth, the Christ would ultimately fulfill his God-given mission as savior of the world.

* * *

As the research team and I considered and reconsidered the structure of this study, we went back and forth trying to determine which part of this research should come first: the Biblical astronomy with its historical and scientific data or the prophecies and people associated with the promised seed. It became evident that the astronomy and its fixing of dates had to be this study's foundation as every succeeding chapter is affected by these dates. However, I am suggesting that you, the reader, determine which approach to reading seems most helpful to you. Some may want to read the book as it is now structured; others may find it more beneficial to read Part II first, followed by Part I, and then, perhaps, Part II again. Whichever way you choose to approach this study, may the result be the same: I want this research on one of the greatest events in all history to bless you mightily, building your believing in God's incomparable integrity as He revealed the coming of His only begotten Son, Jesus Christ, our promised seed.

ACKNOWLEDGMENTS

This book *Jesus Christ Our Promised Seed* came into concretion with the assistance of the scholarship of a group of qualified research men and women. In August of 1979 a research team, consisting of Walter J. Cummins, John Crouch, Gary R. Curtis, Michele C. Curtis, Bernita Jess, Karen W. Martin, Donna Randall, Bo Reahard, and Chip Stansbury, joined me in considering my original research work on the birth of Christ. After the research team's study and discussion, Chip Stansbury and John Crouch, under the supervision of Walter J. Cummins (coordinator of the Research Department of The Way International) continued to refine and expand the research work on this great topic of the coming of the Messiah. John Crouch's scientific contribution to Part I of this study regarding astronomy is most illuminating and exciting in bringing to light the unparalleled accuracy and depth of God's dynamic Word written in the stars.

Acknowledgments

My daughter and long-time editor, Karen Wierwille Martin, along with Michele C. Curtis, reworked the research manuscript for its structure and clarity of communication. The manuscript in its numerous drafts was tirelessly retyped by our Word Processing Department under the supervision of Joann Herman. Camille Kavasansky and Barbara Geer proofread the manuscript, while Way Publications under Tom Plain prepared the copy for publication. Rosalie F. Rivenbark, as coordinator of my publications, oversaw the production of this book and Emogene Allen, coordinator of The Way International Bookstore, prepared *Jesus Christ Our Promised Seed* for marketing. To all who contributed to this work, I am very grateful.

As a follower of God and a confirmed believer in the accuracy of God's Word, I am particularly awed and grateful for the love, the grace, and the goodness of our God in allowing such truths as these unfolded in *Jesus Christ Our Promised Seed* to be heralded again from His Scriptures.

THE CHRONOLOGICAL ORDER OF THE EVENTS SURROUNDING THE BIRTH OF CHRIST

Listed below are the events surrounding the birth of Christ which can be historically and/or astronomically pinpointed.

May, 4 B.C.	During the course of Abia, the angel Gabriel appears to Zacharias serving in the Temple
June, 4 B.C.	Conception of John the Baptist
Dec., 4 B.C.	Gabriel appears to Mary in Nazareth; conception of Jesus Christ; Mary travels to Judea to see her cousin Elisabeth
March, 3 B.C.	Mary returns to Nazareth; John the Baptist is born to Zacharias and Elisabeth
Aug. 12, 3 B.C.	Jupiter and Venus in conjunction in Leo; Magi begin noting their observations of the activity of Jupiter, the king planet
Sept. 11, 3 B.C.	Birth of Jesus Christ; first day of Tishri; sun in Virgo with the "moon beneath her feet"
Sept. 14, 3 B.C.	Jupiter and Regulus in conjunction in Leo

The Chronological Order of Events

Feb. 17, 2 B.C.	Jupiter and Regulus in conjunction in Leo
May 8, 2 B.C.	Jupiter and Regulus in conjunction in Leo
June 17, 2 B.C.	Jupiter and Venus in conjunction in Leo
Aug. 27, 2 B.C.	Massing of planets Jupiter, Mars, Mercury, and Venus in Leo, Jupiter and Mars in conjunction; Magi leave for Jerusalem after this celestial event
Dec., 2 B.C.	Magi arrive in Jerusalem; Jupiter visible over Bethlehem before dawn as the Magi travel there to worship the Christ who is more than one year and three months old; Magi depart for Persia; Joseph, Mary, and Jesus flee to Egypt
Jan. 9, 1 B.C.	Eclipse preceding Herod's death
April 8, 1 B.C.	Archelaus, the new king of Judea, disrupts Passover; Joseph, Mary, and Jesus returning to Judea from Egypt "turn aside" into Galilee and settle in Nazareth

Listed below are the Biblical passages recording the events surrounding the birth of Christ in the order in which they occurred. There is some overlapping in time for some of the events listed.

Luke 1:5-25	Angel's announcement to Zacharias in the Temple of the birth of John the Baptist.

The Chronological Order of Events

Luke 1:26-38	Angel's announcement of the birth of Jesus to Mary in Nazareth
Luke 1:39-56	Mary visits her cousin Elisabeth, mother of John the Baptist, for three months
Luke 1:57-80	Birth of John the Baptist to Zacharias and Elisabeth
Matt. 1:18-24	Joseph is encouraged by an angel of the Lord "to take unto thee Mary thy wife"
Matt. 1:25a; Luke 2:1-20	Jesus Christ is born in Bethlehem
Matt. 1:25b; Luke 2:21	Jesus' circumcision and naming
Luke 2:22-24	Mary's purification and Jesus' presentation to the Lord
Luke 2:25-35	Simeon thanks God for the promised seed
Luke 2:36-38	Anna, a prophetess in the Temple, gives her praise and thanks to God
Matt. 2:1-12	Magi from the East arrive in Jerusalem and proceed to Bethlehem
Matt. 2:13-22	Joseph, Mary, and the child flee from Herod to Egypt
Matt. 2:23; Luke 2:39	After Herod's death Joseph and family return to Nazareth
Luke 2:40	Jesus (to age twelve) "grew, and waxed strong"

The Chronological Order of Events

Luke 2:41-50	Jesus stays behind at the Temple when his parents leave after the Feast of Unleavened Bread
Luke 2:51-52	Jesus (from age twelve to manhood) "increased in wisdom and stature"

CALENDAR OF PERTINENT EVENTS FROM 4 B.C. to 1 B.C.

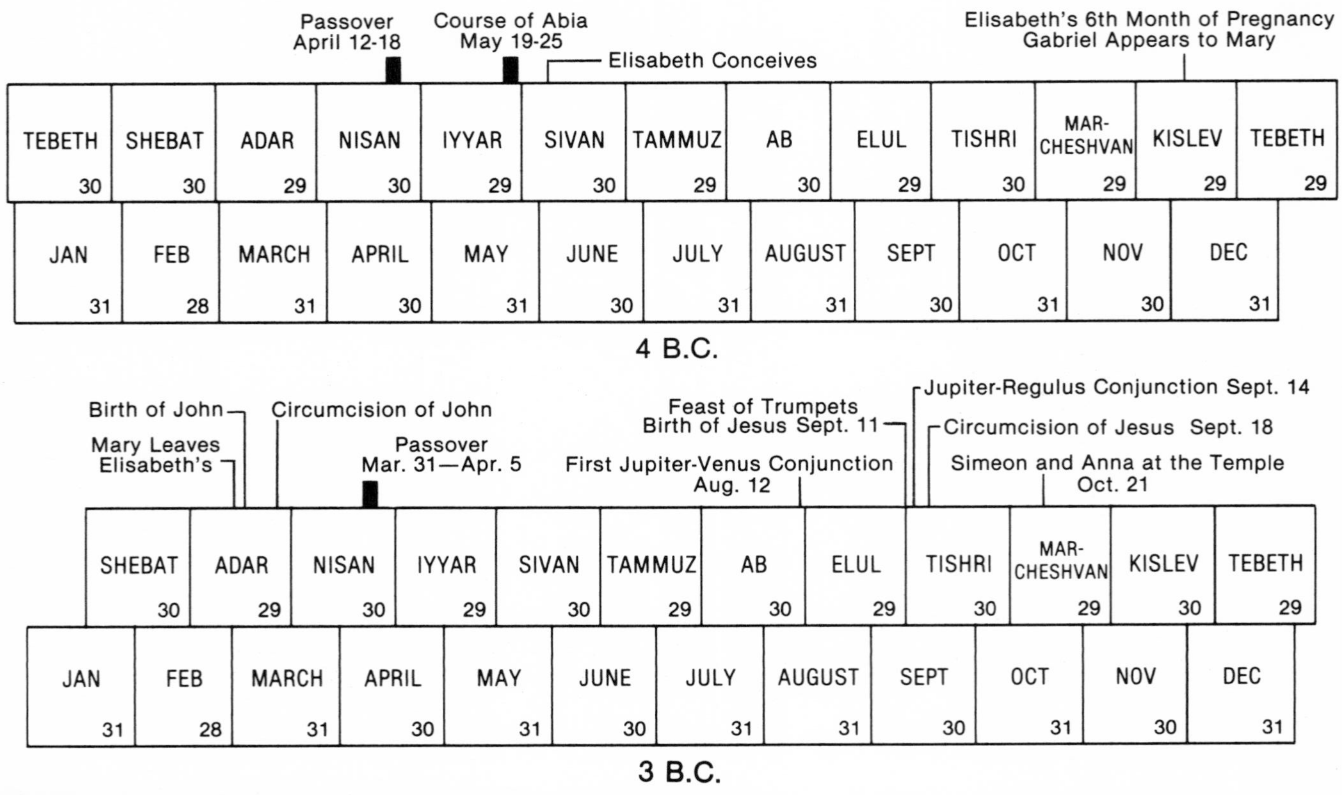

Passover April 12-18

Course of Abia May 19-25

Elisabeth Conceives

Elisabeth's 6th Month of Pregnancy
Gabriel Appears to Mary

TEBETH	SHEBAT	ADAR	NISAN	IYYAR	SIVAN	TAMMUZ	AB	ELUL	TISHRI	MAR-CHESHVAN	KISLEV	TEBETH
30	30	29	30	29	30	29	30	29	30	29	29	29

JAN	FEB	MARCH	APRIL	MAY	JUNE	JULY	AUGUST	SEPT	OCT	NOV	DEC
31	28	31	30	31	30	31	31	30	31	30	31

4 B.C.

Birth of John

Mary Leaves Elisabeth's

Circumcision of John

Passover
Mar. 31—Apr. 5

First Jupiter-Venus Conjunction
Aug. 12

Feast of Trumpets
Birth of Jesus Sept. 11

Jupiter-Regulus Conjunction Sept. 14

Circumcision of Jesus Sept. 18

Simeon and Anna at the Temple
Oct. 21

SHEBAT	ADAR	NISAN	IYYAR	SIVAN	TAMMUZ	AB	ELUL	TISHRI	MAR-CHESHVAN	KISLEV	TEBETH
30	29	30	29	30	29	30	29	30	29	30	29

JAN	FEB	MARCH	APRIL	MAY	JUNE	JULY	AUGUST	SEPT	OCT	NOV	DEC
31	28	31	30	31	30	31	31	30	31	30	31

3 B.C.

GLOSSARY OF ASTRONOMICAL NAMES AND TERMS

Astrology
the pretended art of predicting the future from the motions and positions of heavenly bodies

Astronomy
the science describing the positions, motions, magnitudes, and composition of the heavenly bodies

Aurora Borealis
a luminous phenomenon appearing high in the atmosphere at night towards the north, especially visible in arctic regions; caused by atomic particles ejected from the sun

Celestial Equator
the great circle in the heavens directly over the earth's equator

Celestial Latitude
the angular distance from the ecliptic (see *Latitude, Ecliptic*)

Celestial Longitude
the angular distance from the line of longitude marked by the first point of Aries, which is the position of the sun over the equator at the spring equinox on March 21

Glossary of Astronomical Names and Terms

Celestial North Pole

the point in the heavens directly over the earth's north pole; now located less than a degree from the star Polaris

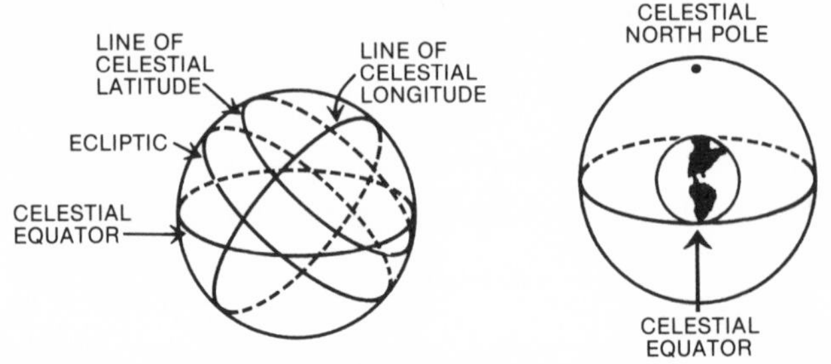

Comet

a luminous heavenly body orbiting the sun which has the appearance of a small, bright head trailed by a tail; orbits range from short parabolic orbits of a few years to near-hyperbolic orbits of thousands of years

Conjunction

a configuration in which heavenly bodies line up along a line of celestial longitude; an imaginary

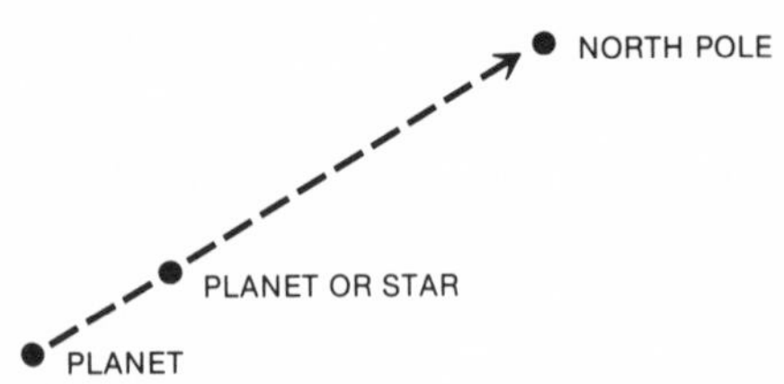

straight line can be drawn through these two celestial bodies to the celestial north pole

Constellation

a configuration of fixed stars around which, since extreme antiquity, an imaginary pictorial representation has been drawn in order to preserve the star names contained therein

Eclipse

the covering of a celestial body by another celestial body, or its shadow; in a solar eclipse, the moon passes between the sun and the earth, and the moon covers the sun, partially or entirely, while in a lunar eclipse, the moon passes through the earth's shadow

Ecliptic

the path that the sun moves through the heavens during the course of a year as it passes through the twelve constellations of the zodiac

Heliacal Rising

the rising of a celestial body in the eastern sky shortly before dawn, before the sun obscures it by its brilliance

Latitude

the angular distance on the surface of the earth north

or south of the equator; lines of latitude circle the earth parallel to the equator

Longitude

the angular distance on the surface of the earth east or west of the standard longitude at Greenwich, England; lines of longitude circle the earth through the north and south poles

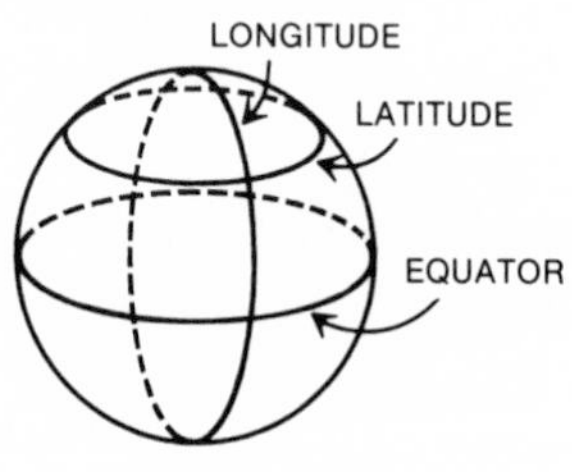

Massing of Planets

the appearance of three or more planets in a constellation

Meridian

an imaginary semi-circle passing directly overhead of the observer and intersecting the horizon directly north and south

Meteor

a small piece of stone or metal in orbit around the sun, which, when it passes into the earth's atmosphere, is heated by friction to incandescence, and appears as a brief, brilliant streak across the sky

North Pole
the northern extremity of the earth's axis (different from *Celestial North Pole*)

Nova
a star that greatly increases its magnitude, then slowly decreases over days and weeks following

Occultation
a smaller celestial body being covered by a larger body, especially the moon passing in front of a star or planet

Planet
a major heavenly body revolving in an orbit about the sun, including the earth; planets visible to the ancients were: Mercury, Venus, Mars, Jupiter, and Saturn; modern telescopes have revealed Uranus, Neptune, and Pluto

Regulus
the brightest star in Leo; in Semitic languages the word *regel* means "foot"

Retrograde Motion
a visual effect in which the planets beyond the earth

appear to reverse their motion, tracing a loop in the sky; occurring because of the change in the line of sight to the planet as the earth passes by the slower-moving outer planets such as Jupiter

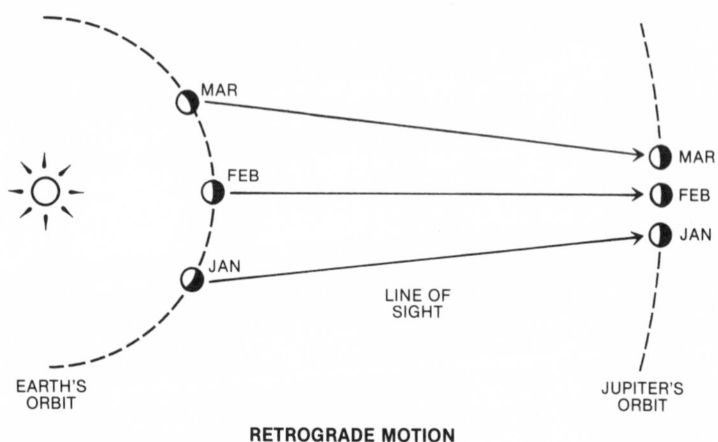

RETROGRADE MOTION

Spica
the brightest star in Virgo; Arabic name is *Al Zimach*, akin to the Hebrew root *ssemah*, translated "sprout, branch"

Triple Conjunction
an outer planet in retrograde motion passes another planet or fixed star three times

Zodiac
the constellations through which the ecliptic passes;

names and pictures of these constellations date from the most remote antiquity; the twelve constellations are: Virgo, Libra, Scorpio, Sagittarius, Capricorn, Aquarius, Pisces, Aries, Taurus, Gemini, Cancer, Leo

Zodiacal Glow

a faint glow lying along the ecliptic from the horizon to about a 30^0 angle above the horizon; origin uncertain

PART I

THE CELESTIAL ANNOUNCEMENT OF THE PROMISED SEED: THE HISTORICAL AND ASTRONOMICAL EVIDENCE

CHAPTER ONE

THE BIBLE AND ASTRONOMY

There is a divinely designed system and order to God's creation. God has numbered and named the stars; He has set them to reveal His marvelous plan of redemption.

> Psalms 147:4:
> He [God] telleth the number of the stars; he calleth them all by *their* names.

In the beginning, when God created the heavens and the earth and set the stars in their courses, He affixed specific names to the stars. The very names of the stars as well as their groupings reveal aspects of God's plan of redemption. This information was given to Adam who taught the patriarchs, and in this manner it was passed on from generation to generation throughout the centuries.

In the study of astronomy's relationship to God's Word, we discover that a knowledge of God and His outline of redemption existed thousands of years before the revelation was given in written form. In both the positioning of the stars and in the star names, the revelation of the grand plan of redemption was given.[1] According to Psalms 147 the very names of the stars were chosen by God; they reveal the significance of God's revelation.

It is sometimes difficult for us who are accustomed to having God's revelation in written form to understand that God can and does communicate to man in more ways than just the written Word. Hebrews 1:1 states that "God. . .at sundry times and in divers manners spake." One of the "divers manners" in which God spoke was through the signs given in the stars. Just as the written Word of God declares God's glory and redemptive plan, so do the heavens.

> Psalms 19:1-6:
> The heavens declare the glory of God; and the firmament sheweth his handywork.
> Day unto day uttereth speech, and night unto night sheweth knowledge.
> *There is* no speech nor language, *where* their voice is not heard.

---

1. More detailed information on this can be found in the following sources: Frances Rolleston, *Mazzaroth*; *or*, *The Constellations* (1863; new ed., London: Rivingtons, 1882); E.W. Bullinger, *The Witness of the Stars* (1893; reprint ed., Grand Rapids: Kregel, 1967); Joseph A. Seiss, *The Gospel in the Stars* (1882; illus. ed., Grand Rapids: Kregel, 1972); and Clyde L. Ferguson, *The Stars and the Bible* (Hicksville, N.Y.: Exposition Press, 1978).

> Their line is gone out through all the earth, and their words to the end of the world. In them hath he set a tabernacle for the sun,
> Which *is* as a bridegroom coming out of his chamber, *and* rejoiceth as a strong man to run a race.
> His going forth *is* from the end of the heaven, and his circuit unto the ends of it: and there is nothing hid from the heat thereof.

A study of the words of this psalm clearly indicates that they denote more than awe for the Creator. In noting both the structure and words used, the whole passage graphically tells of God's revelation placed in the heavens: the stars prophesy, they show knowledge, they tell of God's glory, and they set forth His purposes.[2]

God's creation of the heavens and the earth in their proper order is given in Genesis 1:1. His reestablishing of the heavens and the earth for man, as we know man, begins with Genesis 1:2. After God had called light into existence, He began giving order to all things in the heavens and in the earth.

> Genesis 1:14:
> And God said, Let there be lights in the firmament of the heaven to divide the day from the night; and let them be for signs, and for seasons, and for days, and years.

---

2. For a more detailed view of this psalm see *The Companion Bible* (reprint ed., Grand Rapids: Zondervan, 1974), pp. 737-738.

Days and years are familiar to everyone. The "seasons" mentioned in this verse indicate periods of time, not just spring, summer, fall, and winter.

The word "signs" in Genesis 1:14 is of great significance. It comes from the Hebrew root *avah*, meaning "to mark," and is used of marking someone significant to come. Thus, at the very opening of the written Word, God declares that lights in the firmament of the heaven are signs of important things to come.

The record of Genesis 1:14 anticipates the coming of the one who is explicitly prophesied of in Genesis 3:15, the "seed of the woman," our promised seed.

> Genesis 3:15:
> And I will put enmity between thee and the woman, and between thy seed and her seed; it shall bruise thy head, and thou shalt bruise his heel.

Since the stars declare God's plan of redemption, it is necessary that the stars should herald the coming of the woman's seed, the redeemer. But how does one begin to understand the stars and their signs and how these reveal God's plan?

A person must first be aware that the original names of stars have been providentially preserved down through the centuries in the Semitic languages. The ancient names of the stars have meanings which, when properly understood, make up the foundation of a true Biblical astronomy. Carefully note at the outset that Biblical astronomy differs vastly from the counterfeit "study" of astronomy known as astrology, which purports to interpret celestial events as they influence men's lives. The original revelation of the stars' meaning was God-given, but as the years passed, the true meaning of the stars' revelation was corrupted and perverted into astrology. From such perversions developed many of the widespread myths of the ancient and modern world. The stars of heaven do give God's divine plans when properly understood, but the distortions and practices of astrology are idolatrous and strenuously forbidden in the Scriptures.[3]

Biblical astronomy is the true understanding of the names of the stars as they depict the coming of the one who is the Christ. Just as the sun and moon in their courses mark out the days, months, and years, likewise the stars and planets in their courses mark out the signs concerning God's plan of redemption which culminates in Jesus Christ, the seed of the woman, the Messiah, the promised seed.

The names of the stars give the detailed parts of

---

3. God's Word specifically forbids astrology and worship of the heavenly bodies. Isaiah 47:12-14: "Stand now with thine enchantments, and with the multitude of thy sorceries, wherein thou hast laboured from thy youth; if so be thou shalt be able to profit, if so be thou mayest prevail. Thou art wearied in the multitude of thy counsels. Let now the astrologers, the stargazers, the monthly prognosticators, stand up, and save thee from *these things* that shall come upon thee. Behold, they shall be as stubble; the fire shall burn them; they shall not deliver themselves from the power of the flame: *there shall* not *be* a coal to warm at, *nor* fire to sit before it."

the plan, for the ancient star names were first given by God. Again, carefully observe Psalms 147:4.

> He telleth the number of the stars; he calleth them all by *their* names.

To begin to understand God's message, the ancient names as well as the groupings of the stars and planets need to be studied. The heavens contain twelve conspicuous groupings of stars. Throughout the ancient world these twelve groupings, called "constellations," or "signs of the zodiac," were known and respected as depicting eternal truths. To focus in on one of these constellations and demonstrate its significance, we can see the record in Genesis 49 where Jacob on his deathbed prophesies concerning his twelve sons and their offspring for generations to come.[4] Verses 9 and 10 contain Jacob's words to his son Judah.

> Genesis 49:9 and 10:
> Judah *is* a lion's whelp: from the prey, my son, thou art gone up: he stooped down, he couched as a lion, and as an old lion; who shall rouse him up?
> The sceptre shall not depart from Judah, nor a lawgiver from between his feet [Hebrew: *regel*], until Shiloh come; and unto him *shall* the gathering of the people *be*.

---

4. For a consideration of Jacob's sons as the twelve zodiacal signs see Ferguson, *The Stars and the Bible*, pp. 13-15.

Jacob by inspiration declares that Judah is symbolized by the lion. In the twelve constellations of the zodiac, there is one sign for the lion and that is Leo. Here in Genesis 49, Leo, the lion, and Judah, are being identified with each other. Furthermore, Jacob declares that "the sceptre shall not depart from Judah, nor a lawgiver from between his feet." In astronomical terms this statement is also significant because of the star named Regulus, which is the dominant, brightest star in the constellation of Leo. The Arabic word *regel* means "foot" and is identical in meaning to the Aramaic word *regla* and the Hebrew word *regel*. Thus the brightest star in the constellation of Leo has the Biblical connotation of the foot, tying in with the "from between his feet," of Genesis 49:10. In this one verse alone, the lion of Judah, Leo, is intertwined with a lawgiver coming from between his feet, represented by the king star, Regulus.[5]

Some of the things foretold in the Book of Genesis gain their full interpretation and meaning in the Book of Revelation. So it is with the full identification of the lion with the Messiah who would descend from Judah, which is stated explicitly in Revelation 5:5.

---

5. All ancient civilizations recognized Regulus as the king star, the one and only king star in the zodiac. "Regulus" means "kingly" in Latin. See Richard Hinckley Allen, *Star Names: Their Lore and Meaning* (1899; new ed., New York: Dover Publications, 1963).

> Revelation 5:5:
> And one of the elders saith unto me [the Apostle John, writer of the Book of Revelation], Weep not: behold, the Lion of the tribe of Juda, the Root of David, hath prevailed to open the book, and to loose the seven seals thereof [Christ being the Lion of the tribe of Judah and the Root and offspring of David].

"... The Lion of the tribe of Juda, the Root of David." Clearly here is the conclusive link between Judah, the lion, and the Lord Jesus Christ. Thus, Leo was the specific sign placed in the heavens to communicate part of God's redemptive plan from the great-grandson of Abraham, Judah, through his genealogical line to the Christ.

This example of the offspring of Judah being linked to the constellation Leo is just one of many examples which shows the authority of the stars as signs. The significance of this particular constellation of Leo will be viewed in more detail later in this study, but it is pointed out here to demonstrate that celestial bodies are God-arranged and have definite God-ordained meanings and significance.

By way of the stars, God's blueprint for mankind was known long before it was put into writing. The detailed meaning of the revelation of the heavens may never be fully recaptured in our day and time. However, by studying ancient records, languages, and astronomical terms, and by evaluating them in light of the written Word, enough truth can be seen to demonstrate some of the greatness of God's wonderful revelation.

CHAPTER TWO

WHO WERE THE WISE MEN?

To begin our study of the stars on the specific subject of the coming of the promised one, we start by looking at the record of the wise men, star observers, of Matthew 2 . This record tells that wise men from the East saw a star, "his star," which prompted them to go to Jerusalem seeking the king of the Judeans. Interestingly, these men, Gentiles, had a knowledge of God's true Word as it was revealed in the stars, for they alone came to Bethlehem seeking the king of the Judeans as they alone recognized the celestial announcement of his birth.

We too can know what the heavens revealed at the time of the Messiah's coming. By thoroughly researching what is stated in the Bible, plus studying the astronomical evidence, we find how intricately the Bible and astronomy mesh with regards to "his star" which the wise men sought, making the truth regarding the birth of God's Son within the reach of those who want to know.[1]

What exactly does the Bible record about the wise men and "his star"? Matthew 2 contains this information.

> Matthew 2:1:
> Now when [after] Jesus was born in Bethlehem of Judaea in the days of Herod the king, behold, there came wise men [Greek: *magoi*] from the east to Jerusalem.

The Greek word *magoi* (Aramaic: *mgushe*) is poorly translated by the words "wise men." *Magoi* is a reference to a specific religious caste called Magi or Magians that was prominent in ancient Near Eastern society, especially in Persia. Virtually nothing is popularly known about them today. Who were these people? Why were they knowledgeable of the birth of the Judean king? As far as we know, at the time of Christ's birth no one in Israel was aware of their king's birth through observation of the stars; it was only the Magi of the East who came to know of this event by reading the astronomical message.

Ancient records indicate that the earliest Magi lived

1. Many scholars' works have contributed valuable insight into this field from historical and astronomical points of view. Many possibilities and new information have been brought to light by Ernest L. Martin in *The Birth of Christ Recalculated*, 2d ed. (Pasadena: Foundation for Biblical Research, 1980). His study and suggestions have been most helpful in our research.

in Media and Persia as a religious caste before the time of Zoroaster (ca. 600 B.C.), the founder and prophet of the Zoroastrian religion. Prior to Zoroaster, the Magi religion is thought to have been a type of nature worship.

When Zoroastrianism became prominent in Persia, many Magi adopted it as their own and became the priesthood of that religion. Following the death of Zoroaster the Magi splintered into two major sects: (1) those who continued following the religion of Zoroaster, and (2) those who returned to the ancient forms of nature worship, especially emphasizing sun worship.[2]

During the first century after the birth of Christ, there was a great influx of the Magian sect into the Roman Empire. These Magi were not those loyal to Zoroastrianism; rather, they were those who had further developed their pagan forms of sun worship, magical arts, astrology, and sorcery. From them we derive the terms "magic" and "magician." The influence of this sect of the Magi, the sun worshippers, on religious practices in the Roman Empire still remains in our culture.

Since the Eastern Magi remained faithful to the teachings of Zoroaster, it is significant to note several

2. James Hope Moulton, *Early Zoroastrianism* (1913; reprint ed., Amsterdam: Philo Press, 1972), p. 226; and Moulton, *The Treasure of the Magi* (London: Oxford University Press, 1917), p. 64. See also George Rawlinson, *The Sixth Great Oriental Monarchy* (New York: Dodd, Mead & Co., 1872), pp. 365, 400.

parallels between Zoroaster's teachings and those of the Old Testament.[3] Zoroastrians believed in one supreme God who created the heavens and the earth, who authored all that is good. They also believed in a spiritual adversary who authored evil. They believed in a coming redeemer, a prophet who would be sent by God to save mankind. They strictly forbade the worship of idols. They believed in angels and in devil spirits and the eventual triumph of good over evil. They set forth a system of laws and ethics stressing a strict code of moral behavior.

It is therefore important to remember that the Magi of Matthew 2:1 are said to be "from the east." They were men reputed for their knowledge of religion, astronomy, and the spiritual significance of astronomical phenomena.[4] How did these Magi happen to accurately understand much of the true meaning of the stars? The Book of Daniel records

---

3. These similarities are noted in detail by Peter M. Bernegger in "The Star of Bethlehem—Part 1: The Biblical Record," *The Way Magazine*, November/ December 1978, pp. 6-10. See also Samuel K. Nweeya, *Persia: The Land of the Magi*, 5th ed. rev. (Philadelphia: John C. Winston, 1913), pp. 249-259.

4. McCasland speaks of Philo's distinction between the respected Magi who were reputable for their genuine knowledge in the natural and spiritual realms, and those Magi who were, as Philo termed them, "counterfeit" practitioners of magic. See *The Interpreter's Dictionary of the Bible* (Nashville: Abingdon Press, 1962), s.v. "Magi," by S.V. McCasland. Moulton's *Early Zoroastrianism* (p. 226) and his *Treasure of the Magi* (p. 64) recognize the two groups, and state that those loyal to Zoroaster remained in Persia. In the Peshitta Old Testament, the same Aramaic word for "wise men," *mgushe*, found in Matthew 2:1 occurs, translated in the King James Version as "sorcerers" in Daniel 2:2, and as "soothsayers" in 5:7.

that Judeans during the Babylonian captivity, five hundred years before the birth of Christ, wielded great influence in the royal courts where Magi served. For example, Daniel, Shadrach, Meshach, and Abednego all held high offices in the kingdom of Babylon. Daniel was made "master of the magicians [Magi], astrologers, Chaldeans, *and* soothsayers," according to Daniel 5:11. Judean teaching on the celestial message in the stars was attentively listened to in this Babylonian society which set much importance on celestial motions. That this society excelled in astronomy and astrology can be seen in how the terms "Babylonian" or "Chaldean" have been long synonymous with diviners and observers of the stars.

The truth concerning "his star" became accessible knowledge to the Magi when the Persians took over the Babylonian Empire (Daniel 5:31). As recorded in Daniel 6, at the time of the takeover, Daniel retained the high position he had held under Babylonian rule. He "was preferred above the presidents and [the one hundred and twenty] princes, because an excellent spirit *was* in him" (Daniel 6:3). Daniel was again set over the Magi, and therefore could fully instruct them in the accurate knowledge of Biblical prophecy written in the stars.

Thus, the Judeans in the courts of Nebuchadnezzar and Darius passed on their knowledge of the spiritual significance of the constellations to the Magi who preserved it and hence were aware of the promise of the birth of the Judean king. Suetonius, the Roman historian, mentions that an expectation of a powerful man who would come forth from Judea was commonly held: "a firm belief had long prevailed through the East that it was destined for the Empire of the world *at that time* to be given to someone who should go forth from Judaea."[5]

Of course, certain major questions arise. What was the star the Magi of Matthew 2:1 and 2 saw? How did they know that this specific sign was "his star"? What was the result of the Magi's journey to Jerusalem? We must look again at Matthew 2 as our source of information for answering these important questions.

> Matthew 2:1 and 2:
> Now when [after] Jesus was born in Bethlehem of Judaea in the days of Herod the king, behold, there came wise men from the east [Eastern Magi] to Jerusalem,
> Saying, Where is he that is born King of the Jews [Judeans][6]? for we have seen his star in the east, and are come to worship him.

---

5. Suetonius *Vespasian* 4.
6. The word "Jew" and its variations as used in the King James Version should always be understood as meaning "Judean." The word "Jew" came into vernacular usage relatively late. It was first included in an English Bible in its present form of "Jew" in the eighteenth century. The text reads "Judean" and in our research work we prefer what the text says. For further information see Victor Paul Wierwille, "Jew and Judean," *Jesus Christ Our Passover* (New Knoxville, Ohio: American Christian Press, 1980), Appendix 3, pp. 435-440.

In verse 2 the Greek words translated "in the east" are *en tē anatolē*, literally meaning "in the rising."[7] This phrase refers to the rising of a star shortly before sunrise, called in astronomy the heliacal rising of a star.[8] Since Matthew 2:2 says a "star," the Magi must have been referring to the rising of a star in the eastern sky, a star that arose shortly before dawn, which was visible until obscured by the brilliance of the sun.

We must realize that in ancient times all astronomical bodies (except the sun and moon) were called "stars," including what we know as planets. The Greek and Hebrew words for "star" are used of any luminous, non-terrestrial body. Even today, popular modern usage refers to celestial bodies as "stars." In this study the general term "stars" will likewise be used unless a specific celestial body is being referred to.

The Magi had seen a celestial body in its heliacal rising above the eastern horizon. And, it was not just any star that arose; it was a star that signaled to them the birth of the Judean king. They said it was "his star" who was "born King of the Judeans."

---

7. The word *anatolē* is in the singular form, meaning "rising." In this form it is often used in reference to the rising of the sun or a star. In its plural form, *anatolōn*, it means "risings" and refers to the direction the sun repeatedly rises day after day. Thus, in the plural form it should be rendered "east" as in Matthew 2:1, whereas the singular form in Matthew 2:2 is best translated literally as "rising."

8. Henry George Liddell and Robert Scott, comps., *A Greek-English Lexicon*, rev. Henry Stuart Jones, 9th ed. (1843; Oxford: Clarendon Press, 1940), p. 123.

The Scriptures specifically record one other time the wise men saw this same star after having seen "his star" in the rising.

> Matthew 2:9:
> When they had heard the king, they departed; and, lo, the star, which they saw in the east [in the rising], went before them, till it came and stood over where the young child was.

God's Word clearly records two distinct appearances of the same star, one in Matthew 2:2 and one in Matthew 2:9. The word "east" in both verses is the Greek word *anatolē*, properly translated "rising."

The first recorded appearance of this star in the Bible was observed by the Magi in their homeland. They saw it "in the rising," above the eastern horizon. The second recorded appearance in the Bible was when the Magi left Jerusalem for Bethlehem. On this second occasion the star appeared in a southerly direction from Jerusalem. The star "went before them" and finally "stood over" Bethlehem, the place where the young child was.

Using the information given in these two verses of Matthew 2, many proposals have been set forth as to the identity of "his star." We want to consider these proposals carefully. But before doing so, several popular misconceptions must be corrected.

Most people believe that the star seen by the Magi was exceptionally bright. However, God's Word indicates that only the Magi took special note of it. Its brilliance is never mentioned, only its significance. Whatever the star was, it was important for its meaning, not its brightness.

Another popular misconception is that, after first seeing the star, the Magi immediately followed the star from their eastern homeland to Jerusalem. This is not so. Tradition depicts the Magi arriving in Bethlehem on the night of Christ's birth, finding the newborn "Christ child" in the manger while the shepherds stood by. Yet God's Word clearly demonstrates that the Magi arrived in Bethlehem over a year and three months after Jesus' birth. In Matthew 2:9-11 the Magi found a "young child," in Greek *paidion* and in Aramaic *talya*. These words do not designate a newborn babe. According to Luke 2:16, the shepherds found a newly delivered babe (Greek: *brephos*; Aramaic: *ula*). The Magi found a child in a house, not a babe in a stable. No shepherds are mentioned as being present.

In researching and identifying "his star," we must do away with all our previous misconceptions and base this study on concrete information and evidence from the Bible, history, and astronomy, not on popular artwork, myths, and conjectures.

CHAPTER THREE

BEGINNING TO DATE "HIS STAR"

To discover exactly what "his star" was we begin by examining both chronology and astronomy. Since notable astronomical events happen frequently throughout history, it is necessary to determine the possible time limits within which the star of Matthew 2 appeared. This is crucial, for it has been an erroneous time frame which has caused problems with most proposals regarding the identity of "his star."

God's Word makes it clear in both Luke 1 and Matthew 2 that King Herod the Great was alive and ruling Judea when Jesus Christ was born. So in order to gain a specific point in time to begin in our calculations, we must find a date associated with Herod and work from that point. The noted historian Josephus, who chronicled events in Judea at the time of Christ, recorded that an eclipse of the moon occurred shortly before Herod's death. Precise calculations can be made as to the dates upon which lunar eclipses occur, since eclipses are capable of being mathematically documented with accuracy. Therefore, by fixing the date of this eclipse—and thus the date shortly preceding Herod's death—scholars can examine astronomical events preceding those dates and choose from among these events that which would exactly fit the description of "his star."

To begin to narrow the time frame, it should be noted that all scholars concur that Herod's death occurred sometime between 7 B.C. and 1 B.C. Since his death was preceded by a lunar eclipse, there are four possibilities to consider because four eclipses were visible in Palestine between these two dates. In the past, most scholars have accepted the traditional teaching, without checking the facts in detail, that the eclipse recorded by Josephus occurred on March 13 of 4 B.C. and that Herod died before Passover the following month. However, we want to reevaluate for ourselves all four lunar eclipses visible to an observer in Palestine between 7 B.C. and 1 B.C. The four are:

(1) a total eclipse on March 23, 5 B.C.
(2) a total eclipse on September 15, 5 B.C.
(3) a partial eclipse on March 13, 4 B.C. (previously the most popular candidate)
(4) a total eclipse on January 9, 1 B.C.

A major problem with both the March 23, 5 B.C. (1), and the March 13, 4 B.C. (3) eclipses is that they occurred too close to their respective Passovers. Josephus records a lengthy list of events which took place between the lunar eclipse and Passover during the year that Herod died.[1] It would have been impossible to squeeze all of these events between either of these eclipses and their respective Passover dates.

What were all these events? Josephus noted that Herod executed two high priests at the time of the lunar eclipse, after which Herod's lingering illness was greatly aggravated, so he went to Callirrhoe to the east of Jordan to seek relief in its hot baths. However, the treatments failed and he returned to Jericho. Knowing that the Judean nation cared nothing for him and that his death would be a cause for celebration, Herod sent messengers throughout Judea to bring every principal man in every city and village to Jericho. When they were gathered, Herod had them all confined to the hippodrome (or race-course), intending to have them killed when he died. After all these men had been gathered and confined, envoys from Caesar at Rome arrived giving Herod permission to execute or banish his son, Antipater. Herod had him executed immediately. Herod died five days later. Upon his death, Herod's other son, Archelaus, became king whereupon Archelaus released the prisoners in the hippodrome. Archelaus prepared a lavish funeral for his father and a procession, consisting of Herod's soldiers and servants,

---

1. Josephus *The Antiquities of the Jews* 17.6.5.

marched to the Herodian, a fortified mountain south of Jerusalem, where they buried Herod. Scholars estimate that this funeral procession from Jericho to the Herodian required at least twenty-five days. After the burial, Archelaus then mourned his father for seven more days before returning to Jerusalem and preparing to sail for Rome to have Caesar confirm his reign. But before Archelaus left, a general riot erupted as the Passover was beginning. The tumult was so serious that Archelaus sent in his army to put down the uprising and to send the people home from the Passover.[2]

---

2. Incidentally, the time of the death of Herod can be estimated by examining the events recorded by Josephus, and allowing a minimum time for them to be accomplished. The following list gives a reasonable minimum time for the events between the eclipse of January 9 and Herod's death in 1 B.C.

Symptoms of Herod's disease intensify	7 days
Herod travels to Callirrhoe and receives bath treatments	14 days
Herod returns to Jericho and summons all Judean elders	14 days
Herod executes Antipater and lives for five more days	5 days
	40 days

Forty days after the eclipse of January 9 brings us to February 18, the earliest date that Herod could have died.

Similarly, estimates can be given for the time for the events following Herod's death.

Preparations for Herod's funeral	3 days
Funeral procession from Jericho to the Herodian	25 days
Archelaus officially mourns	7 days
Archelaus returns to Jerusalem and prepares to sail for Rome	7 days
	42 days

Forty-two days before the Passover on April 8 gives February 26 (1 B.C. being a leap year), which is the latest date that Herod could have died.

Even with the uncertainties in the exact time of these events, the time of the death of Herod can be narrowed to within a week.

Since this time-consuming series of events occurred between the lunar eclipse and Passover in the year that Herod died, it would be impossible to compress all of these stated events into the time allotted in the 5 B.C. eclipse, especially since March 23 was the very date of the Passover that year. Furthermore, in 4 B.C. the eclipse was on March 13, and Passover that year was only a month later on April 11—simply not enough time for all the events spoken of by Josephus to have taken place.

Some scholars have proposed that the eclipse of September 15, 5 B.C. was the one mentioned by Josephus, shortly after which Herod died. This date gives a six-month period between Herod's death and the Passover. Josephus records that after Herod's funeral, the new king Archelaus *hasted* to sail to Rome at the same time that the Passover was approaching. The problem with the date of this eclipse is, how could it be said that Archelaus *hasted* to Rome if he had waited six months from the death of Herod in the fall until Passover the following spring? This and other factors discount this eclipse as the one Josephus records.[3]

There is only one remaining lunar eclipse to consider, and that is the total eclipse on January 9,

---

3. Another factor is that Josephus records that Herod stayed in Jericho until his death. Herod would not have subjected himself to residing in Jericho in the intense late summer desert heat preceding September, especially since his illness made him extremely uncomfortable. In winter Jericho would have been pleasant. See also Martin, *Birth of Christ Recalculated*, pp. 50-52.

1 B.C. All the events recorded by Josephus occurring between the lunar eclipse and Passover could and do fit into this three-month time period of January 9 and Passover on April 8 in the year 1 B.C.

There is other evidence also which clearly dates that the birth of Christ occurred *after* 4 B.C. At least sixteen early Christian sources date Christ's birth after 4 B.C., the majority of which date his birth in 3 B.C.[4]

A handful of scholars from the sixteenth century to the present have asserted the authenticity of the January 9, 1 B.C. eclipse as the one Josephus recorded

---

4. Early Sources Dating Christ's Birth

Approximate Date of Source	*Source*	*Date of Christ's Birth*
180 A.D.	Irenaeus	4/3 B.C.
194 A.D.	Clement of Alexandria	3/2 B.C.
198 A.D.	Tertullian	3/2 B.C.
170-240 A.D.	Julius Africanus	3/2 B.C.
170-236 A.D.	Hippolytus of Rome	3/2 B.C.
185-253 A.D.	Origen	3/2 B.C.
325 A.D.	Eusebius of Caesarea	3/2 B.C.
490-585 A.D.	Cassiodorus Senator	3 B.C.

While it is true that early Christian writings may not be the most reliable chronological sources, when their testimonies are so consistent it certainly warrants attention and explanation, especially in this case since *no* Christian church father dates the birth of Christ before 4 B.C., and only one dates it before the Passover of April, 4 B.C. One may add to the above sources Orosius, Chrysostom, Jerome, *The Paschal Chronicle*, Hippolytus of Thebes, Photius (the Patriarch of Constantinople), Zonaras, and Bar Hebraeus (who cited Syrian, Armenian, and Greek sources), all of whom accepted a 3/2 B.C. date for Christ's birth. See Martin, *Birth of Christ Recalculated*, p. 5; Jack Finegan, *Handbook of Biblical Chronology* (Princeton: Princeton University Press, 1964), pp. 222-230.

as preceding Herod's death. Their proposal found little acceptance, because of tradition. In *The Birth of Christ Recalculated*, Ernest Martin presents material so overwhelmingly supportive of this January 9, 1 B.C. eclipse, that students and scholars have been prompted to rethink their assumptions and give the 1 B.C. date serious consideration. The evidence is impressive both historically and astronomically.

Since it has been popularly held that the March 13, 4 B.C. eclipse was the one spoken of by Josephus, most scholars and astronomers looked only at astronomical occurrences before that time in considering possibilities for "his star." Working within that time frame, the triple conjunction of Jupiter and Saturn in 7 B.C. was most impressive. Other candidates were suggested, but the triple conjunction has continued to prevail in the Christmas shows at planetariums throughout the world.[5] But by placing Herod's death early in 1 B.C., other astronomical events between 4 B.C. and 1 B.C. are now being considered by scholars and are swaying scientific thought regarding "his star."

---

5. See Appendix 1, "The Triple Planetary Conjunction of 7 B.C.," pp. 271-273

CHAPTER FOUR

ASTRONOMICAL CANDIDATES FOR "HIS STAR"

Since early 1 B.C. is the latest year in which Jesus could have been born, as Herod would still have been living prior to that time, we must now consider the earliest possible date for his birth. Scholars generally agree that any date before 7 B.C. is much too early because historical evidence cannot be reconciled with an earlier date. So using 7 B.C. to 1 B.C. as the parameters within which the birth of Christ must have fallen, we will examine astronomical events of significance between those two dates, looking for the outstanding candidate fitting the specifications of "his star." The following list catalogs noteworthy celestial occurrences of that time period.

Working within this time frame of 7 B.C. to 1 B.C. and its noteworthy astronomical occurrences, we now must narrow down the candidates by

SIGNIFICANT CELESTIAL EVENTS 7 B.C.—1 B.C.	
May 27, 7 B.C.	Jupiter and Saturn in conjunction in Pisces
Oct. 5, 7 B.C.	Jupiter and Saturn in conjunction in Pisces
Dec. 1, 7 B.C.	Jupiter and Saturn in conjunction in Pisces
Feb. 25, 6 B.C.	Massing of planets Jupiter, Saturn, and Mars in Pisces
March 5, 6 B.C.	Jupiter and Mars in conjunction in Pisces
March 23, 5 B.C.	Total lunar eclipse
March, 5 B.C.	Nova (perhaps comet) appears in Capricorn or Aquila
Sept. 15, 5 B.C.	Total lunar eclipse
March 13, 4 B.C.	Partial lunar eclipse
April, 4 B.C.	Nova (perhaps comet) appears in Aquila
Aug. 12, 3 B.C.	Jupiter and Venus in conjunction in Leo
Sept. 1, 3 B.C.	Mercury and Venus in conjunction in Leo
Sept. 14, 3 B.C.	Jupiter and Regulus in conjunction in Leo
Feb. 17, 2 B.C.	Jupiter and Regulus in conjunction in Leo
May 8, 2 B.C.	Jupiter and Regulus in conjunction in Leo
June 17, 2 B.C.	Jupiter and Venus in conjunction in Leo
Aug. 27, 2 B.C.	Massing of planets Mercury, Venus, Mars, and Jupiter in Leo
Dec. 9, 2 B.C.	Venus and Mars in conjunction in Scorpio
Jan. 9, 1 B.C.	Total lunar eclipse
Aug. 21, 1 B.C.	Jupiter and Venus in conjunction in Virgo

considering them in light of the astronomical specifications designated in Matthew 2. Since the Magi used the expression "star" to describe their astronomical observation of the birth of the Judean king, let us establish exactly what that term meant. In Biblical usage, as well as in popular modern usage, "star" could refer to any luminous body in the sky. Thus the possibilities for "his star" taken from the preceding list could include a nova, a comet, a planetary conjunction, or a planet. Each of these candidates merits consideration. However, this research work proves "his star" was the planet Jupiter.[1]

Was "his star" either a nova or a comet?

The word "nova" is a form of a Latin word meaning "new." A nova is actually a star which suddenly increases in brilliance and then gradually grows fainter. Upon seeing it flare up, the ancients thought a new star was being born, hence the name "nova." A comet is a celestial body that has a long luminous tail and travels in an orbit around the sun which may take anywhere from three to thousands of years to complete.

According to Chinese records, an unusual star appeared in the constellation of either Capricorn or

1. Other transient astronomical events such as zodiacal glow, aurora borealis, eclipses, or meteors are not significant enough to consider.

Aquila in March of 5 B.C. The sources are not clear as to whether this was a nova or comet.[2] Chinese records also indicate the appearance of another nova or comet in the constellation of Aquila in April of 4 B.C.[3]

However, because Matthew 2 specifies two appearances of the same star, these nova or comet appearances cannot qualify as "his star" as they would not be two appearances of the *same* star. They would be appearances of different stars at two different times. A nova will seldom flare up more than once, and very rarely will it repeat its initial brilliance. For these reasons, neither the appearance of a nova or comet in March of 5 B.C., nor another appearance in April of 4 B.C., qualify as the star of Matthew 2.[4]

Was "his star" a planetary conjunction?

A planetary conjunction is the aligning of either

---

2. J. Williams, *Observations of Comets from B.C. 611 to A.D. 1640* (London: Strangeways and Walden, 1871), p. 10; Hsi Tsē-tsung, "A New Catalog of Ancient Novae," *Smithsonian Contributions to Astrophysics* 2 (1958), p. 115; K. Lundmark, "The Messianic Ideas and Their Astronomical Background," *Actes du vii congrès international d'histoire des sciences, Jerusalem* 4 (1953), p. 438.

3. Williams, *Observations of Comets*, p. 10; Finegan, *Handbook of Biblical Chronology*, p. 247.

4. It is also suggested that "his star" was the comet now commonly known as "Halley's Comet" which appeared from August to October of 12 B.C. Evidence which has been put forward to support the Halley's Comet theory is that Luke 2 records an enrollment that took place under Cyrenius, which is spelled "Quirinius" in Latin. A tomb inscription from 10 B.C. refers to a man named Quirinius who sent a

two or more planets, or a planet and a star, in the same part of the heavens along the same degree of celestial longitude. When they are in conjunction, an observer can mentally draw a straight line through these celestial bodies to the celestial north pole.[5] For several days before and after a conjunction, the two bodies are approaching conjunction in the same part of the sky. A conjunction is defined not by the actual positions of heavenly bodies in their orbits around the sun, but deals only with their position in the heavens as an observer on earth views them. To an observer on earth a conjunction occurs at the point of closest approach between the two planets. Normally, two planets in conjunction are clearly distinguishable one from another. Only on extremely rare occasions are the celestial bodies so close together that the two bodies appear to merge as one. Can a conjunction or conjunctions qualify as "his star"? No. The reason being that a conjunction of two planets, even if they

---

census taker to a town in Syria to carry out a census, which may have been taken in 12 B.C. However, a detailed study in chapter 16 demonstrates that this 12 B.C. census could not have been the census of Luke 2.

The proposal that Halley's Comet was "his star" seems unlikely for two reasons: (1) a comet was traditionally regarded as an omen of evil; and (2) setting 12 B.C. as the year of Christ's birth conflicts with historical records. Although some have tried to compress historical records in order to make Christ's birth coincide with this appearance of Halley's Comet, 12 B.C. is simply far too early to synchronize with the historical record surrounding the birth of Christ.

5. See Glossary of Astronomical Names and Terms at the beginning of this book for a pictorial illustration of a conjunction.

merged one over the other, simply cannot be referred to in the singular as a "star."

Between 12 B.C. and 7 A.D. there were hundreds of planetary conjunctions and groupings. However, most of them were either too close to the sun to be observed or were not visible from the Middle East. Others were quite ordinary events that would not attract special attention. The rare triple conjunction of Jupiter and Saturn in Pisces in 7 B.C. was most remarkable, but chronologically would not fit the historical record of events surrounding Christ's birth.

Was "his star" a planet?

The possibility of "his star" being a planet is the most likely. The celestial body whose activity the Magi observed definitely was in motion in the heavens. Stars, used in the strict sense of the word, appear fixed in relation to each other because they are in distant space. The planets of our solar system were termed "wandering stars" (Greek: *planētes asteres*). Planets are so close to us that we are able to follow their motions. A planet in its activity would attract far more attention than a fixed star in distant space. Thus a planet merits our full attention as a candidate for "his star."

Writers have dealt at length with the spiritual significance of the constellations and their respective stars, but little has been said of the significance of the planets from a Biblical point of view. This subject is beset with difficulties because of the numerous meanings which have been assigned to the planets over the centuries. But once one realizes that the planets do have a genuine Godly significance and importance and that this significance must fit within the framework of God's Word, one can begin to work this subject accurately as we consider planets as candidates for "his star."

Mercury, the planet closest to the sun, has long been characterized as the messenger god, the one who delivers messages. In Acts 14:12 Paul as the chief speaker is called Mercurius. This same characteristic of being a message-bearer is attributed to Gabriel, God's archangel, whom God sent to Mary in Nazareth in Luke 1:26.

Venus, the next closest planet to the sun, is known in astronomy as the morning star because of its prominent position and brightness in the dawn sky. Biblically, it is associated with Jesus Christ, "the bright and morning star" in Revelation 22:16.

Mars, the first planet farther away from the sun than Earth is in mythology associated with war. In its genuine spiritual light this characteristic is best seen in the Archangel Michael, whom God commissions to stand and fight for His people. He is spoken of as standing for God's people in Daniel 12:1, and as fighting the Devil in Revelation 12:7.

Still farther away from the sun than Mars is

Jupiter. In mythology Jupiter was the father of gods, the ruler, the king who reigned over all else. Jupiter was associated with royalty. Interestingly, the Hebrew name for the planet Jupiter is *ssedeq*, meaning "righteousness." The Messiah who would come from David's genetic line was to be the "righteous Branch," according to Jeremiah 23:5, who would reign as a king and execute righteousness. His name would be called "the Lord our Righteousness" (Jeremiah 23:5 and 6; Jeremiah 33:15 and 16). Thus Jupiter has characteristics that would associate it with the Messiah, the Christ.

Saturn's significant associations have been obscured more than others, although Saturn is identified as the god responsible for agriculture and the harvest. In astrological lore, Saturn is an evil star signifying death and darkness. Likewise in Jewish tradition, its usual signification is negative, for it is associated with death, destruction, weeping, and grief. It was felt to have a hindering and inhibitive force in its negative aspect, especially when in conjunction with another planet.[6] Perhaps here is a clue to its association with Satan, the fallen archangel. The similarity between the names "Saturn" and "Satan" point to a possible common etymological origin.

---

6. Joel C. Dobin, *To Rule Both Day and Night: Astrology in the Bible, Midrash, and Talmud* (New York: Inner Traditions International, 1977), pp. 79, 166.

No ancient beliefs surrounded Uranus, Neptune, and Pluto, the three remaining planets in our solar system, because being invisible to the naked eye, they were unknown to the ancients.

The above associations and meanings proposed for the planets cannot be affirmed with finality. However, they are very interesting when viewed in a Biblical light.

Could the planet Jupiter be "his star"?

For many years scholars discounted or ignored the outstanding celestial activities of Jupiter in 3 B.C. and 2 B.C. because of their assumption that Herod died in the spring of 4 B.C., shortly after the March 13 eclipse. Thus, only notable astronomical phenomena occurring before 4 B.C. were seriously considered as candidates for "his star." Under those conditions, a triple conjunction of Jupiter and Saturn visible in 7 B.C. was the most viable candidate. Now that it has been demonstrated that the eclipse recorded by Josephus was on January 9, 1 B.C., instead of March 13, 4 B.C., the final proposal that merits our consideration is that Jupiter is "his star," the star of the Messiah, the promised seed. This corresponds to the Biblical description of the star in Matthew 2 as well as with historical details recorded in the Word of God. In looking at the list on page 32 regarding significant celestial events, one is immediately struck by the observation that the planet Jupiter is common to most of these noteworthy astronomical events occurring between May 27, 7 B.C. and August 27, 2 B.C. The following table lists ten conjunctions involving Jupiter with other celestial bodies between these two dates.

What is so remarkable about Jupiter's being "his star"? Jupiter is the largest planet in our solar system, and associated by the ancients with kings. It was the "king planet," a royal planet of great significance.[7]

Since Jupiter was in the sky every night, there must have been some special indication heralding the birth not only of any king, but specifically of a Judean king. If Jupiter were "his star," the fact that the Magi came in search of one who was "born king of the Judeans" indicates that Jupiter must have appeared in a position significant of Judea.

In August of 3 B.C. Jupiter first became visible above the eastern horizon as a morning star. In Matthew 2:2, the Magi referred to this initial appearance when they said they saw it "in the rising." However, they did not immediately leave for Jerusalem on this appearance. It was the extraordinary chain of six major astronomical events involving Jupiter in the constellation Leo that intensified the

---

7. *Encyclopaedia Britannica*, 1954 ed., s.v. "Jupiter." Also see Martin, "Jupiter—The Planet of the Messiah," *Birth of Christ Recalculated*, Appendix III, pp. 173-177.

SIGNIFICANT CONJUNCTIONS OF JUPITER WITH OTHER CELESTIAL BODIES NEAR THE TIME OF CHRIST

DATE	EVENT	DEGREE OF SEPARATION*
May 27, 7 B.C.	Jupiter and Saturn in conjunction in the constellation Pisces	.99
Oct. 5, 7 B.C.	Jupiter and Saturn in conjunction in the constellation Pisces	.99
Dec. 1, 7 B.C.	Jupiter and Saturn in conjunction in the constellation Pisces	.99
March 5, 6 B.C.	Jupiter and Mars in conjunction in the constellation Pisces	.80
Aug. 12, 3 B.C.	Jupiter and Venus in conjunction in the constellation Leo	.23
Sept. 14, 3 B.C.	Jupiter and the star Regulus in conjunction in the constellation Leo	.63
Feb. 17, 2 B.C.	Jupiter and the star Regulus in conjunction in the constellation Leo	1.19
May 8, 2 B.C.	Jupiter and the star Regulus in conjunction in the constellation Leo	1.06
June 17, 2 B.C.	Jupiter and Venus in conjunction in the constellation Leo	.04
Aug. 27, 2 B.C.	Jupiter and Mars in conjunction in the constellation Leo	.14

NOTE: This table's calculations are derived from computer-based tables compiled by Bryant Tuckerman, perhaps the most accurate source for such calculations. See Bryant Tuckerman, *Planetary, Lunar, and Solar Positions: 601 B.C. to A.D. 1969 at Five-Day and Ten-Day Intervals*, 2 vols. (Philadelphia: American Philosophical Society, 1962).

*To give an idea of the distance of separation between the celestial bodies during these conjunctions, .50 degrees is approximately equivalent to the apparent diameter of the moon.

significance of this appearance to the Magi and from which they concluded that the king of the Judeans had been born.

On August 12, 3 B.C., at 5 A.M., Jupiter came into a very close conjunction with Venus in the eastern sky (fig. 1). The spiritual significance of this was that Jupiter, the planet of royalty and kingship, was in conjunction with Venus, a planet that is Biblically used for the Messiah in the expression "the bright and morning star." Furthermore, this conjunction was in the constellation of Leo, the sign of the lion, the constellation associated with the tribe of Judah. And as we know from Jacob's prophecy recorded in Genesis 49, the Messiah was to come out of Judah as the ruler of Israel. So on August 12, 3 B.C., the royal planet of Jupiter was not only in conjunction with Venus, the bright and morning star, but in the constellation of Leo, the constellation which represented the rulership of Judah.

Almost a month later, on September 14, 3 B.C., Jupiter came into conjunction with the star Regulus (fig. 2).[8] Regulus is the brightest star of the constellation Leo and is traditionally called "the heart of the lion" since it is situated in that general area of the

8. Although from an astronomical point of view the conjunction technically occurred on September 14, Jupiter's slow movement and the angle of observation would have made a conjunction apparent to any observer as early as September 12 before dawn. This may be significant in light of an astronomical event which occurred during the day and evening of September 11 which we will study later.

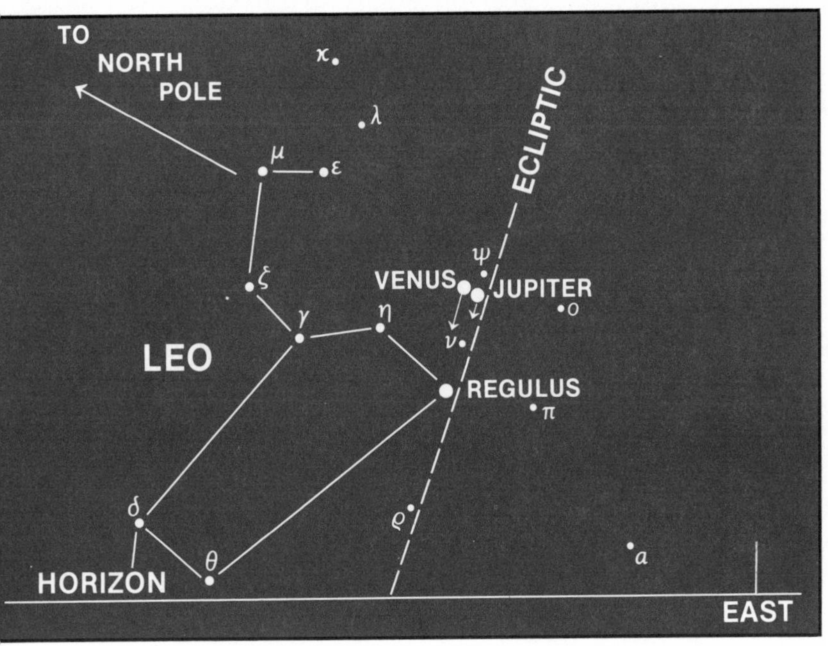

Fig. 1. Jupiter and Venus in Conjunction in Leo
5:00 A.M., August 12, 3 B.C.

This diagram shows what an observer, standing near the latitude of Palestine or Persia, would see facing east on the date August 12, 3 B.C. at 5:00 A.M. The horizontal line represents the horizon, and due east is the small vertical line marked on the horizon. Therefore, Leo at 5:00 A.M. was rising somewhat north of east. Lines connect the major stars that outline the constellation of Leo, and certain other stars are indicated for more completeness (astronomical practice marks the brighter stars in a constellation by Greek letters). The ecliptic is the path the sun moves through in its annual motion. The sun passed through Leo from July 9 until August 17 in Christ's time. Presently it moves through Leo a month later. The direction to the north pole is indicated by the arrow. Arrows are drawn projecting from the planets to indicate the relative direction and speed of their motion.

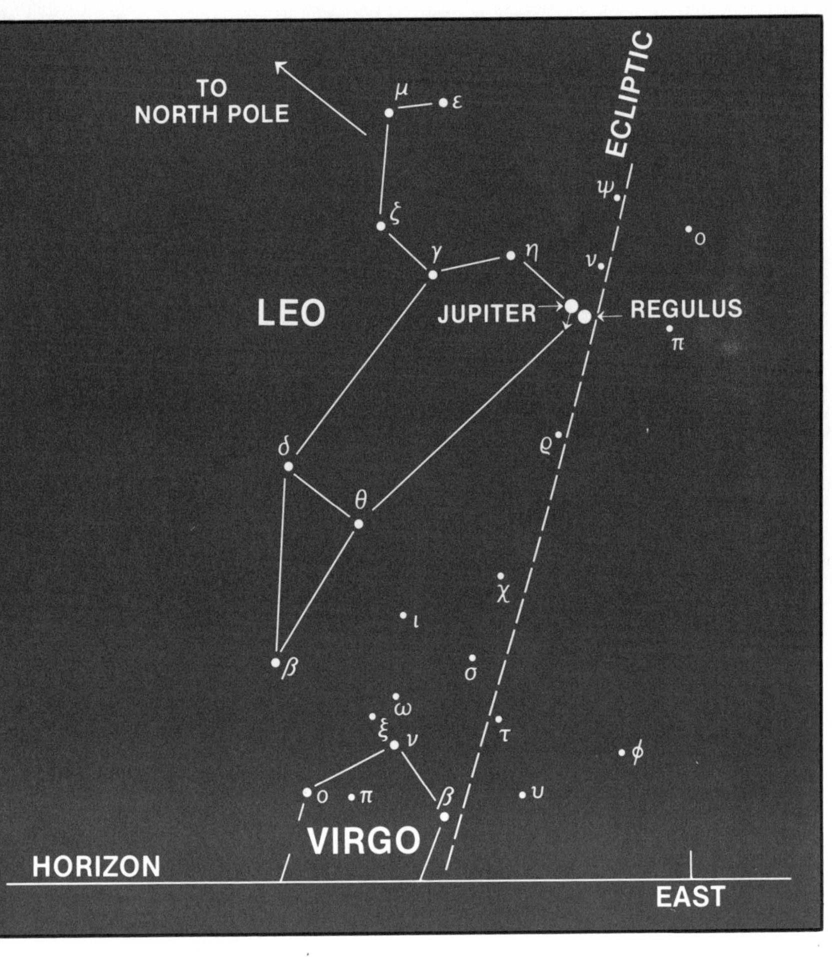

Fig. 2. Jupiter and Regulus in Conjunction in Leo
4:00 A.M., September 14, 3 B.C.

configuration in that constellation. In antiquity Regulus was known as the king star, being associated with rulership and dominion, just as Jupiter was the king planet. Thus on September 14, 3 B.C., the king planet and the king star were in conjunction in the constellation Leo. Looking at figure 2, we see that the view to the observer was similar to that which was seen in August, the month before, but now Leo was higher in the sky, so that by 4:00 A.M., Leo was already well above the horizon, with the first stars of the constellation Virgo beginning to rise.

Five months later, on February 17, 2 B.C., Jupiter and Regulus again came into conjunction in Leo (fig. 3). By early morning, Leo was setting in the west, so that figure 3 shows the horizon with Leo setting somewhat north of due west. The conjunction was not the only astronomical phenomenon at this time—the moon slowly moved into position between Jupiter and Regulus, and literally covered Regulus in a phenomenon called an occultation. This was indeed a momentous event.

A third Jupiter-Regulus conjunction occurred on May 8, 2 B.C. (fig. 4). On this date, Leo was setting in the western sky in the hours prior to midnight. A crescent moon was also visible at this time ahead of Leo, closer to the horizon.

With Jupiter, the planet signifying royalty, and Regulus, the king star of the constellation Leo, coming into conjunction three times in the space of eight months, the Magi in observing Jupiter's celestial travels would have had much to consider as to its spiritual significance.

On June 17, 2 B.C., Jupiter and Venus came into conjunction again. Between their initial conjunction ten months before in August and this one, Venus had disappeared into the light of the sun, but reemerged in the west as an evening star, and slowly began progressing east toward Jupiter, which was slowly traveling west. The two planets were on a remarkable course toward each other, as if for a planned rendezvous. Thus, on the evening of June 17, 2 B.C., Jupiter and Venus met in the western sky (fig. 5). The conjunction occurred at the same time the full moon appeared in the eastern sky. This Jupiter-Venus conjunction was rare indeed, for the two planets were separated by only .04 degrees. To the human eye they appeared to merge into one as a brilliant, dazzling star. Thus, the two brightest planets in the heavens, the king planet and the bright and morning star planet, both of which are scripturally symbolic of the Messiah, had joined together in what was a truly spectacular celestial event. And, as the final crowning point, the conjunction occurred in the constellation of Leo, the lion, the ruler of Israel.

Finally, on August 27, 2 B.C., Jupiter came into a very close conjunction with Mars in the constellation Leo at the same time that Mercury and Venus

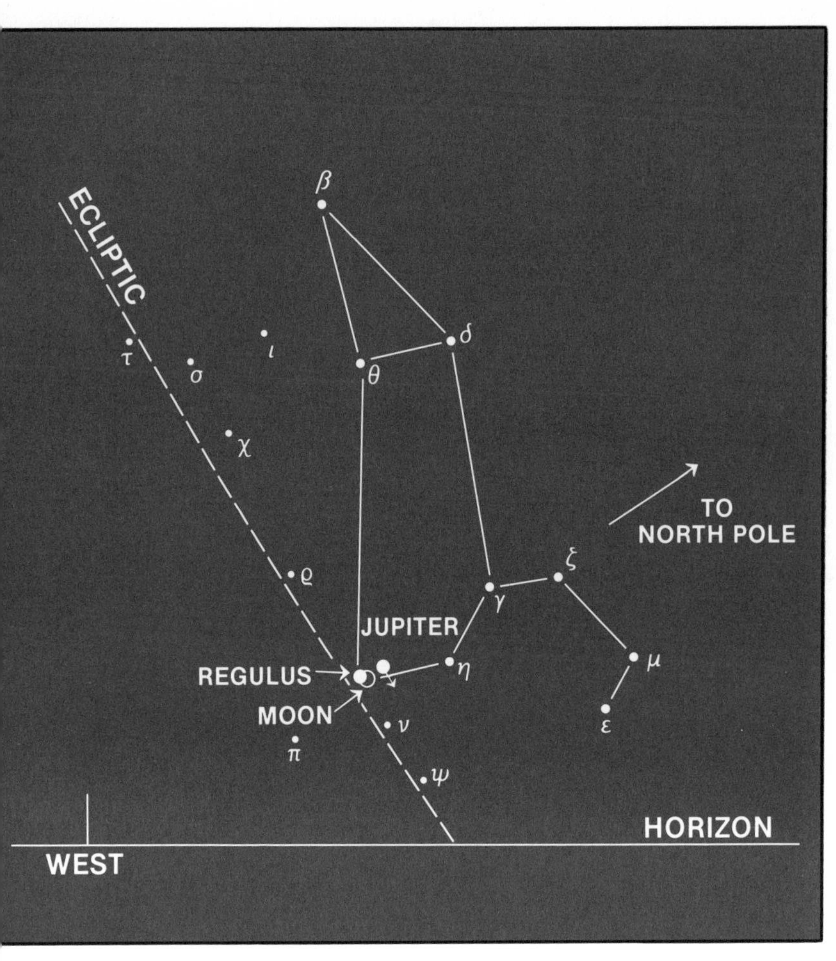

Fig. 3. Jupiter and Regulus in Conjunction in Leo
4:30 A.M., February 17, 2 B.C.

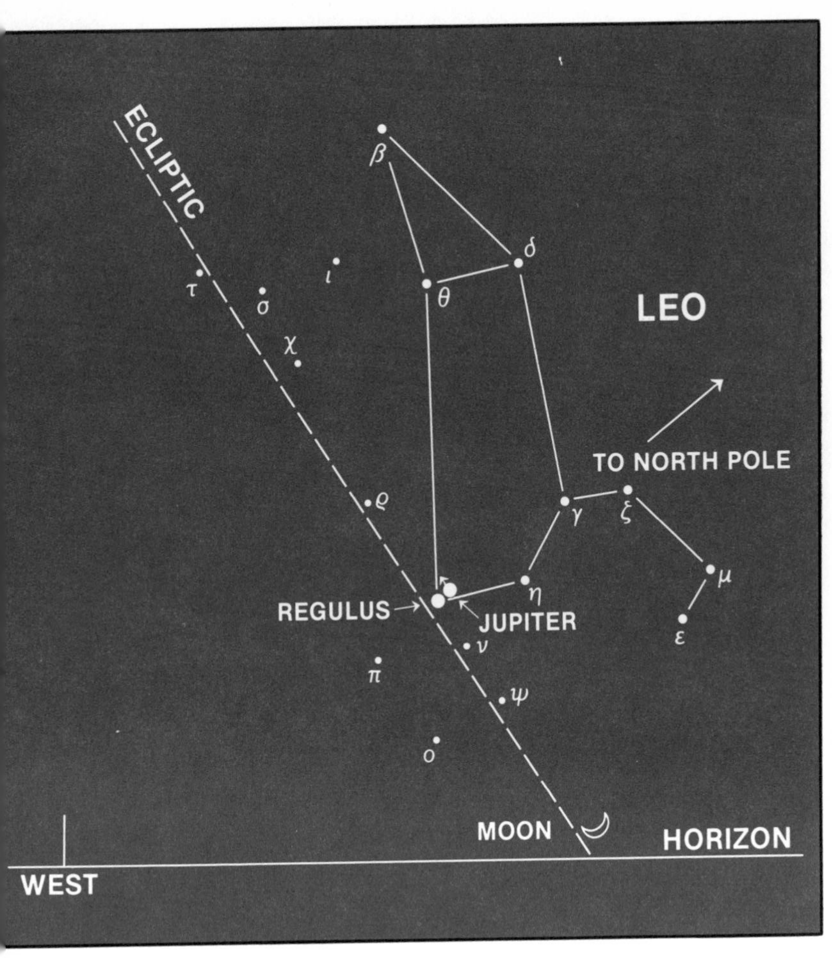

Fig. 4. Jupiter and Regulus in Conjunction in Leo
11 P.M., May 8, 2 B.C.

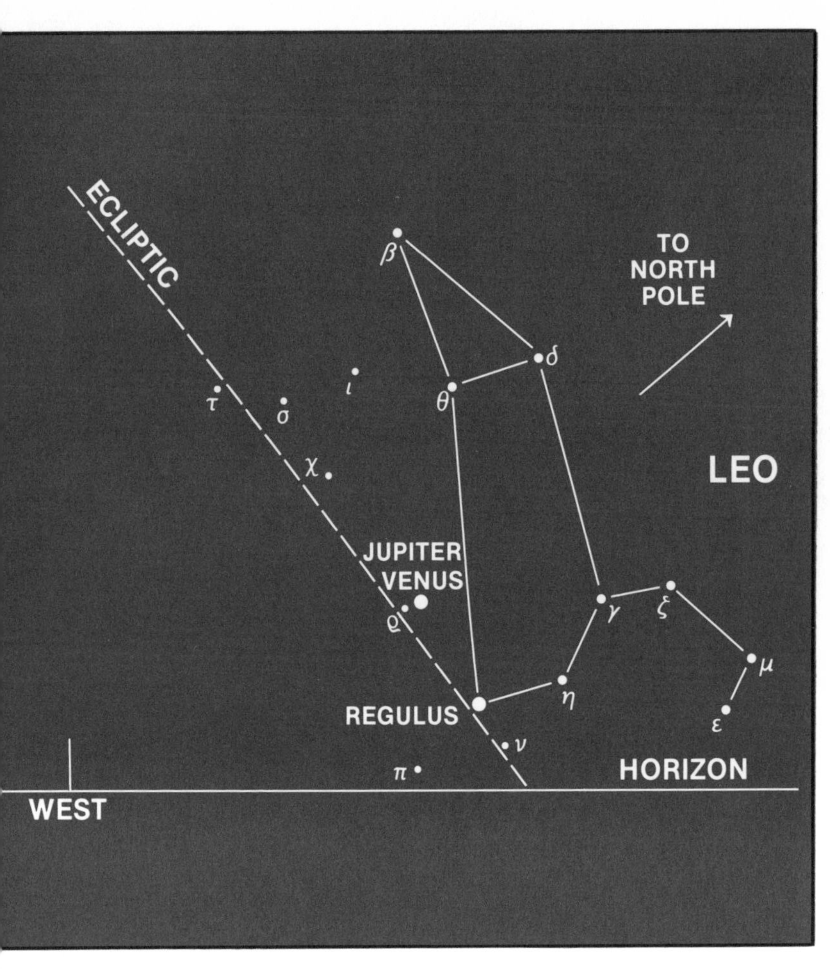

Fig. 5. Jupiter and Venus in Conjunction in Leo
9:30 P.M., June 17, 2 B.C.

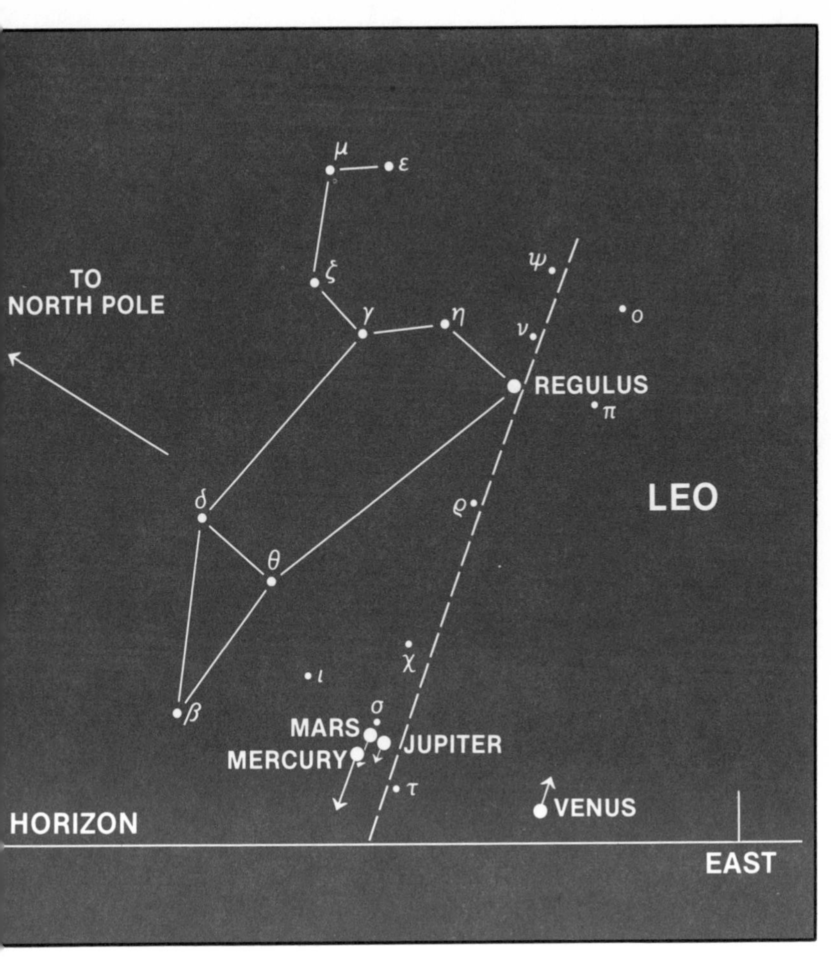

Fig. 6. Massing of Planets Jupiter, Mars, Mercury, and Venus in Leo (Jupiter and Mars in Conjunction) 5:00 A.M., August 27, 2 B.C.

were also visible in that constellation (fig. 6). All this was observable in the early morning in the eastern sky, just as the first conjunction which had occurred in Leo over a year before (see fig. 1 for August 12, 3 B.C. conjunction).

The six astronomical events in Leo that captured the Magi's attention were the following:

1. Jupiter and Venus in conjunction in Leo: August 12, 3 B.C.
2. Jupiter and Regulus in conjunction in Leo: September 14, 3 B.C.
3. Jupiter and Regulus in conjunction in Leo: February 17, 2 B.C.
4. Jupiter and Regulus in conjunction in Leo: May 8, 2 B.C.
5. Jupiter and Venus in conjunction in Leo: June 17, 2 B.C.
6. Massing of planets Jupiter, Mars, Mercury, and Venus in Leo (Jupiter and Mars in conjunction): August 27, 2 B.C.

The final conjunction in Leo with its massing of four planets convinced the Magi that a king had been born in Judea. They began their journey to Jerusalem to find the "king of the Judeans" soon after this event.

When all of these astronomical events are considered in light of God's Word, the proposal of

Jupiter as "his star" is the clear and only true choice. Its royal significance, its Messianic associations, and its repeated appearances in astronomically and scripturally meaningful positions conform to the record in God's Word of the birth of the promised seed.

CHAPTER FIVE

JUPITER AND THE MAGI

The first recorded appearance of "his star" in Matthew 2:2 was "in the rising." This would be in accordance with Jupiter's initial appearance in the eastern morning sky in August, 3 B.C. It is this first appearance of Jupiter that the Magi referred to in Matthew 2:2: "we have seen his star in the east." Ancient astronomers in the course of their regular observations always noted the date a star or planet *first* appeared above the eastern horizon at dawn, called the heliacal rising.

> Matthew 2:2:
> Saying, Where is he that is born King of the Jews [Judeans]? for we have seen his star in the east [in the rising], and are come to worship him.

Watching Jupiter closely after its heliacal rising in August, 3 B.C., the observant Magi began to realize the significance of what they were seeing. A king had been born (Jupiter-Regulus conjunction), a king that would come out of Judah (Leo). This was the long-promised king of the Judeans, the Messiah. He would be the bright and morning star (Venus) for whom mankind had waited for centuries. When this realization flowed together in their understanding, the Magi prepared to travel westward to Judea. Certainly the awesome massing of the planets in August of 2 B.C. was the final motivation.

Because ancient astronomers paid particular attention to the planets when in retrograde motion, which is when they appear to change direction,[1] the Magi would have carefully noted this in Jupiter in 2 B.C. Jupiter went into retrograde motion on November 29, 3 B.C. and on March 29, 2 B.C. (fig. 7). When these motions were followed by continued significant configurations, such as the Jupiter-Venus conjunction in June of 2 B.C. and the massing of the planets in August of 2 B.C., it is understandable that the Magi would conclude with certainty the astronomical message that was being given.

Prompted by this overwhelming evidence, the Magi left their homeland and traveled to Jerusalem. There they received instructions from Herod to seek the child in Bethlehem, only five miles directly south of Jerusalem.[2]

---

1. A. Aaboe, "Scientific Astronomy in Antiquity," in *The Place of Astronomy in the Ancient World*, ed. F.R. Hodson, organized by D.G. Kendall, et al. (London: Oxford University Press, 1974), pp. 21-42.
2. The Magi's arrival in Jerusalem and their dealing with Herod as told in Matthew 2:1-9 is examined in detail in chapter 17, "The Magi," pp. 229-248.

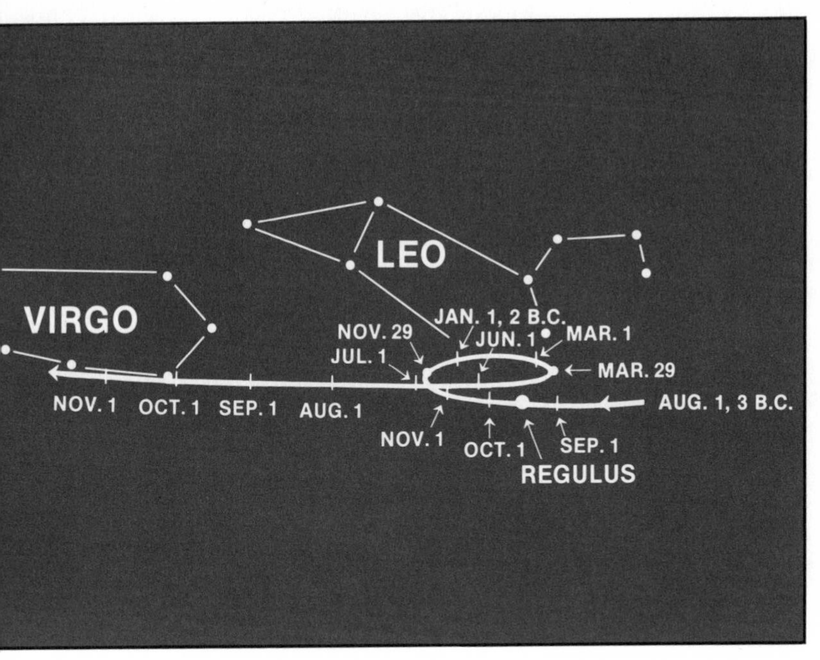

Fig. 7. Path of Jupiter
August, 3 B.C.—November, 2 B.C.

Expanded vertical scale to indicate retrograde motion.

Matthew 2:9:
When they had heard the king [Herod], they departed; and, lo, the star, which they saw in the east, went before them, till it came and stood over where the young child was.

As the Magi left Jerusalem, they saw go before them the same star, Jupiter, which they had seen in the rising. As they traveled south, the star "went before them, till it came and stood" over Bethlehem. How could "his star" so clearly point out Bethlehem to the Magi? There is an astronomical explanation for such a seemingly phenomenal event.

All the visible stars and planets appear to an observer on earth to move westward during the course of a night, similar to the motion of the sun during the day. A star or planet will reach its highest point when it arrives on the meridian, directly south of the observer in the northern hemisphere. This is similar to the sun when it reaches its highest point during the day at noon, when it is on the same meridian as the observer; from this point on, the sun begins to descend in the western half of the sky.

As the Magi left Jerusalem, they saw Jupiter on its nightly course. Looking south they saw it high in the sky, nearing its apex on the meridian of Jerusalem and Bethlehem. As learned astronomers, they knew that Jupiter would slowly progress to its meridian. Indeed, as they traveled, they could see Jupiter slowly moving in the direction of Bethlehem. The very star they had seen "in the rising," which had inspired their journey to Judea, the star they had seen in so many notable configurations—the king planet—was now confirming their destination by approaching its meridian as they traveled towards it.

As the Magi approached Bethlehem (fig. 8), Jupiter finally "stood over" where the child was, the area of Bethlehem. The time period in which the Magi traveled to Bethlehem could only have been between December 4, 2 B.C., when Jupiter could be seen in this position over Bethlehem, and before January 9, 1 B.C., when the events surrounding the death of Herod began. The words "stood over" do not necessarily mean Jupiter stopped; they mean the star had reached its highest point, or "stood." In beholding "his star" as it stood over Bethlehem, the Magi were thrilled with unspeakable joy that they would soon find the one they had come searching for: the king of the Judeans whose star they had seen in the rising, yes, the promised seed.

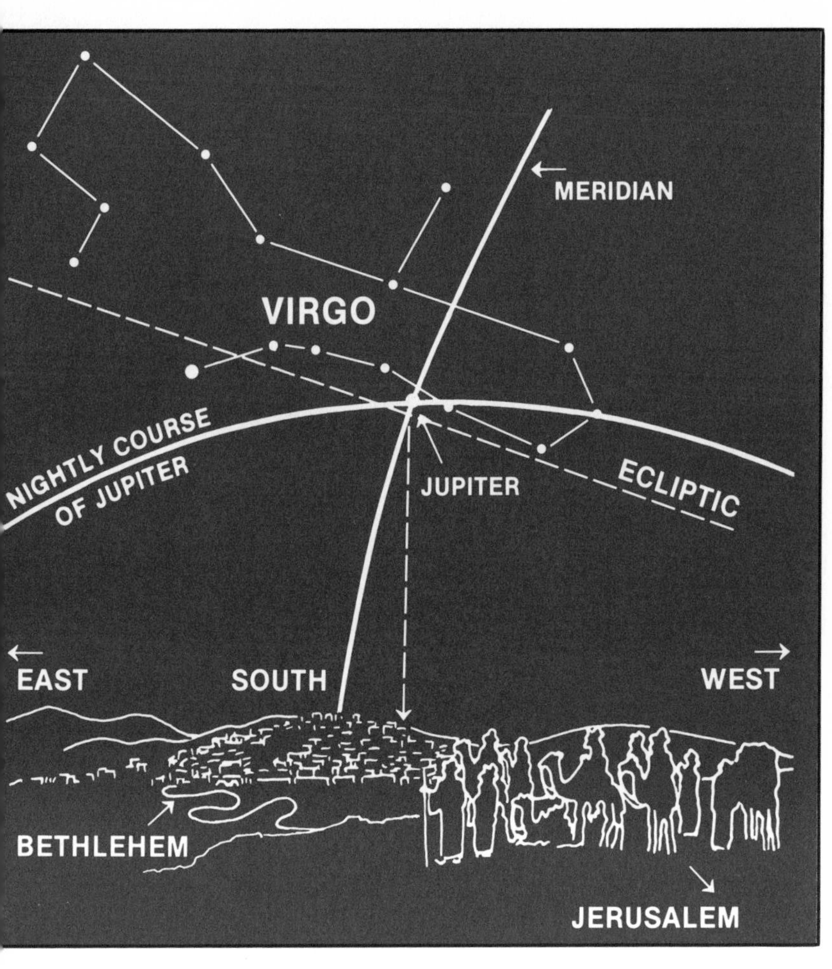

Fig. 8. Magi Approach Bethlehem
6:30 A.M., December, 2 B.C.

CHAPTER SIX

DAY AND TIME OF DAY OF CHRIST'S BIRTH

It is established that the eclipse recorded in Josephus occurred on January 9, 1 B.C., and that it was not long before this that Herod interviewed the Magi concerning the appearance of the star (December of 2 B.C.). When Herod discovered that the Magi would not be returning, he arranged to have the children in Bethlehem killed, and specified that they must be "two years old and under, according to the time which he had diligently inquired of the wise men," Matthew 2:16 tells us. Herod would not have specified two years as the upper limit unless he knew from his diligent inquiry of the Magi that the child was born during 3 B.C.

Biblical, historical, and astronomical evidence converge on 3 B.C. as the year of Jesus Christ's birth. Building on this information of 3 B.C. as the year of Christ's birth, we can look at additional Biblical and astronomical testimony and determine with precision the date of Christ's birth to the day and the hour. The twelfth chapter of the Book of Revelation presents essential information for pinpointing this exact time.

> Revelation 12:1-5:
> And there appeared a great wonder in heaven; a woman clothed with the sun, and the moon under her feet, and upon her head a crown of twelve stars:
> And she being with child cried, travailing in birth, and pained to be delivered.
> And there appeared another wonder in heaven; and behold a great red dragon, having seven heads and ten horns, and seven crowns upon his heads.
> And his tail drew the third part of the stars of heaven, and did cast them to the earth: and the dragon stood before the woman which was ready to be delivered, for to devour her child as soon as it was born.
> And she brought forth a man child, who was to rule all nations with a rod of iron: and her child was caught up unto God, and *to* his throne.

Here in Revelation 12, events past and future are revealed regarding the spiritual warfare between the true God and the Devil. This passage describes a vision which God gave the Apostle John. The vision involves symbols and words full of great truths. Their meaning can be recaptured by a diligent search of God's Word: first and foremost in the written Word and secondarily in the Word written in the stars. Parallel truths can be found in both. This entire passage in Revelation 12 takes on a profoundly significant dimension when analyzed in terms of astronomy.

Revelation 12:1 says, "there appeared a great wonder in heaven." The word "wonder" is the Greek word *sēmeion*. In Greek literature *sēmeion* is used of any kind of sign, but a notable usage is in reference to a sign of the zodiac. This is particularly interesting in the context of Revelation 12 for the sign is said to have appeared "in heaven."

The sign spoken of in verse 1 is a woman. And the only sign of the zodiac that could correspond to this description is the constellation Virgo.[1]

Revelation 12 further specifies that the woman was "clothed with the sun," another celestial body. The sun, as it appears to travel through the ecliptic each year, enters into the mid-body between the neck and the knees of the constellation Virgo, "clothing" her "with the sun," for approximately a twenty-day period. So this one astronomical detail shown in John's vision narrows down the astronomical event he is describing to a twenty-day period during any given year. In the year 3 B.C. the sun was in this position from August 27 through September 15.

The woman in Revelation 12 was not only "clothed

---

1. The woman of Revelation 12:1-5 is described as having a crown of twelve stars on her head. This reference to Virgo as the initial sign of the zodiac indicates her headship of the other eleven signs of the zodiac. See Bullinger, *Witness of the Stars*, pp. 20-22; Seiss, *Gospel in the Stars*, p. 27.

with the sun," but also the moon was "under her feet." With these two specific details, the sun and moon found in Virgo, we can be very precise in our computation of time. In 3 B.C. this configuration of the sun and moon in Virgo occurred on one day only, and that was September 11 (fig. 9).

This configuration of the sun and the moon in the constellation Virgo was observable in Palestine between sunset and moonset, this twilight period being called "night."[2] On September 11, 3 B.C., sunset was at 6:18 P.M. and moonset at 7:39 P.M. Based on the information given in Revelation 12, it was during this eighty-one-minute period that Jesus Christ took his first breath of life and became a living soul, even as Adam did in Genesis 2:7, perhaps even at the beginning of this new day. The description given in Revelation 12:1 exactly chronicles the astronomical occurrence of the evening of September 11, 3 B.C.

Verse 2 of Revelation 12 describes the woman as being in labor, ready to give birth. Verses 3 and 4 recount symbolically the Adversary's fall from heaven and his plan to slay the child as soon as he was born. In verses 4 and 5 the woman's labor finishes and the child is brought forth. Verse 5 refers to the child's birth and ascension to God's throne. Clearly, from

2. This timing is in agreement with the Gospel of Luke in placing Jesus' birth at night. Luke 2:8 says the shepherds watched their flock by night at the time of Jesus' birth.

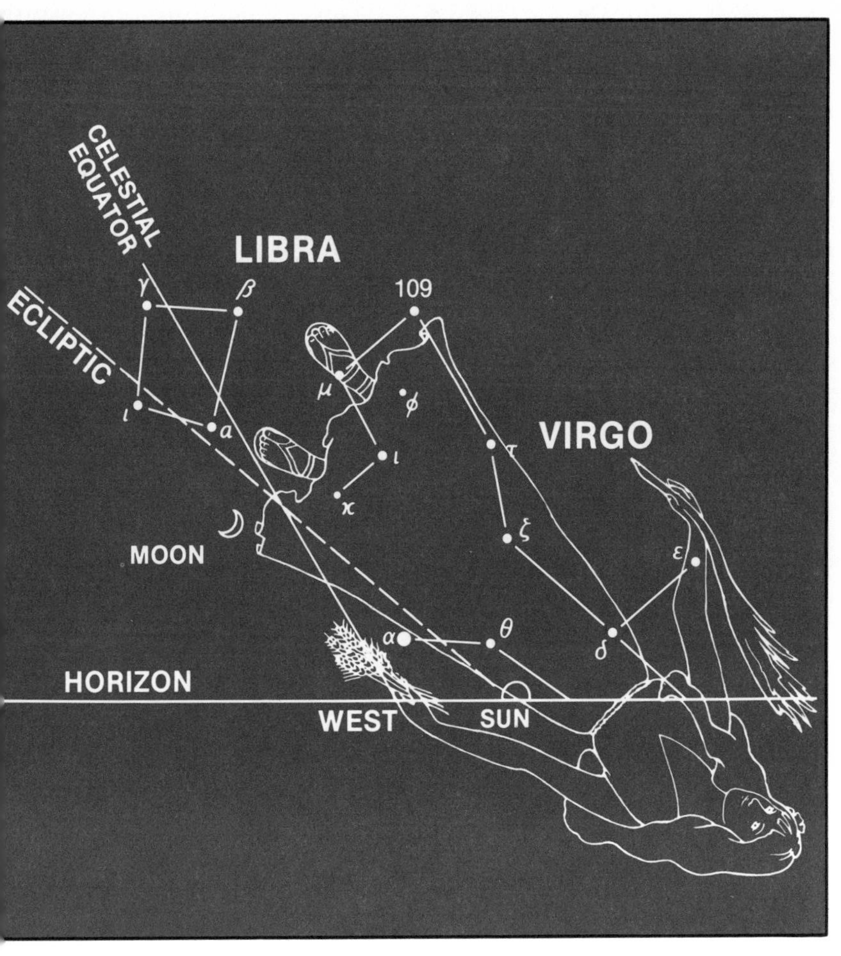

Fig. 9. The "Great Wonder" of Revelation 12:1
Sunset, 6:18 P.M., September 11, 3 B.C.

The diagram shows the sun half-way set. The sun is on the ecliptic, the dotted line, and the solid line is the celestial equator, which is directly overhead at the earth's equator. At this point, the first thin crescent of the moon appears, marking the first of the new month, Tishri.

all these specifics the child can be none other than the Christ, the Messiah, the promised seed.[3]

As if this were not enough evidence, there was yet another significant astronomical display on September 11, 3 B.C. From sunset of September 11 to sunset of September 12 was one day on the Hebrew calendar. Not only did the sign of Revelation 12:1 occur then, but also on this very day Jupiter and Regulus could be seen approaching conjunction before dawn. Although the precise astronomical conjunction occurred on September 14 (fig. 2), the angle of observation and Jupiter's slow apparent motion would have made their close rendezvous obvious as early as the predawn hours of Thursday, September 12, within hours of the Messiah's birth. At this time the king planet (Jupiter) could be seen approaching the king star (Regulus) in the constellation of Leo, the sign of Judah from whose seed the Messiah, the promised seed, the ultimate ruler, came.

According to chronological tables, September 11,

---

3. This heavenly sign mentioned in Revelation 12 should not be confused with "his star," Jupiter, described by the Magi in Matthew 2:2 and 9, although both signs heralded the Messiah's birth. The sign of Revelation 12:1 occurred on the very night of Jesus' birth, when the woman Mary labored and brought him forth, whereas the Magi were observing Jupiter in many significant positions both before and after the birth. Because the sun's entering into Virgo is a normal yearly occurrence, the sun's passing through Virgo in the year of Christ's birth would not have necessarily caught the Magi's attention. It is with the hindsight offered by Revelation 12 that we can see the significance of the activity in Virgo that day.

3 B.C. fell on a Wednesday.[4] Jesus Christ was born on the Hebrew day corresponding to our sunset September 11, Wednesday. Therefore Jesus Christ was born on Wednesday, September 11, 3 B.C., between 6:18 and 7:39 P.M., Palestine time.

September 11 may appear to be of no particular significance to us, but in Biblical and Hebrew reckoning, this month and day held a special significance. On the evening of what we would call September 11, 3 B.C., the new moon first became visible in the west shortly after sunset. Since the Hebrew calendar months began on the evening that the new moon appeared, the evening of September 11 was the first day of a new month. The evening of September 11 to the evening of September 12 in 3 B.C. was the first day of the seventh month, the month of Tishri.

Hence, in Biblical terminology, Jesus was born on the first of Tishri, between 6:18 and 7:39 P.M. On this night the remarkable astronomical configuration described in Revelation 12:1 occurred: Virgo, the Woman, was clothed with the sun and the moon rested under her feet.

---

4. William D. Stahlman and Owen Gingerich, *Solar and Planetary Longitudes for Years -2500 to +2000 by 10-Day Intervals* (Madison: University of Wisconsin Press, 1963), pp. XIII, 307.

CHAPTER SEVEN

THE SIGNIFICANCE OF TISHRI 1

God's timetable is never haphazard or coincidental. Since Jesus was born on Tishri 1 of the Hebrew calendar, it behooves us to check every possible source to determine the significance of that date. Many people are aware that Tishri 1, *Rosh Ha-Shanah* (Rosh Hashanah), is the New Year's Day on the calendar of modern Judaism. But further research needs to be done to search out the significance of this date from a Biblical and historical point of view.

In Exodus 12:2 it is recorded that God told Moses that a springtime month called Nisan "*shall be* unto you the beginning of months." Before this time another month was considered the first month. Evidence shows that originally the first month was Tishri.

According to Genesis 7:11, the flood began on the seventeenth day of the second month. The second month in Noah's time, according to Josephus and others, was Marcheshvan.[1] Furthermore, Josephus states that this reckoning was used by the Israelites in Egypt.[2] Since the month of Marcheshvan follows Tishri on the Judean calendar, it is axiomatic that Tishri was the first month on Noah's calendar and the calendar of Israel before the Exodus.

Genesis 8:13 indicates that Noah entered his six-hundred-first year of life on Tishri 1. Unless Noah had been born on Tishri 1, we can conclude that age reckoning was done from New Year's Day to New Year's Day, Tishri 1 to Tishri 1.[3] This would make sense if the first man, Adam, had been formed, made, and created in Tishri. Old rabbinical tradition said Tishri 1 was the first day of creation.[4] Although consideration must be given to possible exaggeration and guesswork in such a tradition, it is

---

1. Josephus is substantiated on this point by the Aramaic Targum known as Targum Jonathan. The Targum comments of Genesis 7:11 that the second month was Marcheshvan, making Tishri the first month. The Targum notes, of I Kings 8:2, that Tishri was the first month of the year prior to the exodus from Egypt. See *The Jewish Encyclopedia*, 1901-1906 ed., s.v. "New Year," by J.D. Eisenstein; and Abraham P. Bloch, *The Biblical and Historical Background of the Jewish Holy Days* (New York: KTAV, 1978), p. 18.
2. Josephus *Antiquities* 1.3.3.
3. If Tishri were the first month on Noah's calendar, Nisan must have been the seventh month. Genesis 8:4 says the ark came to a rest on the seventeenth day of the seventh month, Nisan 17. This is the exact date centuries later of Jesus Christ's resurrection. See Wierwille, "The Eighteenth of Nisan," *Jesus Christ Our Passover*, pp. 311-348.
4. *Rosh Ha-Shanah* IIa. According to M'Clintock and Strong's *Cyclopaedia*, Tishri 1 "came to be regarded as the birthday of the world" (10:568). Theodor H. Gaster, in his *Festivals of the Jewish Year*

quite plausible and probable that the six days of Genesis 1 occurred in Tishri.

When God instructed Moses, according to Exodus 12, to change the calendar so that the spring month of Nisan would become the first month, the other Hebrew months were consistently renumbered making Tishri the seventh month.[5] Although Tishri was no longer the first month, Tishri 1 retained many of its New Year characteristics, which is not surprising or unusual. Since its founding, the United States has had January, the first month, as the beginning of the calendar year; yet July, the seventh month, has been for the United States government the official beginning of the fiscal year. The situation in Israel after Exodus 12 was similar.

In commenting on the calendar change of Exodus 12, Josephus states that Nisan was made the

---

states, "Judaism regards New Year's Day [Tishri 1] not merely as an anniversary of creation—but more importantly—as a renewal of it. This is when the world is reborn" (p. 109). Alfred Edersheim in his *The Temple: Its Ministry and Services* (reprint ed., Grand Rapids: Wm. B. Eerdmans, 1958), p. 295 fn., states, "The Jews hold that the world was created in the month Tishri."

5. According to traditional reckoning, the Hebrew and Babylonian months began at the time the new moon was visible. Therefore, the two calendars would often correspond. But the intercalary months were added differently in Judea so that the barley harvest would not come too early or too late for the wave offering at Passover time. As a result, the Hebrew first month would occasionally begin one month earlier than the first month on the Babylonian calendar. See Richard A. Parker and Waldo H. Dubberstein, *Babylonian Chronology 626 B.C.—A.D. 45*, 2d ed. (Chicago: University of Chicago Press, 1946), pp. 1,4, 23,24; Finegan, *Handbook of Biblical Chronology*, pp. 33-40.

first month of the sacred year, especially as it related to the religious festivals, since Passover and the Feast of Unleavened Bread were celebrated then. Tishri, seven months later, culminated the festal period of the year with the final harvests and the Feast of Tabernacles (Leviticus 23).[6]

While God was establishing a new calendar order to Moses, He commanded that Tishri 1 be designated as the Day of Trumpets. The word "trumpets" in Hebrew is *shofar*, literally "rams' horns."

> Leviticus 23:23-25:
> And the Lord spake unto Moses, saying,
> Speak unto the children of Israel, saying, In the seventh month, in the first *day* of the month, shall ye have a sabbath, a memorial of blowing of trumpets, an holy convocation.
> Ye shall do no servile work *therein*: but ye shall offer an offering made by fire unto the Lord.

> Numbers 29:1-6:
> And in the seventh month, on the first *day* of the month, ye shall have an holy convocation; ye shall do no servile work: it is a day of blowing the trumpets unto you.
> And ye shall offer a burnt offering for a sweet savour unto the Lord; one young bullock, one ram, *and* seven lambs of the first year without blemish:
> And their meat offering *shall be of* flour mingled with

---

6. Josephus also says Tishri retained its status as the beginning of the civil year especially as related to business and agricultural practices. See Josephus *Antiquities* 1.3.3.

> oil, three tenth deals for a bullock, *and* two tenth deals for a ram,
> And one tenth deal for one lamb, throughout the seven lambs:
> And one kid of the goats *for* a sin offering, to make an atonement for you:
> Beside the burnt offering of the month, and his meat offering, and the daily burnt offering, and his meat offering, and their drink offerings, according unto their manner, for a sweet savour, a sacrifice made by fire unto the Lord.

Now it should be noted that trumpets were blown and special offerings were made at the beginning of every month (Numbers 10:10; 28:11-15; Psalms 81:3). But a comparison will show that the trumpet-blowing and offerings of Tishri 1 were singled out and were more extensive than for any other month. Edersheim says that in Jesus' time, "During the whole of New Year's Day [Tishri 1], trumpets and horns were blown in Jerusalem from morning to evening."[7]

Just as age was reckoned from Tishri 1 to Tishri 1 during Noah's time, so were the regnal years of the Judean kings. In other words, the years of the reign of the kings, such as David and Solomon, were counted from Tishri 1 to Tishri 1.[8]

Thus it is interesting to observe that the blowing of

---

7. Edersheim, *The Temple*, pp. 297-298.
8. This is thoroughly documented by Edwin R. Thiele in his work *The Mysterious Numbers of the Hebrew Kings*, rev. ed. (Grand Rapids: Wm. B. Eerdmans, 1965), pp. 28-31, 161-163.

trumpets, associated with Tishri 1, was also part of the coronation ceremony for a new king, as II Kings shows.

> II Kings 11:12-14:
> And he brought forth the king's son, and put the crown upon him, and *gave him* the testimony; and they made him king, and anointed him; and they clapped their hands, and said, God save the king.
> And when Athaliah heard the noise of the guard *and* of the people, she came to the people into the temple of the Lord.
> And when she looked, behold, the king stood by a pillar, as the manner *was*, and the princes and the trumpeters by the king, and all the people of the land rejoiced, and blew with trumpets. . . .

Edersheim understands the blowing of trumpets to have maintained this royal and Godly significance in Christ's time.

> And so every season of 'blowing the trumpets,' whether at New Moons, at the Feast of Trumpets or New Year's Day [Tishri 1], at other festivals, in the Sabbatical and Year of Jubilee, or in the time of war, was a public acknowledgment of Jehovah as King.[9]

In this regard, Tishri 1, the Day of Trumpets, came to be recognized as the day when Israel was to reaffirm its acknowledgment that Jehovah was the one great and true King over all.

9. Edersheim, *The Temple*, p. 290.

> The Sovereignty of God is a dominant theme of the occasion [and] it is one of the cardinal features of New Year's Day [Tishri 1].[10]

The association of the blowing of a trumpet with kingship is also made in the Book of Revelation. Revelation 8:2 speaks of the seven angels with seven trumpets. The first six angels blow their trumpets in Revelation 8:6, 7, 8, 10, 12; 9:1 and 13. Finally, the seventh angel sounds the trumpet.

> Revelation 11:15-17:
> And the seventh angel sounded; and there were great voices in heaven, saying, The kingdoms of this world are become *the kingdoms* of our Lord, and of his Christ; and he shall reign for ever and ever.
> And the four and twenty elders, which sat before God on their seats, fell upon their faces, and worshipped God,
> Saying, We give thee thanks, O Lord God Almighty, which art, and wast, and art to come; because thou hast taken to thee thy great power, and hast reigned.

The purpose of the introductory crescendo of the first six trumpets leading up to the sounding of the seventh was to bring complete attention to the sovereignty of God. That it was the seventh trumpet that sounded is highly significant. Recall that the first of

---

10. Gaster, *Festivals of the Jewish Year*, p. 115. Furthermore, other scholars believe that Psalms 47, 93, 96, 97, 98, and 99—especially those psalms beginning with "The Lord [Jehovah] reigneth"—were an important part of the ancient Tishri 1 celebrations.

each month, beginning with Nisan, was to be observed with the blowing of trumpets. But Tishri 1 was the seventh new moon, the beginning of the seventh month, and the great Day of Trumpets.[11] As this was a time of blowing trumpets and of celebrating the lordship of Jehovah in the Old Testament, so the seventh trumpet in Revelation will herald the lordship of God and His Son. Thus, Tishri 1 with the blowing of the trumpets noted the birth of the king of kings. What an appropriate and notable day for Jesus Christ to have been born! What perfect alignment of history when we consider that Jesus Christ was born on Tishri 1, New Year's Day of Adam's reckoning. It was the first day of the seventh month, the last festal month of Moses' calendar. It was the day beginning the regnal years of the kings of Judah. It was the great Day of Trumpets celebrating Jehovah as the one True God.

---

11. According to the traditional reckoning of the Hebrew calendar, each month began at the time of the new moon. Psalms 104:19 says, "He appointed the moon for seasons. . . ." The words normally translated "month" mean "moon" or "new moon," showing a relationship between the month and the moon or the period of a lunation. If so, beginning with Nisan as the first month, Tishri 1 would be the seventh new moon, much of its special significance being drawn from this relation to the number seven. Edersheim's comment in his book *The Temple*, pp. 294-295, is pertinent in this regard: "Quite distinct from the other new moons, and more sacred than they, was that of the *seventh* month, or *Tishri*, partly on account of the symbolical meaning of the seventh or sabbatical month, in which the great feasts of the Day of Atonement and of Tabernacles occurred, and partly, perhaps, because it also marked the commencement of the civil year, always supposing that, as Josephus and most Jewish writers maintain, the distinction between the sacred and civil year dates from the time of Moses."

On that very day, Tishri 1, September 11, 3 B.C., Jesus Christ, God's only begotten Son, was born in Bethlehem. Unknown to the people, the trumpet sounds which blew from morning to evening in Jerusalem heralded God as the King over all and His Son as the promised king under the King, God. Yes, the Messiah, the promised seed, the second Adam, had been born.

CHAPTER EIGHT

ASTRONOMY AND THE BIRTH OF CHRIST

In summary, the significant celestial events heralding the birth of Jesus Christ began in August of 3 B.C., when Jupiter the king planet became visible above the eastern horizon as a morning star, seen by the Magi "in the rising." On August 12, Jupiter came into conjunction with Venus, the bright and morning star, in the constellation of Leo, the sign of Judah.

Virgo was the constellation signifying the woman and her seed as prophesied in Genesis 3:15. And on September 11, 3 B.C., the sun was positioned in the midst of Virgo while the new moon was directly under Virgo's feet—this configuration corresponding exactly to the description in Revelation 12 regarding the Messiah's birth. This stellar arrangement was visible in Palestine from sunset at 6:18 P.M. until moonset at 7:39 P.M. Thus it was during this eighty-one-minute period on the night of September 11,

3 B.C. that Jesus Christ was born in a stable in Bethlehem.

Although Jupiter and Regulus reached conjunction on September 14, to the naked eye their approach would have been observable in the predawn sky on September 12. This appeared in the same night sky of Tishri 1, as had the sign of Virgo earlier in the evening.

On September 14, 3 B.C., Jupiter came into conjunction with the king star—Regulus—the heart of the lion, in the constellation Leo. Jupiter and Regulus came into conjunction two more times a few months later, on February 17, 2 B.C. and May 8, 2 B.C.

Then Jupiter again came into conjunction with Venus in Leo on June 17, 2 B.C., when the two planets dramatically merged in a rare close conjunction to form one brilliant star in the western night sky. On August 27, 2 B.C., Jupiter came into conjunction with Mars in another significant astronomical arrangement.

Having watched Jupiter from the time they first saw it "in the rising," the Magi were in awe of Jupiter's multiple celestial displays and the significance of these. They knew Jupiter to be "his star," the star of the long-promised king who would reign in Judea. Thus, they journeyed to Jerusalem, the capital of Judea and the location of the throne of the promised king.

As the Magi departed from Jerusalem after speaking with King Herod, they again observed Jupiter's movement, this time in relation to themselves. Jupiter was rising in its nightly course to the meridian over Bethlehem. The timing was perfect, precise. The Magi went to Bethlehem sometime after December 4, 2 B.C., because only after that date was Jupiter visible crossing the meridian over Bethlehem before dawn obscured it. There in the home of Joseph and Mary they found the child, presented gifts, paid him homage, and departed to their homeland.

On January 9, 1 B.C., an eclipse occurred. Between the time of this eclipse and Passover that spring, April 8, Herod succumbed to disease and died a horrible death.[1]

Scriptures and historical facts begin to pattern harmoniously and fit so beautifully when we

---

1. Josephus describes Herod the Great's demise in graphic detail: "But now Herod's distemper greatly increased upon him after a severe manner, and this by God's judgement upon him for his sins: for a fire glowed in him slowly, which did not so much appear to the touch outwardly, as it augmented his pains inwardly; for it brought upon him a vehement appetite to eating, which he could not avoid to supply with one sort of food or other. His entrails were also exulcerated, and the chief violence of his pain lay on his colon; an aqueous and transparent liquor also had settled itself about his feet, and a like matter afflicted him at the bottom of his belly. Nay, further, his privy-member was putrified, and produced worms; and when he sat upright he had a difficulty of breathing, which was very loathsome, on account of the stench of his breath and the quickness of its returns; he had also convulsions in all parts of his body, which increased his strength to an insufferable degree." Josephus *Antiquities* 17.6.5.

recognize that the birthdate of Jesus was in the early fall of 3 B.C. Herod would still have been alive. Jesus' thirtieth birthday and the beginning of his ministry would then have been in 27 A.D., which aligns itself with the scriptural and historical indications as to the time his ministry began. Finally, the planet Jupiter's significance and celestial travels mesh dramatically with the star seen by the Magi as described in Matthew 2.

The accuracy of God's Word never ceases to move the heart of any person who hungers to know the truth and seek out its wealth of riches. With an awesome pageantry of celestial displays, God heralded the birth of His only begotten Son, the promised seed, the second Adam, as the king who would occupy the throne of David forever. With Christ's birth occurring on Tishri 1, a day filled with trumpet-blowing and gladness, the Hebrews unknowingly rejoiced as the promised seed, the seed originally promised in Genesis 3:15, was born.

PART II

THE PROPHECIES AND PEOPLE ASSOCIATED WITH THE PROMISED SEED: THE BIBLICAL RECORD

CHAPTER NINE

PROPHECIES ABOUT THE PROMISED SEED

To comprehend the significance of the birth of our Lord Jesus Christ, one must have a knowledge of Old Testament prophecies relating to him. Who was prophesied to be the Christ, the Messiah? What would be the Messiah's mission? In this study we will examine several scriptural prophecies of the promised one, beginning in the Book of Genesis. The first reference to him is found in Genesis 3:15 where God is speaking to the Adversary, the Devil, after the disobedience of Adam and Eve.

> Genesis 3:15:
> And I [God] will put enmity [a condition of separation and hostility] between thee [the serpent, the Devil] and the woman, and between thy seed and her seed; it [the seed of the woman] shall bruise thy [the serpent's, the Devil's] head, and thou shalt bruise his [the seed of the woman's] heel.

This single verse sets forth the central theme of all the Scriptures, the red thread of the redeemer which is interwoven throughout the Old and New Testaments. An offspring of the woman is promised who will ultimately destroy the Adversary and his works. This prophecy was passed down from generation to generation. As the peoples of the earth migrated from the Tower of Babel to populate the earth's surface, they carried this knowledge with them. This prophecy's meaning became distorted or lost by some, but others kept the truth of it embedded in their hearts so that they looked for a coming redeemer, a coming seed of the woman, the Messiah.

As time progressed, God further delineated the genealogical line from which this redeemer would come. God promised Abraham that the Messiah would be his offspring. In Genesis 21:12 God told Abraham that "in Isaac shall thy seed [the Christ] be called."

Abraham had other sons;[1] however, it would be from Isaac that the promised seed would descend. God's promise to Abraham continued the implementation of the promise which God had made centuries

1. Abraham had a total of eight sons in his lifetime. The number of daughters is not stated. He had one son by Hagar, the bondwoman, named Ishmael; one son by Sarah, named Isaac; and six sons by Keturah, whom Abraham married after Sarah's death. See Genesis 16:16; 21:1-5; and 25:1-2.

before in Genesis 3:15. Paul, in writing the epistle to the Galatians, also testified to this truth.

> Galatians 3:16:
> Now to Abraham and his seed were the promises made. He saith not, And to seeds, as of many; but as of one, And to thy seed, which is Christ.

Thousands of years after God had made His promise to Abraham, the Apostle Paul looked back and, by revelation, declared that the promise in Genesis 21:12, "in Isaac shall thy seed be called," referred to the Messiah, Jesus Christ, the promised seed.

The Prophet Moses led Israel out of the bondage of Egypt and toward the Promised Land. Not only did Moses give God's law to the Hebrews, but Moses also prophesied of a coming prophet whom Israel must follow.

> Deuteronomy 18:15 and 18:
> The Lord thy God will raise up unto thee a Prophet from the midst of thee, of thy brethren, like unto me [Moses]; unto him ye shall hearken;
> I [the Lord] will raise them [the children of Israel] up a Prophet from among their brethren, like unto thee [Moses], and will put my words in his mouth; and he shall speak unto them all that I shall command him.

So this coming Messiah would be raised up from

among the brethren and would be a prophet like unto Moses.[2]

Not only would the Messiah be a prophet of the stature of Moses, he would also be a priest after the order of Melchizedek. Psalms 110:4 prophesied of the coming priest.

> Psalms 110:4:
> The Lord hath sworn, and will not repent, Thou *art* a priest for ever after the order of Melchizedek.

Hebrews 5:6 announces the fulfillment of the prophecy when it says, "Thou [Christ] *art* a priest for ever after the order of Melchisedec." The promised seed was to be both a prophet and a priest.

In addition to prophet and priest, the Messiah was to be king. Starting with Abraham, the genealogy of the Messiah follows with Isaac and then on to his son Jacob, who was renamed Israel. Jacob had twelve sons who eventually fathered the twelve tribes of the Biblical nation called Israel. One of those twelve sons was Judah. It was from Judah, as prophesied by Jacob on his deathbed, that the scepter, the symbol of rulership, would not depart.

---

2. This prophecy in Deuteronomy 18 is what is referred to in John 6:14 when it says, "Then those men, when they had seen the miracle that Jesus did, said, This is of a truth that prophet that should come into the world." Acts 3:22 and Acts 7:37, in context, clarify Moses' prophecy in Deuteronomy 18 as a reference to Jesus Christ.

Genesis 49:10:
The sceptre shall not depart from Judah, nor a lawgiver from between his feet, until Shiloh come; and unto him *shall* the gathering of the people *be*.

Many years after Jacob spoke these words, the rulers of God's people emerged from the tribe of Judah,[3] beginning with King David. The phrase "until Shiloh come" refers to the Messiah's coming.[4] The Messiah would become the final ruler of Israel, and he would be from the tribe of Judah.

So the children of Israel had the hope of a coming ruler, a Messiah descending from Judah, sent from God to deliver them. That this hope was real to the people of Israel can be seen in a prophecy about Israel given by Balaam to the ruler of Moab. Balaam declares this revelation when the children of Israel, wandering in the wilderness, ventured near Moab.

Numbers 23:21:
He [the Lord] hath not beheld iniquity in Jacob [the nation Israel], neither hath he seen perverseness in

---

3. Psalms 60:7: ". . .Judah *is* my lawgiver."
4. The phrase "until Shiloh come" is a point of controversy among translators. Most are agreed that Shiloh is not a proper name as it is used here. However, the Hebrew, the Aramaic, and other ancient versions all indicate that the phrase refers to a coming Messiah and his dominion. Brown, Driver, and Briggs in their *Hebrew and English Lexicon* suggest "he whose it is" comes or "that which belongs to him" comes. George M. Lamsa translates the Aramaic as "until the coming of the One to whom the sceptre belongs" in *The Holy Bible from Ancient Eastern Manuscripts* (Nashville, Tenn.: A.J. Holman, 1957).

> Israel: the Lord his God *is* with him [Israel], and the shout of a king *is* among them.

The "shout of a king" was Israel's joyous expectation of a coming Messiah. How meaningful this hope was to them!

> II Samuel 7:12,13,16:
> And when thy [David's] days be fulfilled, and thou shalt sleep with thy fathers, I [the Lord] will set up thy seed after thee, which shall proceed out of thy bowels, and I will establish his kingdom.
> He shall build an house for my name, and I will stablish the throne of his kingdom for ever.
> And thine house and thy kingdom shall be established for ever before thee: thy throne shall be established for ever.

> I Kings 8:25:
> Therefore now, Lord God of Israel, keep with thy servant David my [Solomon's] father that thou promisedst him, saying, There shall not fail thee a man [David would have descendants] in my sight to sit on the throne of Israel. . . .

> Psalms 132:11:
> The Lord hath sworn *in* truth unto David; he will not turn from it; Of the fruit of thy body [Aramaic: *karsa*, belly, loins] will I set upon thy throne.[5]

---

5. See Acts 2:30: ". . . that of the fruit of his [David's] loins [*karsa*, belly, loins], according to the flesh, he would raise up Christ [the Messiah] to sit on his throne."

Jeremiah 33:17:
For thus saith the Lord; David shall never want [or, there shall not be cut off from David] a man to sit upon the throne of the house of Israel.

Psalms 89:3 and 4:
I [the Lord] have made a covenant with my chosen, I have sworn unto David my servant,
Thy seed will I establish for ever, and build up thy throne to all generations. Selah.

God promised David that He would establish David's throne forever. The Messiah was to come out of the royal line of David and his son Solomon, and would sit on that throne forever. This Messiah is described in Isaiah 11:1 and 10 as "a rod out of the stem of Jesse," and "a root of Jesse," Jesse having been the father of David. What tremendous promises these were to David and all the children of Israel.

Besides being a descendant of David, the Messiah was to be born in a definite place, as prophesied in the Book of Micah.

Micah 5:2:
But thou, Bethlehem Ephratah, *though* thou be little among the thousands of Judah, *yet* out of thee shall he come forth unto me *that is* to be ruler in Israel; whose goings forth [forthcoming] *have been* from of old, from everlasting.

In God's omniscience He foreknew and foreordained from before the foundation of the world that the Messiah would come. The Messiah's coming began being revealed to man as early as Genesis 3:15. Because of God's promises mankind anticipated the Messiah's coming. By the time of Micah, as recorded above, all Israel could know God's promises of a Messiah, and that he would be a royal descendant of David, of the tribe of Judah, of the lineage of Abraham. The Prophet Micah then revealed that, of all the cities of Judah, the Messiah would come out of a little town named Bethlehem.

* * *

So far we have observed a number of key scriptures telling of God's promise of a Messiah, a redeemer. However, passage after passage could be cited from the Old Testament that in some way alludes to or foreshadows the coming savior. The sacrifices, the offerings, the law, the tabernacle, the Temple—God used these and many other things to illustrate and prepare His people for their coming Messiah. Indeed, the Scriptures as a whole, when rightly divided and understood, pertain to the Christ. From Genesis 3:15 through Revelation 22:21, Jesus Christ is the underlying subject, the red thread, of the Word of God. The written Word makes known the Christ, and the Christ makes known God.

When you understand this, that the Messiah, the promised seed, is the central subject of the Bible from Genesis 3:15 to Revelation 22:21, you then begin to perceive the many ways he is revealed in God's Word. Even historical events are recorded in such a way as to show the coming Messiah and his work.

An example of this is found in Hosea 11:1 where God's Word says, "...I [God] loved him, and called my son out of Egypt." From the context it is clear that this is a reference to God's having called Israel, the nation He had adopted as His son, out of the bondage of Egypt. The scriptural record of that historical event is also a prophecy concerning Jesus Christ. The fulfillment of the prophecy is recorded in Matthew 2:13-15.[6]

Another example is the well-known prophecy of Isaiah 7:14: "...Behold, a virgin [the Hebrew is *almah*, meaning simply 'a young woman'] shall conceive, and bear a son, and shall call his name

---

6. Matthew 2:13-15: "And when they were departed, behold, the angel of the Lord appeareth to Joseph in a dream, saying, Arise, and take the young child and his mother, and flee into Egypt, and be thou there until I bring thee word: for Herod will seek the young child to destroy him. When he arose, he took the young child and his mother by night, and departed into Egypt: And was there until the death of Herod: that it might be fulfilled [with the result that it was fulfilled] which was spoken of the Lord by the prophet, saying, Out of Egypt have I called my son."

Immanuel [meaning 'God with us']." A study of Isaiah 7 and 8 shows that this prophecy had an immediate fulfillment in Isaiah's time, besides its ultimate fulfillment in Christ.

God worked in the course of human events according to His divine plan so that, uniquely, Isaiah himself and his sons were, according to Isaiah 8:18, "for signs and for wonders in Israel." Chapters 7 through 9 of Isaiah show how Isaiah's sons communicated God's revelation to Israel. Isaiah 7:3 tells of a son named Shearjashub whose name foretold how a remnant would return from captivity. Isaiah had another son named Mahershalalhashbaz. This name is explained in Isaiah 8:4 as indicating that Assyria would spoil Israel and Syria, enemies of Judah.

As God revealed His will by these two sons of Isaiah, so Isaiah 7:14 from context would then refer to a son of Isaiah, whose name was Immanuel.[7] The birth of Isaiah's son Immanuel was a fulfillment of the prophecy given in Isaiah 7, but not its only fulfillment. This prophecy and the event it foretold

---

7. Isaiah 7:10-16: "Moreover the Lord spake again unto Ahaz, saying, Ask thee a sign of the Lord thy God; ask it either in the depth, or in the height above. But Ahaz said, I will not ask, neither will I tempt the Lord. And he said, Hear ye now, O house of David; *Is it* a small thing for you to weary men, but will ye weary my God also? Therefore the Lord himself shall give you a sign; Behold, a virgin shall conceive, and bear a son, and shall call his name Immanuel. Butter and honey shall he eat, that he may know to refuse the evil, and choose the good. For before the child shall know to refuse the evil, and choose the good, the land that thou abhorrest shall be forsaken of both her kings."

are also used by God to communicate great truth concerning the coming Messiah, in whom the prophecy had its ultimate fulfillment, as recorded in Matthew 1.[8]

> Matthew 1:23:
> Behold, a virgin shall be with child, and shall bring forth a son, and they shall call his name Emmanuel, which being interpreted is, God with us.

Since Matthew 1:23 says, "they shall call his name Emmanuel," why is the Christ never called by this name throughout the rest of the Gospels? There are instances in God's Word where God will give a name to a man, yet that man is known to men by another name. This is true with Solomon.

> II Samuel 12:25:
> And he [God] sent by the hand of Nathan the prophet; and he called his [Solomon's] name Jedidiah, because of the Lord.

God called Solomon by the name Jedidiah, though he is not popularly known by that name. Even today in our Western culture, a man can have one or more middle names, yet they may be written down only as initials, if he chooses to write them at all. So, Jesus

---

8. There is a more detailed discussion of this principle of prophecy and Isaiah 7 and 8 in *The Companion Bible*, pp. 939-943, and Appendix 103, pp. 147-148.

Christ could be given another name by God that was not generally known among men. Furthermore, there is no Hebrew text or ancient version of Isaiah 7:14, from which Matthew 1:23 is quoted, that gives "they" as the subject of the verb "call." In Matthew 1:23, a few Greek manuscripts read "you will call," while some Latin manuscripts read "he will call." In view of these variations, the only necessity in fulfilling this prophecy was that Mary and Joseph include the name Emmanuel.

In considering prophecy that foretells, it should be noted that such prophecy is generally not fully understood until the time it starts to come to pass and reaches its fulfillment. Yet many have tried to interpret Biblical prophecies in the light of experience and conjecture, which is why so much prophecy concerning future events has been distorted by guesswork and spiritualizing.

While we should never forget that Christ is the subject of the Scriptures, we must guard against drifting into typology and the misapplication of a scripture's intended meaning. The immediate or literal meaning of a passage must be understood before its relationship to Jesus Christ can be properly comprehended.

While we can be certain of those prophecies that are recorded in the Scriptures, there are other prophecies which were simply spoken and not written. For example, Matthew 2:23.

Matthew 2:23:
And he came and dwelt in a city called Nazareth: that it might be fulfilled which was spoken by the prophets, He shall be called a Nazarene.

This prophecy is not found in the Old Testament; nevertheless, spoken prophecies are revelation and are fulfilled.

Other dynamic examples of prophecies foretelling the Messiah are the five passages which tell of the coming "branch." The Hebrew word for "branch" is *ssemah*. The word *ssemah* is used only twelve times in God's Word, and in five instances it pertains specifically to the Messiah. A more precise translation of *ssemah* is "that which springeth up," "a sprout," "a shoot," or "an offspring." A *ssemah* is a young shoot newly sprouted from the ground.

We need to study these five uses of *ssemah* as they relate to the Messiah for we will gain important knowledge. First, let's look at Jeremiah 23.

Jeremiah 23:5:
Behold, the days come, saith the Lord, that I will raise unto David a righteous Branch [*ssemah*, offspring], and a King shall reign and prosper, and shall execute judgment and justice in the earth.

This "righteous Branch" would be a descendant of David. He would inherit the throne of David and, as such, would be a king. It is this aspect of the

Messiah which this verse designates. So one of the important qualities of the Messiah, this righteous branch or offspring, is that he would be a king.

Another use of *ssemah* is found later in Jeremiah.

> Jeremiah 33:14 and 15:
> Behold, the days come, saith the Lord, that I will perform that good thing which I have promised unto the house of Israel and to the house of Judah.
> In those days, and at that time, will I cause the Branch [*ssemah*, offspring] of righteousness to grow up unto David; and he shall execute judgment and righteousness in the land.

Again Jeremiah foretells of the Messiah as a descendant of David, one who would execute judgment and righteousness as a king. This is the second prophecy in which the coming branch, the *ssemah*, is portrayed as a king descended from David.

Zechariah foretells another aspect of the offspring.

> Zechariah 3:8:
> Hear now, O Joshua the high priest, thou, and thy fellows that sit before thee: for they *are* men wondered at: for, behold, I will bring forth my servant the BRANCH [*ssemah*].

In this scripture, the coming branch or *ssemah* is called a servant. The position of a servant would be another aspect and characteristic of the Messiah.

Zechariah also foretells a third characteristic of the *ssemah*, that the coming branch would be a man.

> Zechariah 6:12:
> And speak unto him, saying, Thus speaketh the Lord of hosts, saying, Behold the man whose name *is* The BRANCH [the *ssemah*]; and he shall grow up out of his place, and he shall build the temple of the Lord.

"Behold the man whose name *is* The BRANCH. . . ." The fourth and final aspect of "the branch" is recorded by Isaiah.

> Isaiah 4:2:
> In that day shall the branch [*ssemah*] of the Lord be beautiful and glorious, and the fruit of the earth *shall be* excellent and comely for them that are escaped of Israel.

Here the Messiah is prophesied to be "the branch of the Lord." That is the fourth great aspect of this Messiah. With this verse we have seen all the uses of *ssemah* which pertain to the Messiah. The coming branch, the offspring, was prophesied in these scriptures as having four characteristics: the promised Messiah was to be a *king*, a *servant*, a *man*, and *the Son of God*. In studying these four characteristics in light of the four Gospels, one arrives at significant and illuminating truths.[9]

---

9. For a more detailed study of this subject, see Wierwille, "Why Four Gospels?" *Jesus Christ Our Passover*, Appendix 5, pp. 445-453.

By careful scrutiny we can see that the Gospel of Matthew emphasizes the kingly qualities of the Christ, the Messiah who fulfilled the Old Testament prophecies. That is why the genealogy in Matthew begins with Christ's royal genealogy from Abraham down through David and Solomon to Mary, tracing the royal lineage forward[10] to Jesus the Christ, and clearly demonstrates his qualifications for inheriting the throne of David as a king.

The term "Kingdom of Heaven" is found thirty-two times in Matthew's Gospel, while it is not found once in any of the other three Gospels. The Kingdom of Heaven was the reign of God's anointed king on earth. The Kingdom of Heaven is a segment of the overall Kingdom of God of which God is King.[11] There are ten parables which are unique to Matthew, all of which depict aspects of life which are associated with a king. Many of the events recorded in Matthew emphasize Jesus' position as God's anointed king. The phrase "son of David," emphasizing his royal lineage, occurs more frequently in Matthew than in any other Gospel.

---

10. According to *The Companion Bible*, pp. 1304 and 1440, Matthew's genealogical order is appropriate for a king. In contrast, the genealogy in the Gospel of Luke begins with Jesus, and Joseph (who reared him), and goes backward through his ancestry to Adam. This order is appropriate for him as a man, not royalty.

11. Victor Paul Wierwille, "*Ekklēsia*: Bride or Body?" *The New, Dynamic Church* (New Knoxville, Ohio: American Christian Press, 1971), pp. 3-22.

In studying the Gospel of Mark, we can see that this Gospel emphasizes Jesus Christ as a servant willing to accept responsibility in serving and helping others. Mark records no genealogy. This is significant because a servant does not gain his position by descent. The Gospel of Mark basically begins with Christ's ministry. The word translated "lord" or "sir" (Greek: *kurios*) is used seventy-three times of Christ in the other three Gospels, but only three times in the Gospel of Mark. Mark puts great stress on Jesus' actions in the service of God to his fellow man.

The Gospel of Luke portrays Jesus Christ as a man, a human being with needs, emotions, and feelings like any other man. Thus, Jesus Christ the perfect man is Luke's overall emphasis. Luke 3:23-38 records Jesus' legal ancestry as a man, through Joseph who reared him, all the way back to Adam, the first man. This genealogy, unlike the royal genealogy in the Gospel of Matthew, begins with Jesus and goes chronologically in reverse, as is normally done in a commoner's genealogy. The entire Gospel of Luke emphasizes Jesus Christ's relationship with the common man. He is depicted as a friend of publicans and sinners. There are eleven parables unique to Luke which emphasize the particularly human aspects of his life.

Of the four Gospels, the one that clearly stresses

Jesus Christ's position as the Son of God is the Gospel of John.

> John 1:14,18,34:
> And the Word [Greek: *logos*] was made flesh, and dwelt [tabernacled] among us, (and we beheld his glory, the glory as of the only begotten of the Father,) full of grace and truth.
> No man hath seen God at any time; the only begotten Son, which is in the bosom of the Father, he hath declared *him*.
> And I saw, and bare record that this is the Son of God.

> John 3:16:
> For God so loved the world, that he gave his only begotten Son. . . .

> John 20:31:
> But these are written, that ye might believe that Jesus is the Christ, the Son of God. . . .

In the Gospel of John, the word "father" is used almost three times as often as in any other Gospel. It is frequently used in describing God's relationship to Jesus Christ. In this Gospel, rather than opening with a long, detailed genealogy, John simply calls Jesus "the Son of God." Some of Jesus' great miracles, such as the healing of the blind man (John 9) and the raising of Lazarus (John 11), are recorded in the Book of John. The phrase "laid down his life" is found only in John, where it is used six times. Jesus Christ "laid down his life" as the Son of God; no one could have taken it from him.

In considering the five Old Testament prophecies of the coming "branch," or *ssemah*, it is interesting that two of them emphasize that he would be a king ruling from the throne of David. There are two books in the New Testament which emphatically show Jesus Christ as the king. One is the Gospel of Matthew; the other is the Book of Revelation which foretells Christ's glorious return as the king of kings and lord of lords.[12] What a wonderful truth from God's marvelous Word!

Thus, the emphasis of each Gospel now comes into clear focus. In Matthew, Jesus Christ is the king, the ruler of Israel. In Mark, Jesus Christ is the servant, a leader willing to accept responsibility in serving and helping others. In Luke, Jesus Christ is the perfect man, a human being with human qualities. In John, Jesus Christ is the Son of God with power.

The coming of Jesus Christ is clearly foretold throughout the Old Testament. The word "Christ" comes from the Greek word *christos* meaning "anointed." The Greek *christos* is translated from the Aramaic word *mshicha* and the Hebrew *mashiah*, both of which mean "anointed." From these words, *mshicha* and *mashiah*, English derives the word

---

12. In Revelation 5:5 Jesus Christ is called "the Lion of the tribe of Juda, the Root of David." In Revelation 22:16 he is called "the root and the offspring of David."

"Messiah." To say "Jesus Christ" is to say "Jesus the Messiah" or "Jesus the Anointed One."

In Biblical times kings were anointed with oil before coronation. Priests also were anointed when being set apart in their service for the Lord. To be anointed with oil represented one's being anointed with the presence of God, being chosen by God, and designated for a special service for Him. As the Messiah, Jesus was God's anointed king over Israel. He was the Lord's chosen one, the prophesied and promised seed of the Old Testament. Jesus Christ himself declares this.

> Luke 24:27:
> And beginning at Moses and all the prophets, he [Jesus Christ] expounded unto them in all the scriptures the things concerning himself.

> Luke 24:44:
> And he [Jesus Christ] said unto them, These *are* the words which I spake unto you, while I was yet with you, that all things must be fulfilled, which were written in the law of Moses, and *in* the prophets, and *in* the psalms [writings], concerning me.

> John 5:39:
> Search the scriptures [Old Testament scriptures]; for in them ye think ye have eternal life: and they [Old Testament scriptures] are they which testify of me [Jesus Christ].

The hope that God gave to Israel was the hope of a coming Messiah: he would be their prophet, he would be their priest, he would be their king. As the Messiah, he would be a man, he would be a servant, and he would be the Son of God. Toward him all of history was directed for he was the promised seed.

CHAPTER TEN

THE GENEALOGY OF JESUS CHRIST

As the Messiah, Jesus Christ had to fulfill certain genealogical requirements promised in the Old Testament, among them, (1) he had to be a descendant of Adam; (2) he had to be a descendant of Abraham; and (3) he had to be a descendant of King David. The Old Testament further stipulated that the Messiah's royal lineage would trace its way through King David and Solomon. Finally, besides being the son of Adam, Abraham, and David, the Messiah would also have to be the Son of God. That Jesus Christ had all of these qualifications will become indisputably clear in studying his conception and genealogy.

Jesus Christ's genealogy, as with all people, was determined by his mother and her predecessors and his Father. So in researching God's Word for the great truths of Jesus Christ's genealogy, we need to begin by noting certain details regarding his conception.

Matthew 1:18:
Now the birth of Jesus Christ was on this wise: When as his mother Mary was espoused to Joseph, before they came together, she was found with child of the Holy Ghost [Holy Spirit].

"Before they came together" means that before Joseph and Mary had sexual intercourse Mary was already pregnant, and the child she was carrying was conceived in her by God, who is the Holy Spirit.[1] Therefore, from a physical, genetic point of view, Jesus Christ's Father was God and his mother was Mary. Joseph, Mary's husband, became Jesus Christ's human father by the circumstances in which he found himself, but not by his genetic contribution. Joseph by God's direction accepted the responsibility of rearing Jesus as a son in his household.

There is no question that the Bible teaches divine conception, that God was literally Jesus Christ's Father. In any conception there are two necessary elements: the egg and the sperm. The egg is supplied by the mother, who in this case was Mary. The sperm is supplied by the father, who in this case was God, who is the Holy Spirit. Being Spirit,[2] God did not, of course, have sexual intercourse with Mary,

---

1. Matthew 1:20: "...that which is conceived in her is of the Holy Ghost [Holy Spirit]." Luke 1:35: "...The Holy Ghost [Holy Spirit] shall come upon [over] thee, and the power of the Highest shall overshadow [cover] thee: therefore also that holy thing which shall be born of thee shall be called the Son of God."
2. John 4:24: "God *is* a Spirit...."

for spirit cannot cohabit with flesh. Rather, by divine creation, God put seed within Mary. That is how Mary, who had never had sexual relations, had Jesus Christ conceived within her. This is the miracle of Jesus Christ's conception. Theoretically, God could have created seed within any woman in history, for all women conceive in the same manner, however only Mary fulfilled all the prerequisites necessary in order to carry the promised seed. God said He would have an only begotten Son, and He chose Mary in whom to create the seed that would give birth to that one Son.

There are several genetic and physical considerations involved with Jesus Christ's divine conception. The Bible teaches that all men since Adam are born "dead in sins."[3] Man is conceived and born with a sinful nature. Psalms 51:5 states, "Behold, I was shapen in iniquity; and in sin did my mother conceive me." Romans 5:12 states, "Wherefore, as by one man [Adam] sin entered into the world, and death by sin; and so death passed upon all men, for that all have sinned."

Not only is man born spiritually separated from God, he is born physically with sin, corruption, and impurities in his blood and in his soul life. This soul life which is the natural life of man, and attested to by a person's breathing, is found in the blood.

---

3. Ephesians 2:5: "Even when we were dead in sins. . ."

> Leviticus 17:11:
> For the life of the flesh *is* in the blood....

While the mother and father both make genetic contributions to the flesh and blood of a child, the soul life in the blood is contributed by the sperm, the seed. It comes from the male side. In the conception of Jesus Christ, this truth is pointedly stated in Hebrews.

> Hebrews 2:14:
> Forasmuch then as the children are partakers [Greek: *koinōneō*, to share fully] of flesh and blood, he [Jesus Christ] also himself likewise took part [Greek: *metechō*, to take a part or portion] of the same [flesh and blood]...

All children share fully of both the flesh and blood, genetically passed on to them since Adam and Eve the first man and woman, but Jesus Christ took only one part. He did not share "fully." Here in Hebrews 2:14, the figure of speech *metonymy* of the adjunct is found, in which the word "blood" is used to represent the soul life in the blood. This usage of "blood" is common in the Bible, especially when it is used with the term "flesh," which here is used for the physical part of man as opposed to the soul part. In partaking of the flesh and blood, all people have inherited their bodies and their soul life from Adam and his descendants. This soul life in the blood is corrupt with a sinful nature inherent within it.[4]

This is why it is necessary to understand from Hebrews 2:14 that Jesus Christ "took part of the same." What part did he take? He did not *share* fully in both the flesh and blood of man. Physically, according to the flesh, part of Jesus' genetic makeup came from Mary. However, the soul life in his blood was not inherited from Mary, Adam, or any other human being. The life of the flesh is in the blood, according to Leviticus 17:11, and the life within the flesh of man, within his blood, is corrupt. But Jesus Christ's came from God. That is why Jesus Christ's soul life was conceived without sin or corruption.

As we have seen, natural life, which is called "soul life," is in the blood. Sin is transmitted through this soul life, in other words, through the blood, and not through the flesh. That is why Hebrews 2:14 is such a tremendous statement. How marvelously God arranged for a child to be conceived that would be completely a man, having complete freedom of will, but also having a sinless nature.[5]

With masterful foresight God prepared for the sinless birth of His Son, Jesus Christ, from the very beginning. In order to produce a sinless man

---

4. See Victor Paul Wierwille, "Body, Soul, Spirit," *The Word's Way* (New Knoxville, Ohio: American Christian Press, 1971), pp. 45-56.
5. See Wierwille, "The Conception of Jesus Christ," *The Word's Way*, pp. 157-174.

descended from Adam, God provided a way whereby Jesus would have a human body derived from Adam's line, yet uncontaminated by Adam's sinful soul life. To accomplish this, God created the sperm containing a perfect soul life which impregnated the egg in Mary's fallopian tube. This sperm, being perfect,[6] carried only dominant characteristics and did what any sperm would do to an egg. Therefore, the dominant characteristics of the genes determining the makeup of Jesus Christ came from his Father, God.

The miracle of the birth of Jesus Christ was his divine conception in Mary. His birth was *not* miraculous, for like any infant he developed within Mary's womb and was born according to natural processes. But, the *miracle* of his divine conception enabled man's redeemer to come into the world as a sinless, perfect human being, yet having the freedom of will to sin or not to sin; to believe or not to believe God. God did not go beyond any of His previously instituted laws to bring His Son into the world.

Understanding all of this, many scriptures con-

---

6. Arthur C. Custance suggests that, from a scientific point of view, the germ plasm of the egg cell seems to be normally unaffected by corruption as it is passed down from generation to generation. He discusses reasons for believing that the germ plasm in the egg contributed by Mary (or most other women) would result in a perfect human being if (and only if) it were united with a perfect sperm from the male side. See Arthur C. Custance, *The Seed of the Woman* (Brookville, Ontario: Doorway Publications, 1980), pp. 210-232, 264-267.

cerning Jesus' descent from the lineage of David become much more meaningful. That is why the following scriptures are so accurate.

> Acts 2:30:
> . . . that of the fruit of his [David's] loins, according to the flesh, he would raise up Christ . . .

> Romans 1:3:
> Concerning his [God's] Son Jesus Christ our Lord, which [who] was made of the seed of David according to the flesh.

These verses do not say Jesus Christ was of the seed of David "according to flesh *and blood*." That would be totally inaccurate. These verses all say "according to the flesh," for Christ's soul life in his blood came from God. It did not come from David or David's descendant, Mary. But physically, according to the flesh, Jesus Christ can properly be said to be of the seed of David. That is the great accuracy of these key verses of scripture.

With this basic understanding of the unique conception of Jesus Christ, we will find the records of his genealogy most illuminating. Let us begin with the genealogy given in the Gospel of Matthew.

> Matthew 1:1:
> The book of the generation of Jesus Christ, the son of David, the son of Abraham.

Matthew documents that Jesus Christ was a descendant of both David and Abraham. According to the Old Testament prophecies, these were two indispensable requirements of the promised Messiah. As we have seen, genetically Jesus Christ had two parents: Mary and God. Jesus Christ's human genetic background is traced in the Gospel of Matthew through Mary. This genealogy from Mary is the focus of the first chapter of Matthew.

> Matthew 1:2-16:
> Abraham begat Isaac; and Isaac begat Jacob; and Jacob begat Judas and his brethren;
> And Judas begat Phares and Zara of Thamar; and Phares begat Esrom; and Esrom begat Aram;
> And Aram begat Aminadab; and Aminadab begat Naasson; and Naasson begat Salmon;
> And Salmon begat Booz of Rachab; and Booz begat Obed of Ruth; and Obed begat Jesse;
> And Jesse begat David the king; and David the king begat Solomon of her *that had been the wife* of Urias;
> And Solomon begat Roboam; and Roboam begat Abia; and Abia begat Asa;
> And Asa begat Josaphat; and Josaphat begat Joram; and Joram begat Ozias;
> And Ozias begat Joatham; and Joatham begat Achaz; and Achaz begat Ezekias;
> And Ezekias begat Manasses; and Manasses begat Amon; and Amon begat Josias;
> And Josias begat Jechonias and his brethren, about the time they were carried away to Babylon:
> And after they were brought to Babylon, Jechonias begat Salathiel; and Salathiel begat Zorobabel;

> And Zorobabel begat Abiud; and Abiud begat Eliakim; and Eliakim begat Azor;
> And Azor begat Sadoc; and Sadoc begat Achim; and Achim begat Eliud;
> And Eliud begat Eleazar; and Eleazar begat Matthan; and Matthan begat Jacob;
> And Jacob begat Joseph the husband of Mary, of whom was born Jesus, who is called Christ.

This last verse, Matthew 1:16, stirs up controversy when it states that "Jacob begat Joseph the husband of Mary" because this contradicts a statement in Luke.

> Luke 3:23:
> . . .Joseph, which was *the son* of Heli.

Matthew says Joseph's father was Jacob, whereas Luke says Joseph's father was Heli. How can this apparent discrepancy be reconciled? The two Josephs surely cannot be the same person if the Word of God is right. Furthermore, Matthew 1:16 declares Joseph to be the husband of Mary. Certainly she did not have two husbands named Joseph. Comparing the records as given by Matthew and Luke, it is only logical and reasonable that they must be speaking of two different people named Joseph. Further investigation shows this difficulty in reconciling the two Gospel records has been in fact caused by a serious mistranslation in Matthew.

> Matthew 1:16:
> And Jacob begat Joseph the husband [Greek: *andra*; Aramaic: *gavra*] of Mary. . . .

The word "husband" is the Greek word *andra*, from the root word *anēr*. The word *anēr* simply means "a male person of full age and stature," in contrast to a child or a female. It is used of men in various relationships, but its specific usage must always be derived from the context. Indeed *anēr* can be and is translated "husband" in some contexts, but its normal translation is "man."[7]

In Matthew 1:16, Joseph is the *anēr*, "the man" of Mary. The Aramaic word translated in English "husband" is *gavra*. *Gavra* means "mighty man." In Biblical culture the father who is the head of the household is "the mighty man." The son would not be considered "the mighty man" of the household until the father died, at which time the younger person would become the head of the household. Therefore, the English phrase "Joseph the husband" in Matthew 1:16 is properly translated from the Aramaic as "Joseph the mighty man [*gavra*, the father] of Mary."

---

7. In the King James Version some translations into English of the Greek word *anēr* include: "man" (I Corinthians 13:11), "prophet" (Luke 24:19), "fellows" (Acts 17:5), "murderer" (Acts 3:14), and "husband" (Romans 7:2). Although *anēr* is Biblically used in many different contexts, its primary meaning is always used in reference to an adult male, a man.

This truth is substantiated even further in Matthew 1:19 where the word "husband" is properly translated in the King James Version. There, this word which refers to Mary's husband Joseph is *bala* in Aramaic. It is not *gavra*, as in Matthew 1:16. That is because Matthew 1:16 speaks of Joseph who was Mary's father, her *gavra*, while in contrast, Matthew 1:19 speaks of Joseph who was Mary's husband, her *bala*. Hence, Mary's father's name was Joseph, and Mary's husband's name also was Joseph.

We have utilized Greek, Aramaic, the recorded genealogies, and ancient custom to demonstrate that the word "husband" in Matthew 1:16 should be rendered "father." However, if all of this evidence were not enough, there is yet one more safeguard supplied by God's Word which proves that the Joseph of Matthew 1:16 was Mary's father.

> Matthew 1:17:
> So all the generations from Abraham to David *are* fourteen generations; and from David until the carrying away into Babylon *are* fourteen generations; and from the carrying away into Babylon unto Christ *are* fourteen generations.

Counting carefully in the record of the Gospel of Matthew 1:2-16, we note that the first two groups each contain fourteen generations, in accordance with verse 17. However, the third group would have only thirteen generations if the Joseph of Matthew 1:16 were the husband of Mary. In order for Matthew 1:17 to delineate fourteen generations for the third group, verse 16 must read "Joseph the father of Mary." How wonderfully God protected this truth by the revelation of Matthew 1:17.

The following table lists the genealogy given in Matthew 1 and shows the three groups of fourteen generations.

THE ROYAL GENEALOGY OF JESUS CHRIST FROM MATTHEW 1

From Abraham to David (14 generations)

1.	Abraham	8.	Aminadab
2.	Isaac	9.	Naasson
3.	Jacob	10.	Salmon
4.	Judas	11.	Booz
5.	Phares	12.	Obed
6.	Esrom	13.	Jesse
7.	Aram	14.	David (the king)

NOTE: The names in this genealogy are spelled somewhat differently from the way they are spelled in the Old Testament because Old Testament spelling is a transliteration from Hebrew while the New Testament spelling is a transliteration from Greek.

From David to the carrying away to Babylon (14 generations)*

1. Solomon
2. Roboam
3. Abia
4. Asa
5. Josaphat
6. Joram
7. Ozias
8. Joatham
9. Achaz
10. Ezekias
11. Manasses
12. Amon
13. Josias
14. Jechonias

From the carrying away to Babylon unto Christ (14 generations)

1. Salathiel (born after carrying away)
2. Zorobabel
3. Abiud
4. Eliakim
5. Azor
6. Sadoc
7. Achim
8. Eliud
9. Eleazar
10. Matthan
11. Jacob
12. Joseph (father of Mary)
13. Mary
14. Jesus

*This second group of fourteen generations purposely omits four of David's descendants in this line. They are Ahaziah (II Kings 8:24—9:27 and II Chronicles 22:1-9) the son of Joram (number 6), Ahaziah's son Joash (II Kings 11:2—12:20 and II Chronicles 24:1-22), Joash's son Amaziah (II Kings 14:1-19 and II Chronicles 25), and Jehoiakim (II Kings 23:34—24:6 and II Chronicles 36:1-8) the son of Josias (number 13). One possible reason for their omission could be idolatry and other wickedness, since certain generations had names deleted for this reason. (Note Exodus 20:4 and 5 and Deuteronomy 29, especially verse 20.) The omission was not an oversight on Matthew's part, as he must have been well aware of their place in the genealogies clearly set forth in the Old Testament. God inspired the setting forth of the generations as they appear in Matthew 1.

The preceding list demonstrates Jesus Christ's royal lineage through his mother, Mary. The descendants listed postdating David were rightful heirs to David's throne. The genealogy of Matthew 1:2-16 clearly shows Jesus Christ's genetic and legal claim to inherit the throne of David. It gives the Messiah's standing in the House of David by birth. He was the long-awaited promised seed, the Christ, the true king of Israel.

Besides the royal genealogy of Jesus Christ given in Matthew, the Gospel of Luke records Jesus' genealogy from the viewpoint of him as a commoner, taking his roots back through David to Adam.

> Luke 3:23-38:
> And Jesus himself began to be about thirty years of age, being (as was supposed) the son of Joseph, which was *the son* of Heli,
> Which was *the son* of Matthat, which was *the son* of Levi, which was *the son* of Melchi, which was *the son* of Janna, which was *the son* of Joseph,
> Which was *the son* of Mattathias, which was *the son* of Amos, which was *the son* of Naum, which was *the son* of Esli, which was *the son* of Nagge,
> Which was *the son* of Maath, which was *the son* of Mattathias, which was *the son* of Semei, which was *the son* of Joseph, which was *the son* of Juda,
> Which was *the son* of Joanna, which was *the son* of Rhesa, which was *the son* of Zorobabel, which was *the son* of Salathiel, which was *the son* of Neri,
> Which was *the son* of Melchi, which was *the son* of Addi,

which was *the son* of Cosam, which was *the son* of Elmodam, which was *the son* of Er,
Which was *the son* of Jose, which was *the son* of Eliezer, which was *the son* of Jorim, which was *the son* of Matthat, which was *the son* of Levi,
Which was *the son* of Simeon, which was *the son* of Juda, which was *the son* of Joseph, which was *the son* of Jonan, which was *the son* of Eliakim,
Which was *the son* of Melea, which was *the son* of Menan, which was *the son* of Mattatha, which was *the son* of Nathan, which was *the son* of David,
Which was *the son* of Jesse, which was *the son* of Obed, which was *the son* of Booz, which was *the son* of Salmon, which was *the son* of Naasson,
Which was *the son* of Aminadab, which was *the son* of Aram, which was *the son* of Esrom, which was *the son* of Phares, which was *the son* of Juda,
Which was *the son* of Jacob, which was *the son* of Isaac, which was *the son* of Abraham, which was *the son* of Thara, which was *the son* of Nachor,
Which was *the son* of Saruch, which was *the son* of Ragau, which was *the son* of Phalec, which was *the son* of Heber, which was *the son* of Sala,
Which was *the son* of Cainan,[8] which was *the son* of

---

8. There is no record of this Cainan of Luke 3:36 in the Old Testament. Genesis 11:12 indicates that Sala was the immediate and direct son of Arphaxad. Although most manuscripts include Cainan in verse 36, the error may have come in when an early scribe copying this section of Luke allowed his eye to drop to the Cainan of Luke 3:37 and mistakenly copied the name in verse 36 as well. Another possibility is that later scribes added it from the Septuagint, a Greek version of the Old Testament which erroneously lists "Cainan" as a son of Arphaxad. The Codex Bezae omits "which was *the son* of Cainan" in verse 36; the third-century papyrus known as p^{75} appears to support the omission.

Arphaxad, which was *the son* of Sem, which was *the son* of Noe, which was *the son* of Lamech,
Which was *the son* of Mathusala, which was *the son* of Enoch, which was *the son* of Jared, which was *the son* of Maleleel, which was *the son* of Cainan,
Which was *the son* of Enos, which was *the son* of Seth, which was *the son* of Adam, which was *the son*[9] of God.

Note that Luke 3:23 includes the phrase "as was supposed." Jesus Christ was not really the son of Joseph by birth. People just supposed that he was because Joseph was Mary's husband, and she gave birth to Jesus. The Father of Jesus Christ was God. However, Joseph accepted Jesus Christ into his household to be reared and treated as a son.

The genealogy in Luke 3 demonstrates that Joseph, like his wife Mary, was a descendant of the House of David. A person's standing in a family was normally recognized by the lineage of the father. From a human point of view, Jesus needed patrilineal credentials in order to function in a soci-

9. In Luke 3:23-38 we observe that the words "*the son*" are consistently italicized throughout the genealogy from Joseph back to Adam and God. The words do not occur in the Greek, but they are appropriately supplied as the expression "David which was of Jesse" normally implies that David was the son of Jesse. The addition of "*the son*" is an accurate aid to our understanding.

The Aramaic texts of this passage include the word *bar*, meaning "son of," in each place where the King James Version italicizes the words "*the son*." The single exception is Luke 3:38 where we read in the King James Version, "Adam, which was *the son* of God." Here the Aramaic does not use the word *bar*. Instead, it simply uses the words *adam dmen alaha* which literally translates as "Adam who was of [from] God."

ety built upon a paternal genealogy. He would not be accepted in the Judean society without a pedigree traceable through *both* parents. Since few would believe that on his Father's side he needed no pedigree, his Father being God, he had to have socially acceptable credentials through the human being whom society considered to be his father, Joseph. Since Joseph assumed the responsibility for Jesus as his son, it was Joseph's line that gave Jesus full legal standing in the House of David. Whereas Joseph's genealogy listed in Luke 3 gave Jesus his standing in the House of David by the assumed responsibility of Joseph, it was in truth the genealogy listed in Matthew 1 which gave Jesus Christ true standing in the House of David with the right to inherit his throne by the family line and genetic contribution of Mary.

The genealogy given in Luke 3 is not Jesus Christ's royal lineage. Matthew 1 indicates his royal lineage from Solomon and others who sat on David's throne (Matthew 1:6 and 7). Luke 3 demonstrates Jesus' lineage through another son of David, Nathan, who was not a king (Luke 3:31). This is why the genealogies in Matthew 1 and Luke 3 are identical up to David, but not from David on to Mary and Joseph.

The following table is a listing from the genealogy of Joseph as given in Luke 3:23-38.

THE LEGAL GENEALOGY OF JESUS CHRIST FROM LUKE 3

GOD

1. Adam
2. Seth
3. Enos
4. Cainan
5. Maleleel
6. Jared
7. Enoch
8. Mathusala
9. Lamech
10. Noe
11. Sem
12. Arphaxad [Cainan*]
13. Sala
14. Heber
15. Phalec
16. Ragau
17. Saruch
18. Nachor
19. Thara
20. Abraham
21. Isaac
22. Jacob
23. Juda
24. Phares
25. Esrom
26. Aram
27. Aminadab
28. Naasson
29. Salmon
30. Booz
31. Obed
32. Jesse
33. David
34. Nathan
35. Mattatha
36. Menan
37. Melea
38. Eliakim
39. Jonan
40. Joseph
41. Juda
42. Simeon
43. Levi
44. Matthat
45. Jorim
46. Eliezer
47. Jose
48. Er
49. Elmodam
50. Cosam

*For explanation see footnote 8 on p. 127.

51. Addi
52. Melchi
53. Neri
54. Salathiel
55. Zorobabel
56. Rhesa
57. Joanna
58. Juda
59. Joseph
60. Semei
61. Mattathias
62. Maath
63. Nagge
64. Esli
65. Naum
66. Amos
67. Mattathias
68. Joseph
69. Janna
70. Melchi
71. Levi
72. Matthat
73. Heli (father of Joseph)
74. Joseph (husband of Mary)
75. Jesus (as it was supposed, the son of Joseph)

The story of Jesus Christ's genealogy is now complete. Both lineages—that of Mary, in the Gospel of Matthew, and that of Joseph, in the Gospel of Luke—have Abraham and David common to their ancestry. Since Joseph assumed the responsibility as Jesus' father, this gave Jesus during his earthly walk a legal standing in the House of David. But as Mary's son by birth, Jesus had more than legal standing in the House of David; because of Mary's genealogy, Jesus Christ was descended from the royal line of the House of David, so that he could genetically and legally inherit the throne of David. Being conceived by the Holy Spirit (who is God) Jesus was the true and only begotten Son of God, the *ssemah* or offspring of the Lord.

Jesus was the offspring of Mary and God. Thus he

was born with no sinful nature in him, yet he was totally a man, a male child who would have to mature and learn in order to complete his God-ordained mission. As the offspring of both God and Mary, the Christ came into the world fulfilling all the genealogical requirements of the promised seed: he would be a descendant of Adam, of Abraham, and of David. He would also be the only begotten Son of God, the promised seed, God's perfect plan for man's redemption.

CHAPTER ELEVEN

ZACHARIAS AND THE ANGEL

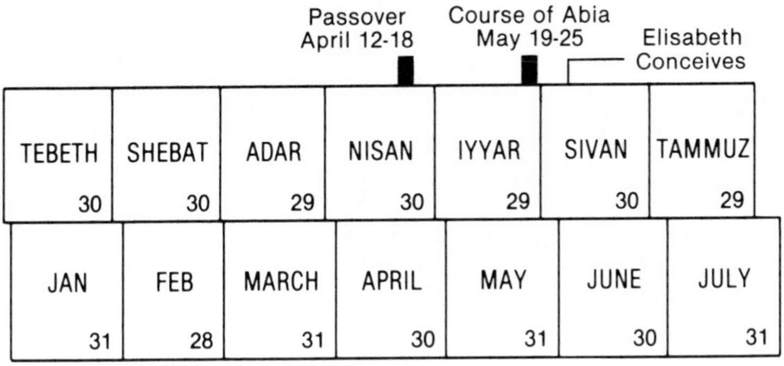

Passover April 12-18 | Course of Abia May 19-25 | Elisabeth Conceives

TEBETH	SHEBAT	ADAR	NISAN	IYYAR	SIVAN	TAMMUZ
30	30	29	30	29	30	29
JAN	FEB	MARCH	APRIL	MAY	JUNE	JULY
31	28	31	30	31	30	31

4 B.C.*

In order to get a full and accurate comprehension of the historical context of Jesus Christ's coming, we must take note of the prophet who preceded him by six months. This person was John the Baptist—a prophet of God, a priest, and a relative of Jesus. The Word of God not only tells us about this man, but it goes to relatively great lengths to set the backgrounds

*This calendar gives significant Biblical events in the year 4 B.C. The Hebrew months are given alongside our modern months. Because the Hebrew months were determined by the moon, their dates according to our calendar would shift from year to year.

and spiritual qualities of John's parents, Zacharias and Elisabeth. This record begins in the first chapter of the Gospel of Luke.

> Luke 1:5:
> There was in the days of Herod, the king of Judaea, a certain priest named Zacharias, of the course of Abia: and his wife *was* of the daughters of Aaron, and her name *was* Elisabeth.

Herod the Great, the king of Judea, was of Idumean[1] descent. He governed Judea by the consent of the Roman government. The events recorded in the first part of Luke occur during the latter years of Herod's reign.

Luke 1 tells that the man who would become the father of John was named Zacharias. He was a priest, which means he was a Levite, and, even more specifically, a direct descendant of Aaron. His wife, Elisabeth, was also descended from Aaron. Elisabeth's name was the same as that of Aaron's wife.[2]

Luke 1:5 tells that as a priest, Zacharias was "of the course of Abia." Now what exactly does a "course" of a priest mean? In the Old Testament as recorded in I Chronicles 23:6—24:19, King David,

---

1. In the Old Testament, Idumea is known as Edom, the home of Esau's descendants. It is located just south of the Dead Sea.
2. Exodus 6:23: "And Aaron took him Elisheba, daughter of Amminadab, sister of Naashon, to wife; and she bare him Nadab, and Abihu, Eleazar, and Ithamar." The name "Elisheba" is the Hebrew equivalent of "Elisabeth."

in giving order to the priesthood, divided the priests into twenty-four groups according to families. I Chronicles 24:19 says that these priestly courses were "the orderings of them in their service to come into the house of the Lord."

Each group of priests of a certain family lineage constituted one course, or service. That course would be assigned to come to the Temple for a specified week twice a year. Besides these two weeks, all priests of all twenty-four courses came and served in the Temple together during the three great annual feasts: the Feast of Unleavened Bread, the Feast of Pentecost, and the Feast of Tabernacles.

When the courses were originally instituted by David, the course of Abia meant those that were descended from Abijah. But by Jesus' time this had changed. The reason for this change was that only four of the original twenty-four courses of families returned to Jerusalem from the Babylonian captivity.[3] So in reestablishing the order to the Temple service upon returning from Babylon, these four family groups were divided into twenty-four courses, each course being assigned one of the original course names from the time of David. Zacharias was of the course of Abia ("Abijah" in the Old Testament), which was the eighth course according to I Chronicles 24:10.

---

3. See Ezra 2:36-39.

The twenty-four courses were ordered in the following manner: the first course would begin its term of service on the weekly sabbath before the first of Nisan, the first Hebrew month,[4] which began in either March or April. By calculating with the aid of chronological tables,[5] the priests of the course of Abia would have been in their first term of annual service according to our months in the last week of May in 4 B.C. So at that time Zacharias, as a priest of the eighth course, would be in Jerusalem at the Temple for a week to minister before the Lord.

> Luke 1:6:
> And they [Zacharias and Elisabeth] were both righteous before [Greek: *enōpion*, in the presence of] God, walking in all the commandments and ordinances of the Lord blameless.

The Greek word "ordinances" is *dikaiōmasin* meaning "legal requirements." Zacharias and Elisabeth were a special couple in that they were both righteous in God's presence because they faithfully carried out all the commandments and legal require-

---

4. Martin, *Birth of Christ Recalculated*, pp. 132-135, 139-142; J. Van Goudoever, *Biblical Calendars* (Leiden: E.J. Brill, 1959), p. 274; and John Lightfoot, *A Commentary on the New Testament from the Talmud and Hebraica: Matthew—I Corinthians*, 4 vols. (1859; reprint ed., Grand Rapids: Baker Book House, 1979), 3:8-11. It is notable as a parallel that the monthly courses of service in the kingdom of David began in Nisan (I Chronicles 27:1 and 2).

5. Parker and Dubberstein, *Babylonian Chronology*, p. 45.

ments of the Lord. In their private lives, however, they had suffered a major disappointment.

> Luke 1:7:
> And [But] they had no child, because that Elisabeth was barren, and they both were *now* well stricken in years.

In Biblical times it was considered a great disgrace not to have a child, especially not to have a son to be the family heir. Easterners believed that the blessing of childbearing had been withheld from childless couples because of a husband and wife's sin. Thus the disgrace was doubly painful to one who was a priest. Elisabeth, because she was barren, became the subject of reproach. And since Elisabeth was now "well stricken in years," all hope of her having a child seemed to be gone.

> Luke 1:8 and 9:
> And it came to pass, that while he [Zacharias] executed the priest's office before God in the order of his course [course of Abia],
> According to the custom of the priest's office, his lot was [it fell to him by lot] to burn incense when he went into the temple of the Lord.

Because of the number of priests involved in each course, every individual priest such as Zacharias would be assigned by lot a specific task on a certain day. The task allotted to Zacharias, according to Luke 1:9, was a great honor for a priest, an opportunity which might come once in a lifetime, if at all. Zacharias, by lot, was given the assignment on this particular day to go alone into the Holy Place and burn incense at the altar of incense.[6] This was the most highly regarded service in the daily ministry of the Temple, because the ascending smoke of the incense symbolized that prayers for Israel were being lifted to God Himself.[7] This priestly task was an awesome privilege and responsibility.

---

6. The Greek word for "temple" in Luke 1:9 is *naos*. It refers to the Temple proper, excluding the outer courts and surrounding area. The *naos* was the actual Temple building which included the Holy Place and the Holy of Holies (the innermost part). The Holy of Holies was entered into only by the high priest and only once a year on the Day of Atonement. The Holy Place was also a very special area and included the altar of incense, where Zacharias went while the people waited outside.

Edersheim describes the daily casting of lots. "It was done in this manner. The priests stood in a circle around the president, who for a moment removed the head-gear of one of their number, to show that he would begin counting at him. Then all held up one, two, or more fingers—since it was not lawful in Israel to count persons—when the president named some number, say seventy, and began counting the fingers till he reached the number named, which marked that the lot had fallen on that priest." Edersheim, *The Temple*, p. 150. See also Lightfoot, *New Testament from the Talmud and Hebraica*, 3:15-16.

The ritual of the burning of incense is also described by Edersheim in *The Temple*, pp. 157-171; and in his *The Life and Times of Jesus the Messiah* (rev. ed., 2 vols. in 1., Grand Rapids: Wm. B. Eerdmans, 1971), 1:137-141.

7. Note Revelation 8:3 and 4: "...and there was given unto him much incense, that he should offer *it* with the prayers of all saints upon the golden altar which was before the throne. And the smoke of the incense, *which came* with the prayers of the saints, ascended up before God...."

> Luke 1:10 and 11:
> And the whole multitude of the people were praying without at the time of incense.
> And there appeared unto him [Zacharias] an angel of the Lord standing on the right side of the altar of incense.

It was customary for people in the Temple area to gather and silently pray outside the Holy Place while the incense was being burned. This was a very special time, a most solemn period of silence throughout the Temple area.[8]

It was at this time of offering incense that Zacharias, alone in the Holy Place, saw the angel on the right side of the altar. In the Biblical culture the right side always represented blessing and power, whereas the left side represented cursing. Also note that in the Word of God angels are never described as having wings and hovering or singing. This angel which appeared to Zacharias was standing by the altar.

> Luke 1:12 and 13:
> And when Zacharias saw *him* [the angel], he was troubled, and fear fell upon him.
> But the angel said unto him, Fear not, Zacharias. . . .

Zacharias was troubled; he was startled and awed by this unexpected appearance. The message the

---

8. Edersheim, *The Temple*, pp. 167-168; *Life and Times*, 1:138.

angel had for Zacharias took him by surprise and made him wonder.

> Luke 1:13:
> . . . for thy prayer [for Israel] is heard; and thy wife Elisabeth shall bear thee a son, and thou shalt call his name John [meaning, "Jehovah shows favor"].

Zacharias was praying for Israel. God heard that prayer and was going to answer by giving him and his wife a son. This child would be sent by God as a blessing to Israel as a result of Zacharias' prayer. It is significant that Zacharias learned of the prayer's answer while the smoke of the incense, representing the prayers to God for Israel, was yet ascending before him. For Zacharias to learn that he and his wife would have a son was a tremendous revelation and blessing to the aged priest, but the angel had even more to declare concerning the greatness of this son.

> Luke 1:14 and 15:
> And thou [Zacharias] shalt have joy and gladness; and many shall rejoice at his birth.
> For he shall be great in the sight of [or, in the presence of] the Lord, and shall drink neither wine nor strong drink; and he shall be filled with the Holy Ghost [holy spirit], even from his mother's womb.

The child, John the Baptist, was not promised to

be great in the sight of the world, but in the sight of God he would be very great; for of all men, only John was filled with holy spirit from his mother's womb.

> Luke 1:16 and 17:
> And many of the children of Israel shall he turn to the Lord their God.
> And he shall go before [*enōpion*, in the presence of] him [God] in the spirit and power of Elias [Elijah], to turn the hearts of the fathers to the children, and the disobedient to the wisdom of the just; to make ready a people prepared for the Lord.

The angel said that the child would grow up to be a great prophet, going forth in the presence of God, calling God's people to turn back to His Word. He would turn the hearts of the fathers to the children. This meant not only a child's parents, who are the first to instruct the child, but also his teachers, who were often called "fathers," just as the students were often called "sons."[9] The hearts of men would again be turned to give the instruction of the Word to the "sons." The disobedient would again turn to seek wisdom. That was John the Baptist's ministry. It was much like the ministry of Elijah in the Old Testament. The words "spirit and power" are the figure

---

9. Elijah was called "father" by Elisha in II Kings 2:12. Likewise, Paul called himself "father" with respect to teaching the Corinthians in I Corinthians 4:15. Also see *The Companion Bible*, Appendix 74, A.1., p. 109.

of speech *hendiadys* in which two nouns are used, but one thing is meant. One of the nouns is used to augment the other to the superlative degree. In other words, John the Baptist, as a great prophet, would walk with the same "powerful spirit" with which Elijah had walked. John would operate that same powerful spirit as Elijah had in calling Israel back to God.

People are "prepared for the Lord" when they are ready to receive God's Word. The word "Lord" here refers to God, not Jesus Christ; John prepared the people for God. Christians often call John "the forerunner" of Jesus Christ. This term is accurate if it is understood to mean that his ministry preceded Jesus Christ's. However, the term "forerunner" can also be used of all the prophets throughout the Old Testament. As all great prophets of old, John would prepare people to receive God's Word by proclaiming it.[10] There had been no written revelation to Israel since the Prophet Malachi who lived four hundred years previous to the birth of John. Spiritual darkness hung like a cloud over Israel. It is no small wonder that God needed to raise up a great prophet

---

10. Because of John's ministry, many people were prepared to receive God's Word. Since Jesus Christ was God's Word in the flesh and John's ministry immediately preceded his, it was only natural that many people were prepared to receive Jesus Christ. As a great prophet, John recognized that Jesus was God's promised Messiah and he indeed declared it. See Matthew 3:11-17; John 1:26-36; 3:28-36.

to prepare people for Him. Zacharias' child was to be that prophet.

> Luke 1:18:
> And Zacharias said unto the angel, Whereby [''by what'' or ''how''] shall I know this? for I am an old man, and my wife well stricken in years.

Zacharias was an aged man. His wife, Elisabeth, was also ''well stricken in years,'' literally this means ''advanced in her days.''

> Luke 1:19 and 20:
> And the angel answering said unto him, I am Gabriel, that stand in the presence of God; and am sent to speak unto thee, and to shew thee these glad tidings.
> And, behold, thou shalt be dumb, and not able to speak, until the day that these things shall be performed, because thou believest not my words, which shall be fulfilled in their season.

The angel revealed that Zacharias' unbelief would not prevent the child's birth from coming to pass. Elisabeth would still bear him a son who would become a great prophet.

> Luke 1:21:
> And the people waited for [were expecting] Zacharias, and marvelled that he tarried so long in the temple.

The people, as they reverently waited outside the

Holy Place, began to wonder why Zacharias did not come out of the Temple after a customary length of time. He had been at the altar of incense much longer than usual,[11] for a reason unknown to the people.

> Luke 1:22:
> And when he [Zacharias] came out, he could not speak unto them: and they perceived that he had seen a vision [this is how the angel appeared to him] in the temple: for he beckoned unto them, and remained speechless.

When Zacharias finally emerged from the Holy Place to stand on top of the steps which led down to the court of the Temple, the other priests and people were waiting for him to pronounce the Lord's blessing. But, as the angel had declared, Zacharias was not able to speak. So he made signs to them, and they realized that he had seen a vision while in the Holy Place.

> Luke 1:23:
> And it came to pass, that, as soon as the days of his ministration were accomplished, he departed to his own house.

---

11. The priest, after burning the incense in the Holy Place, normally came out and pronounced a blessing on the people. This would precede the daily meat offering, and be a time of joy and praise. This blessing would be similar to Numbers 6:24-26: "The Lord bless thee, and keep thee: The Lord make his face shine upon thee, and be gracious unto thee: The Lord lift up his countenance upon thee, and give thee peace."

Zacharias returned to his home in the hill country of Judah following the completion of his ministration, his week of service at the Temple during the course of Abia. Soon afterwards, his wife Elisabeth conceived according to the promise of the angel.

> Luke 1:24 and 25:
> And after those days his wife Elisabeth conceived, and hid herself five months, saying,
> Thus hath the Lord dealt with me in the days wherein he looked on *me*, to take away my reproach among men.

Zacharias would have been in Jerusalem serving in the Temple during the last week of May of 4 B.C. After he completed his course, he would have returned home in early June of 4 B.C. Upon his return, Elisabeth conceived a son. The promise from God declared by the angel of the Lord to Zacharias that he and Elisabeth would have a son began to come into fruition.

God's Word says that Elisabeth hid herself for the first five months of her pregnancy. She did not conceal herself because she was afraid. Nor was she trying to conceal her pregnancy from others. Indeed, she "hid" herself for the first five months (meaning to "conceal in retirement," or "seclude") simply to have privacy from everyone and everything going on around her during the first part of her pregnancy.

Elisabeth states, "Thus hath the Lord dealt with me in the days wherein he looked on *me*, to take away my reproach among men." Elisabeth's "reproach among men" was that she had no child. Yet God enabled her to conceive by Zacharias even though she had been barren and was getting to be advanced in her years. God took away her reproach, her censure, among men. When all others had reproached her, the Lord had not. He alone had watched over her, looking for the day when He could enable her to conceive by Zacharias. Now Elisabeth in turn would dedicate this time of the early part of her pregnancy to God, recognizing the Lord's special favor in allowing her to have the child. During these five months she would enjoy quiet fellowship with God in grateful worship for what He had done. She would keep herself without distraction as she carefully nurtured the baby developing within her womb.

This concludes the record from Luke 1 of the revelation to Zacharias concerning John's birth and Elisabeth's subsequent conception. It is in this context, after the conception of John the Baptist, that God's great plans continue to unfold as He sends His messenger Gabriel to a town in Galilee to bring news to a relative of Elisabeth. The announcement of another baby was imminent.

CHAPTER TWELVE

MARY AND THE ANGEL

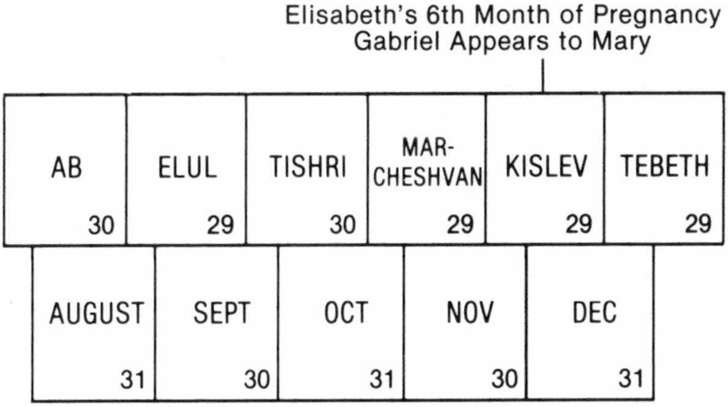

Elisabeth's 6th Month of Pregnancy
Gabriel Appears to Mary

AB	ELUL	TISHRI	MAR-CHESHVAN	KISLEV	TEBETH
30	29	30	29	29	29

AUGUST	SEPT	OCT	NOV	DEC
31	30	31	30	31

4 B.C.*

After God's messenger Gabriel announced to Zacharias the coming of a son to him and his wife, Elisabeth conceived and went into seclusion for five months. Moving in chronological order, as the record unfolds in Luke 1, Gabriel is sent on another mission—this time to a young woman named Mary in a town in Galilee. There Gabriel announced to Mary that she would bear the Christ, the Messiah to

*This calendar gives significant Biblical events in the year 4 B.C. The Hebrew months are given alongside our modern months. Because the Hebrew months were determined by the moon, their dates according to our calendar would shift from year to year.

Israel. Again this truth is disclosed in the Gospel of Luke.

> Luke 1:26:
> And in the sixth month [of Elisabeth's pregnancy] the angel Gabriel was sent from God unto a city of Galilee, named Nazareth.

Previously Gabriel had spoken to the priest, Zacharias, in the Temple in the city of Jerusalem. Now Gabriel delivers God's message in a Galilean city named Nazareth.[1] Since Elisabeth conceived in June of 4 B.C., her sixth month of pregnancy would be in December. Therefore, it was at this time that Gabriel appeared to Mary in Nazareth.

> Luke 1:27:
> To a virgin espoused to a man whose name was Joseph, of the house of David; and the virgin's name *was* Mary.

To understand this verse, we need to look into Oriental marriage customs, including "espousal." Because marriage customs of the East were very different from our own, terms must be understood in light of Eastern culture.

---

1. The name Nazareth is related to the Hebrew word *nesser* meaning "sprout" or "shoot," according to Brown, Driver, and Briggs (*Hebrew and English Lexicon*, p. 666) and other Hebrew scholars. It is also related to the Aramaic word *nassarta* which means "young twig" or "spring branch, shoot, sprout." Carolo Brockelmann, *Lexicon Syriacum* (Edinburgh: T. & T. Clark, 1895), p. 443.

The marriage procedures of that time can be divided into five stages: (1) the prearrangements, (2) the betrothal ceremony, (3) the wedding ceremony, (4) the initial coming together for sexual intercourse, and (5) the honeymoon.[2]

The first stage, or prearrangements, took place before the betrothal, often years before. The women of the prospective groom's family generally arranged the marriage. The mother and aunts selected an appropriate girl to be the future bride of the young man. Much care was taken in this selection. Then arrangements were made with the girl's parents for the dowry and the future marriage.[3]

After the bride had been chosen, the next stage was the betrothal ceremony. This was not the wedding, but a preliminary to it. The betrothal ceremony took place as long as a year before the wedding, although sometimes several years elapsed between these two events.[4] This occasion was very solemn. The bride would be veiled, as it was considered improper for a groom to look upon the face of

---

2. Bo Reahard, "The Espousal of Mary and Joseph," *The Way Magazine*, January/February 1976, pp. 9-11.
3. James Neil, *Everyday Life in the Holy Land*, 4th ed. (1913; reprint ed., London: Church Missions to Jews, 1930), pp. 223-225; K.C. Pillai, *Light Through an Eastern Window* (New York: Robert Speller & Sons, 1963), pp. 1-3; George H. Scherer, *The Eastern Colour of the Bible* (London: National Sunday School Union, n.d.), p. 97.
4. G.M. Mackie, *Bible Manners and Customs* (London: A. & C. Black, 1903), p. 122; James M. Freeman, *Manners and Customs of the Bible* (reprint ed., Plainfield, N.J.: Logos International, 1972), p. 330.

the bride until the wedding ceremony was performed.

During the betrothal ceremony, the two families gathered for a large feast. Afterwards, they went out into a garden. There the couple sat in a special place. The girl held her hands out to the young man and he would drop ten pieces of silver into them. At this moment God was believed to kindle love in their hearts for each other.[5]

At the time of the betrothal, a payment or dowry was made by the groom's family to the bride's family for the privilege of marrying their daughter. The Aramaic root word for "betroth" means "to barter." After a betrothal with its dowry, the girl was considered promised, vowed, and purchased as the young man's wife.[6]

This betrothal involved a much stronger commitment than engagement does in our culture. Indeed, betrothal was an actual marriage commitment. A betrothal could only be disannulled by divorce or death. For all intents and purposes, the betrothed man and woman were considered husband and wife from the time of the betrothal,[7] though they did not

---

5. Pillai, *Light Through an Eastern Window*, pp. 3-5. The ten pieces of silver are referred to in Luke 15:8.

6. See J. Payne Smith, ed., *A Compendious Syriac Dictionary* (1903; reprint ed., Oxford: Clarendon Press, 1957), pp. 271-272. Also, see George M. Lamsa, *Gospel Light*, rev. ed. (Philadelphia: A.J. Holman, 1936), pp. 6-9; Samuel Burder, *Oriental Customs* (Philadelphia: William W. Woodward, 1804), p. 271; also, Neil, *Everyday Life in the Holy Land*, p. 230.

7. Reahard, "Espousal," p. 11; H. Clay Trumbull, *Studies in Oriental Social Life* (Philadelphia: John D. Wattles & Co., 1894), p. 26.

come together for intercourse until after the wedding ceremony.

The man and woman would not begin living together until after the wedding, which occurred as much as a year after the betrothal. During this interval, the man and woman would be preparing themselves for the wedding and the experience of living together as husband and wife. These preparations included the making of the wedding garments[8] and the selection of the attendants.

When the time for the wedding ceremony came, there would be a great joyous gathering of family and friends. The wedding could last as long as ten days and there would be much singing, rejoicing, and feasting. An elder or holy man, usually a priest, would officiate.[9]

When the wedding was over, the couple did not, as in our culture, immediately come together as a man and wife in sexual relations. Rather, the priest would designate a time, normally within a week after the wedding ceremony, when the couple would have their first sexual intercourse. Until this time of their "first coming together," the bridegroom would be attended by a man and the bride by a woman.[10]

---

8. Freeman, *Manners and Customs*, p. 330.
9. Pillai, *Light Through an Eastern Window*, pp. 7-20; Scherer, *Eastern Colour*, p. 97.
10. K.C. Pillai, *The Orientalisms of the Bible* (Fairborn, Ohio: Munkus Publishing Co., 1969), pp. 52-53; Pillai, *Light Through an Eastern Window*, pp. 20-21; Reahard, "Espousal," pp. 10, 25.

With this coming together as husband and wife having sexual intercourse, the man and woman began their honeymoon. This honeymoon would last for one year and would be dedicated to the development of a marriage relationship as the couple learned to live with one another.[11]

At the time Gabriel appeared to Mary it was December of 4 B.C. Mary was betrothed to Joseph. She had been purchased to be his bride and was committed to him. However, they had not yet gone through the wedding ceremony, nor had they begun living together.

> Luke 1:26 and 27:
> And in the sixth month [of Elisabeth's pregnancy] the angel Gabriel was sent from God unto a city of Galilee, named Nazareth,
> To a virgin espoused to a man whose name was Joseph, of the house of David; and the virgin's name *was* Mary.

Mary is called a "virgin" in Luke1:27. The Greek word for "virgin" is *parthenos*, meaning "a young woman." At this time Mary had certainly not had any sexual relations with Joseph or with any other

---

11. See Deuteronomy 24:5: "When a man hath taken a new wife, he shall not go out to war, neither shall he be charged with any business: *but* he shall be free at home one year, and shall cheer up his wife which he hath taken." The phrase "free at home" indicates that the man would be free from military service during the year. Also see Pillai, *Light Through an Eastern Window*, pp. 20-22; and his *Orientalisms of the Bible*, pp. 56-57.

man. In Biblical culture, a young woman was assumed not to have had any sexual relations until she began living with her husband. That is why *parthenos* was often used in reference to a girl who had not had sexual intercourse.

However, *parthenos* can also be used of a young woman who has had sexual relations with a man.[12] This is clear from the Septuagint, a Greek translation of the Old Testament.

> Genesis 34:1-4:
> And Dinah the daughter of Leah, which she bare unto Jacob, went out to see the daughters of the land.
> And when Shechem the son of Hamor the Hivite, prince of the country, saw her, he took her [Dinah], and lay with her, and defiled her.
> And his soul clave unto Dinah the daughter of Jacob, and he loved the damsel [*parthenos*], and spake kindly unto the damsel [*parthenos*].
> And Shechem spake unto his father Hamor, saying, Get me this damsel to wife.

---

12. Deuteronomy 22:14-17 uses the word *parthenos* (in the Septuagint) regarding a "maid" and "*the tokens of* the damsel's virginity." According to Gerhard Delling, while profane sources sometimes do use *parthenos* in reference to a girl who has not had sexual relations, he states that even then "there is no more stress on this than when we speak of a 'girl' or 'young woman' (which is in innumerable instances the best rendering)." Delling further states that "many times it is used in the Septuagint simply to mean 'girl.'" See Gerhard Kittel and Gerhard Friedrich, eds. *Theological Dictionary of the New Testament*, 10 vols., trans. and ed. G.W. Bromiley (Grand Rapids: Wm. B. Eerdmans, 1964-76), 5:826-837.

In the above record it is clear that Dinah is called a *parthenos* even after having had sexual intercourse. A verse in II Corinthians implies the same.

> II Corinthians 11:2:
> For I am jealous over you with godly jealousy: for I have espoused you to one husband, that I may present *you as* a chaste virgin [*parthenos*] to Christ.

The use of the word "chaste" implies that it is possible to be a defiled *parthenos*, one that is not chaste.

Thus, *parthenos* does not always indicate the woman has not had sexual relations. *Parthenos* simply emphasizes her young, marriageable age as does the English word "maiden."[13] This same basic truth holds for the Hebrew word *bthulah* and the Aramaic word *bthulta*[14] as can be seen from their usage in Genesis 24:16, Deuteronomy 22:19, Esther 2:17 and 19, and Joel 1:8. Joel 1:8 says, ". . .like a virgin [*bthulah*] girded with sackcloth for the husband of her

---

13. Hence, *parthenos* in Luke 1:27 is translated as "girl" in *The New English Bible*. J.B. Phillips' translation renders it "young woman," as does C.F. Kent in *The Shorter Bible*.

14. See Charles D. Isbell, "Does the Gospel of Matthew Proclaim Mary's Virginity?" *Biblical Archaeology Review* 3 (June 1977): 18, 18 fn. Isbell states, "Hebrew *bethulah* did not, when used alone, denote virginity. . . . Not only Hebrew *bethulah*, but the cognate word in Akkadian, Aramaic, Ugaritic, etc., functions similarly as well." Isbell shows that "there is simply no single word in the languages of the ancient Near East which carries in and of itself the idea of *virgo intacta* [virgin who had had no sexual relations]." Such an implication must be drawn from context.

youth.'' A young, childless wife was considered and called a virgin.

In Luke 1:27, Mary was betrothed to Joseph but had not yet gone through the wedding ceremony. We know that Mary had not had sexual relations with any man. She was a young woman of the lineage of David betrothed to a man who was also descended from David. This is the revelation of Luke 1:27 when read with Biblical understanding.

Next Luke records that the angel addressed the young woman and blessed her.

> Luke 1:28:
> And the angel came in unto her, and said, Hail, *thou that art* highly favoured, the Lord *is* with thee: blessed *art* thou among women.

The words ''highly favoured'' are the one Greek word *kecharitōmenē*. The angel, in essence, was saying, ''Hail, you who have been highly favored by God. The Lord is with you. Blessed are you among women.'' Of all the women who had ever lived, it would be Mary who would conceive and give birth to mankind's promised seed. Certainly she received God's high favor. What a tremendous young woman Mary was.

> Luke 1:29:
> And [But] when she saw *him* [the angel], she was

> troubled at his saying, and cast in her mind what manner of salutation this should be.

The word "and" should be "but" according to the Greek and Aramaic manuscripts. The words "when she saw *him*" should be deleted according to most critical Greek texts. The word "saying" is the Greek word *logos*, meaning "word." The first part of this verse should then read, "But she was troubled at his word."

Very humanly, Mary was troubled when she first heard the angel's declaration. She did not understand what Gabriel meant. Therefore the angel exhorted her to rid herself of fear and reassured her that she was favored of the Lord God.

> Luke 1:30 and 31:
> And the angel said unto her, Fear not, Mary: for thou hast found favour with God.
> And, behold, thou shalt conceive in thy womb, and bring forth a son, and shalt call his name JESUS.

Mary was told that she would become pregnant with a son and was instructed to name him "Jesus." The Aramaic for "Jesus" is *yeshu*; the Greek word is *Iēsous*; the corresponding Hebrew word is *yehoshua*, translated "Joshua." Jesus, or Joshua, means "the Lord our savior" or "the Lord is salvation." This was to be the name of the son Mary would have. The angel prophesied further concerning Jesus.

Luke 1:32:
He [Jesus] shall be great, and shall be called the Son of the Highest: and the Lord God shall give unto him the throne of his father David.

This child Mary would bear was to be called "the Son of the Highest," that is, the Son of God. God would also give him "the throne of his father [ancestor] David." Again we see the wonderful truth that Jesus Christ was descended from David and could rightfully inherit David's throne by virtue of his being born of Mary.

Luke 1:33:
And he [Jesus] shall reign over the house of Jacob for ever; and of his kingdom there shall be no end.

Note how wonderfully the angel's words agree with the Old Testament prophecies. The angel's message was a tremendous revelation, but Mary could not understand how all the things the angel was telling her could come about.

Luke 1:34:
Then said Mary unto the angel, How shall this be, seeing I know not a man?

Mary and Joseph were betrothed, but the wedding ceremony had not yet occurred. Mary had not begun living with her husband Joseph; nor had she had sexual intercourse and therefore could not possibly be pregnant. The angel responded to Mary's question by explaining that the child would be divinely conceived.

> Luke 1:35:
> And the angel answered and said unto her, The Holy Ghost [Holy Spirit] shall come upon thee, and the power of the Highest shall overshadow thee: therefore also that holy thing which shall be born of thee shall be called the Son of God.

This child would not be conceived in her by a man, but by God, the Holy Spirit. Therefore, the child would be called the Son of God.

In verse 31, the angel said that Mary would conceive in her womb. The "womb" figuratively represents all the internal female organs associated with reproduction by the figure of speech *synecdoche*. "The Holy Spirit shall come upon thee" simply expresses the truth that God, not a man, would impregnate the egg in Mary by creating a sperm within her fallopian tube at the proper moment of ovulation so that fertilization would occur. But from that point on, the fetus developed according to natural processes as in any other pregnancy. This was the miraculous, divine conception of Jesus Christ.

> Luke 1:36:
> And, behold, thy cousin [Greek: *sungenēs*, kinswoman] Elisabeth, she hath also conceived a son in her old age:

> and this is the sixth month [December] with her [Elisabeth], who was called barren.

In order for Mary to be a relative of Elisabeth, a Levite, somewhere in Mary's ancestry there had to have been a Levite. Mary's paternal bloodline was Judean, not Levitical, as given in the genealogy of Mary in Matthew 1. Therefore, somewhere in Mary's maternal bloodline there was a Levitical ancestor. Whoever it was, that person was directly related to the family of Elisabeth. This is how Mary and Elisabeth were related to each other. Since Mary and Elisabeth were kinswomen, Mary knew that Elisabeth had been barren and was "in her old age." Now she learned of Elisabeth's pregnancy. What unexpected, exciting news that was.

The angel was revealing all these truths to Mary when Elisabeth was in her sixth month of pregnancy, in December of 4 B.C. The angel Gabriel then ended his message to Mary with a statement that authoritatively and appropriately concluded the glorious news he had just spoken.

> Luke 1:37:
> For with God nothing [not anything spoken] shall be impossible [Greek: *adunatēsei*, shall be void of power].

The word "nothing" in verse 37 is translated from the Greek words *ouk pan rhēma, ouk* meaning "not" and *pan rhēma* meaning "anything spoken." Nothing that Gabriel had spoken to Mary would be impossible. God was fully capable of seeing that it all came to pass. He stood behind every syllable of the message Mary had heard.

> Luke 1:38:
> And Mary said, Behold the handmaid of the Lord; be it unto me according to thy word. And the angel departed from her.

The word "handmaid" in Luke 1:38 and 48 is the Greek *doulē*, the feminine form of *doulos*, slave. Its only other occurrence in the New Testament is in Acts 2:18: "And on my servants [*doulos*] and on my handmaidens [*doulē*] I will pour out in those days of my Spirit; and they shall prophesy." This is a quote from Joel 2:29 where the Hebrew word *shifhah* is employed. This Hebrew term is used of female servants who were treated as members of the family, servants such as Hagar was to Sarah (Genesis 25:12), and Zilpah was to Leah (Genesis 29:24), and Bilhah was to Rachel (Genesis 29:29).

Another Hebrew word *amah* is used of a female servant who was not considered a part of the family but rather as a servant among servants. I Samuel 25:41 says, ". . . *Let* thine handmaid [*amah*] *be* a servant [*shifhah*] to wash the feet of the servants of my lord." Mary was more than a female servant, she was a handmaid, one of the family, bearing God's only begotten Son.

In I Samuel 1, Hannah was barren. She referred to herself as a female servant (*amah*, a servant of servants) of the Lord in verses 11 and 16 while petitioning the Lord for a son. But when the petition was granted, she referred to herself as the handmaid (*shifhah*, one of the family) in verse 18. With the granting of this request, Hannah became the mother of the Prophet Samuel. So Mary referred to herself as a handmaid, one of the family, literally believing God's Word as Hannah had done. "...Be it unto me according to thy Word." Perhaps it was at the moment she uttered these words that she conceived.

Mary's response to the angel's declaration was one of great believing. She alone fulfilled the requirements for being the savior's mother. Mary was of the proper lineage, and in the right place at the right time in order to allow God's perfect timetable to be fulfilled. Mary not only had the proper credentials, but she believed the angel's words and conceived the promised seed, the Messiah.

CHAPTER THIRTEEN

MARY AND ELISABETH

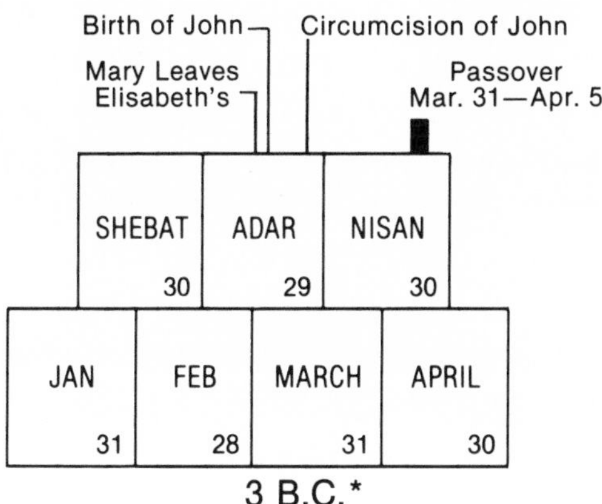

3 B.C.*

Mary, a young woman betrothed to Joseph, was now pregnant with the promised seed, "the Son of the Highest." From a divine viewpoint she had been favored; however, from a human point of view, she was in a serious predicament. Mary was not yet married to Joseph and thus not living with him. How could she explain her pregnancy to

*This calendar gives significant Biblical events in the year 3 B.C. The Hebrew months are given alongside our modern months. Because the Hebrew months were determined by the moon, their dates according to our calendar would shift from year to year.

Joseph, to her parents, to the religious leaders, or to anyone else and make them understand and believe? Mary was in a great dilemma.

According to Old Testament law, a betrothed woman could be stoned to death if she were discovered to have had sexual intercourse with someone prior to her coming together with her husband in their designated first intercourse.[1] The best treatment a betrothed, pregnant woman could hope for was to be given a written bill of divorcement and sent away in disgrace, resulting in total humiliation for herself and her family.[2] The betrothed, pregnant Mary now found herself in this perplexing situation.

However, there was one place where she could possibly find consolation and understanding. Since the angel had spoken to Mary of Elisabeth, a kinswoman who had miraculously conceived in her old age, she was the obvious choice for Mary to confide in: a relative, an older woman, the wife of a priest, and one who was also bearing a child promised by the Lord.

Furthermore, it would have been perfectly acceptable for Mary to visit Elisabeth a few months before her wedding. In the Biblical culture, the older women in the family always gave the young brides-

1. See Deuteronomy 22:13,14,20-24.
2. Deuteronomy 24:1: "When a man hath taken a wife, and married her, and it come to pass that she find no favour in his eyes, because he hath found some uncleanness in her: then let him write her a bill of divorcement, and give *it* in her hand, and send her out of his house."

to-be instruction concerning married life. Mary would have had no difficulty in explaining to her parents her desire to visit Elisabeth.

> Luke 1:39 and 40:
> And Mary arose in those days, and went into the hill country with haste, into a city of Juda;
> And entered into the house of Zacharias, and saluted [greeted] Elisabeth.

In Biblical culture, this visit to a kinswoman would never take place after the wedding ceremony, because Joseph and Mary would have been in their honeymoon year. Joseph was not with Mary for they were still betrothed, not yet married. Culturally a couple would not be allowed such a trip together before their wedding and their time of coming together. Mary was very earnest in her desire to see Elisabeth, for it says she traveled "with haste," which means she left as soon as she conveniently could, leaving her home without delay.

> Luke 1:41-43:
> And it came to pass, that, when Elisabeth heard the salutation [greeting] of Mary, the babe [John] leaped in her womb; and Elisabeth was filled with the Holy Ghost [holy spirit]:
> And she [Elisabeth] spake out with a loud voice, and said, Blessed *art* thou among women, and blessed *is* the fruit of thy womb.

And whence *is* this to me, that the mother of my Lord should come to me?

The word "Lord" in verse 43 in Greek is *kurios*; in Aramaic it is *marya*. Both the Aramaic and Greek words are used of anyone who is a master or owner of servants or property. Therefore, the word "lord" is Biblically used of God, of Jesus Christ, and of any man with servants or property. The phrase "mother of my Lord" does not mean Mary was the mother of God. Elisabeth simply recognized that Mary's child was sent by God to be her lord, her master, her spiritual superior.

Imagine the relief from anxiety, the encouragement, the spiritual uplifting Elisabeth's words must have given Mary. Elisabeth, by her five senses, had no previous knowledge of Mary's pregnancy. Yet, as soon as Mary greeted her, Elisabeth by inspired utterance proclaimed with exuberance the blessing of the child in Mary's womb. The baby in Elisabeth's womb literally jumped for joy. The angel had promised that John would be filled with the holy spirit even from the womb. Elisabeth continued prophesying concerning Mary and the child.

Luke 1:44 and 45:
For, lo, as soon as the voice of thy salutation sounded in mine ears, the babe [John] leaped in my womb for joy.

And blessed *is* she [Mary] that believed: for there shall be a performance of those things which were told her from the Lord [through His messenger Gabriel].

Elisabeth's inspired declaration was emphatic. Elisabeth's prophecy corroborated that all that the angel had told Mary would come to pass. Mary's concerns could all be put to rest, for God would arrange everything and see that all was accomplished. All was in God's hands. Elisabeth's words blessed Mary in such a wonderful way that Mary's heart overflowed with comfort and praise.

Luke 1:46-48:
And Mary said, My soul doth magnify the Lord,
And my spirit hath rejoiced in God my Saviour.
For he [God] hath regarded the low estate [humility, meekness] of his handmaiden [Greek: *doulēs*, female bondservant]: for, behold, from henceforth all generations shall call me blessed.

Mary was indeed a woman of God. Mary described herself as "the handmaid of the Lord." All generations would call her blessed. She was not to be called "the blessed virgin" or "the blessed mother of God." These titles are unscriptural and inaccurate. They cause people to misunderstand how human Mary and the wonderful child she bore were. Furthermore, the erroneous titles degrade the God whom Mary served.

The great qualities of Mary's character included believing and humility. She meekly accepted God's Word concerning her unusual pregnancy, knowing full well that her culture would criticize and directly oppose it. Her meekness, her humility, were some of the wonderful attributes of Mary that God noted. Mary humbly gave God the praise and glory for all He did as she spoke to Elisabeth.

> Luke 1:49-55:
> For he that is mighty hath done to me great things; and holy *is* his name.
> And his mercy *is* on them that fear [reverence] him from generation to generation.
> He hath shewed strength with his arm; he hath scattered the proud in the imagination of their hearts.
> He hath put down the mighty from *their* seats, and exalted them of low degree [humility, meekness].
> He hath filled the hungry with good things; and the rich he hath sent empty away.
> He hath holpen his servant Israel, in remembrance of *his* mercy;
> As he spake to our fathers, to Abraham, and to his seed for ever.

All undue concerns were now totally lifted from Mary. She knew that God Almighty was over everything, and that she had nothing to fear for God was taking care of her. He had helped Israel in the past by remembering His covenant with Abraham and his seed. Now God was again helping Israel by performing a great work in a humble young woman from Galilee. Mary's heart was full of praise and awe.

> Luke 1:56:
> And Mary abode with her [Elisabeth] about three months, and returned to her own house.

In the information given concerning the visit of Mary and Elisabeth, there is no indication of Joseph's presence. However, since Mary was betrothed to Joseph, she would soon be married and begin living with him; therefore, she returned to her home in Nazareth.

Luke 1:56 says that Mary stayed with Elisabeth "about three months." Having arrived at Elisabeth's home in December of 4 B.C., Mary had to have returned to Nazareth in March of 3 B.C. Since Elisabeth was in her sixth month of pregnancy when Mary arrived, Mary returned to her own home when Elisabeth was in her ninth month and about to be delivered of her son John.

CHAPTER FOURTEEN

THE BIRTH OF JOHN THE BAPTIST

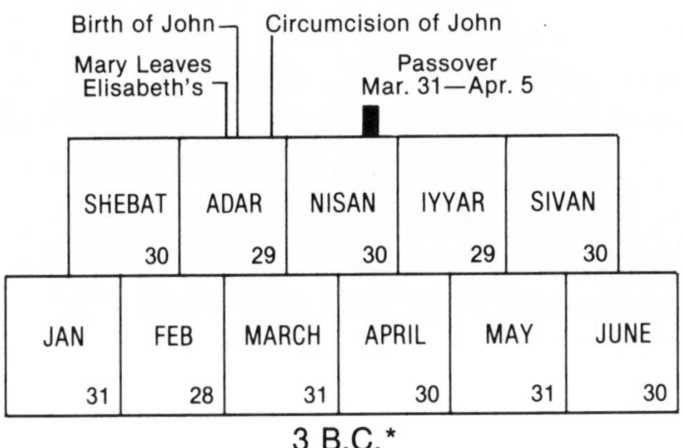

When Mary left the house of Zacharias, Elisabeth was in her ninth month of pregnancy. Having conceived the previous June, Elisabeth gave birth in March. The many promises the angel had made concerning the child which Elisabeth was carrying were being fulfilled according to and in

*This calendar gives significant Biblical events in the year 3 B.C. The Hebrew months are given alongside our modern months. Because the Hebrew months were determined by the moon, their dates according to our calendar would shift from year to year.

their proper time. It must have been very exciting for Elisabeth as the time of her delivery approached.

> Luke 1:57 and 58:
> Now Elisabeth's full time came that she should be delivered; and she brought forth a son.
> And her neighbours and her cousins heard how the Lord had shewed great mercy upon her; and they rejoiced with her.

Elisabeth, the aged woman who had been disgraced by her childlessness, not only gave birth, but gave birth to a son. Of course, the neighbors and relatives were overjoyed by this. Everyone was excited for both the child and his parents. However, in the excitement at the time of his circumcision, confusion arose regarding the naming of the infant. Neighbors and relatives wanted to name the child Zacharias after his father.

> Luke 1:59:
> And it came to pass, that on the eighth day they [the neighbors and relatives] came [to Zacharias and Elisabeth's home] to circumcise the child; and they [the neighbors and relatives] called him Zacharias, after the name of his father.

Here in Luke 1:59 "called" should be translated "would have called" or "tried to call."[1] The

1. The word "called" is *ekaloun* in Greek. It is the conative imperfect tense of the root word *kaleō*. The conative imperfect tense means the ac-

neighbors and relatives assumed the first and only son would be named after the father or some other ancestor in order to carry on the family name as was the tradition.

> Luke 1:60 and 61:
> And his mother [Elisabeth] answered and said, Not *so*; but he shall be called John.
> And they said unto her, There is none of thy kindred that is called by this name.

Elisabeth obviously did the speaking because her husband was still unable to speak. Even though it meant spurning tradition and showing disregard for the neighbors and relatives, she was intent on obeying the angel's command to Zacharias; so she called the baby John. The neighbors and relatives who were insisting that the child be named for a relative simply could not believe that Elisabeth knew what she was doing, so they beckoned to Zacharias, the father, the one ultimately responsible for naming the child.

> Luke 1:62 and 63:
> And they made signs to his father, how he would have him called.
> And he asked for a writing table [tablet or slate], and wrote, saying, His name is John. And they marvelled all.

---

tion is begun but not completed. See A.T. Robertson, *Word Pictures in the New Testament*, 6 vols. (Nashville: Broadman Press, 1930-1933), 2:17.

Zacharias, like Elisabeth, obeyed the angel's word rather than the wishes of the relatives and neighbors. Having motioned for a writing slate, he plainly wrote, "His name is John." The witnesses were incredulous.

> Luke 1:64:
> And his [Zacharias'] mouth was opened immediately, and his tongue *loosed*, and he spake, and praised God.

For over nine months Zacharias had been unable to speak. He had been dumb since his conversation with Gabriel while burning incense in the Holy Place. Now, having obeyed God's Word by naming the child John, he was set free. The angel had said, as recorded in Luke 1:20, that Zacharias would be unable to speak "until the day that these things shall be performed." Now that "these things" had been performed, Zacharias' tongue was loosed and his first words were in praise to God for His wonderful blessings. Zacharias' deliverance and his words of praise stirred every hearer and filled them with awe.

> Luke 1:65 and 66:
> And fear [reverence] came on all that dwelt round about them: and all these sayings were noised abroad throughout all the hill country of Judaea.
> And all they that heard *them* laid *them* up in their hearts, saying, What manner of child shall this be! And the hand of the Lord was with him.

The news of Zacharias and Elisabeth's baby's birth became well known throughout that entire part of Judea. Surely this was a child who would do great things for God. The hand of the Lord God was with John throughout his childhood.

Zacharias now had a promised son, John. He also would have known that the promised seed, the Messiah, would be born within six months, since Mary had visited Elisabeth and him for three months. With great rejoicing and reverence and hope in his heart, Zacharias prophesied regarding God's promises to Israel and that his son would be a prophet for the God of Israel.

> Luke 1:67 and 68:
> And his [John's] father Zacharias was filled with the Holy Ghost [holy spirit], and prophesied, saying,
> Blessed [eulogized, praised] *be* the Lord God of Israel; for he hath visited and redeemed his people.

This says that God had visited[2] and redeemed His people Israel. Who had just been born? John the

---

2. The word "visited" in Greek is *epeskepsato* (Aramaic: *sar*, visited), from the word *episkeptomai* meaning "to look upon." This term, *episkeptomai*, can be used idomatically in the sense of "to visit," which is the literal meaning of *sar*, the Aramaic word used in Luke 1:68. Here it is used in the sense of "visited." However, this does not mean that John or Jesus were literally God. The idiom is used figuratively in the Old Testament when God has blessed His people in a remarkable way. See Genesis 21:1; 50:24; and Ruth 1:6. It is interesting that the word "visit" in these verses is translated from the Hebrew word *paqad* which also means "to look over."

Baptist. How did God visit His people? By the birth of Zacharias' son, John the Baptist. Later God would be with His people by the birth of His only begotten Son, Jesus Christ.

Zacharias continued to prophesy, being inspired by the Holy Spirit.

> Luke 1:69-78:
> And [God] hath raised up an horn of salvation for us in the house of his servant David;
> As he spake by the mouth of his holy prophets, which have been since the world began:
> That we [Israel] should be saved from our enemies, and from the hand of all that hate us;
> To perform the mercy *promised* to our fathers, and to remember his holy covenant;
> The oath which he sware to our father Abraham,
> That he would grant unto us, that we being delivered out of the hand of our enemies might serve him without fear,
> In holiness and righteousness before [*enōpion*, in the presence of] him, all the days of our life.
> And thou [the baby John], child, shalt be called the prophet of the Highest [God]: for thou [John] shalt go before the face of the Lord [the Lord God] to prepare his [God's] ways;
> To give knowledge [God's knowledge] of salvation unto his [God's] people [Israel] by the remission [forgiveness] of their sins,
> Through the tender mercy of our God; whereby the dayspring [sunrising] from on high hath visited [*epeskepsato*, as in verse 68] us.

As a great prophet, John would give Israel a knowledge of the salvation and forgiveness of sins that was available in his day.[3] Whenever God has a prophet declaring His Word with such boldness, God can be a new sunrise to His people. The Prophet John lifted the cloud cover of darkness to show the first rays of light on a bright new spiritual day for Israel.

Israel had come through four hundred years of spiritual darkness, because there was no recorded prophet of God during that time. John would declare God's Word as light breaking through that darkness. That is why God, through the ministry of John, is here described as the sunrising from on high for the children of Israel. The next verse further expands on this wonderful truth.

---

3. Luke 3:3: "And he [John] came into all the country about Jordan, preaching the baptism of repentance for the remission [forgiveness] of sins." The word translated "remission" in Luke 1:77 and Luke 3:3 is the Greek word *aphesis* which can be translated either "remission" or "forgiveness" according to the context. Remission of sins specifically refers to the one-time cleansing of all sins that happens to a person at the time of the new birth. Forgiveness relates to the mending of broken fellowship. After the new birth, a Christian can receive forgiveness by simply confessing his sin (I John 1:9). In the Old Testament there were sacrifices and offerings to atone for sins, but there was no one-time offering for the cleansing of sin, hence the word remission does not apply there. The Book of Hebrews contrasts the yearly offerings of the Old Testament, which could not take away sins, with Jesus Christ who offered himself as a one-time sacrifice for sins and thereby perfected forever those that are sanctified (Hebrews 10:3, 4, 12-14). Therefore, the word *aphesis* in reference to events before the new birth made available at Pentecost should always be translated "forgiveness."

Luke 1:79:
To give light [God would give His light by way of John's ministry] to them that sit in darkness and *in* the shadow of death, to guide our feet into the way of peace.

What a tremendous man of God this John was promised to be!

Luke 1:80:
And the child [John] grew, and waxed strong in spirit [waxed strong spiritually], and was in the deserts [the wilderness areas, the uninhabited areas] till the day of his shewing [his appearance, his showing forth] unto Israel.

Since the beginnings of man, John was the only person ever known to have been given holy spirit while in his mother's womb. Even Jesus Christ did not receive holy spirit until he was about thirty years old. That is the magnitude of the statement in God's Word that John waxed strong spiritually. John was spiritually very powerful.[4]

What a tremendous impact John made when he finally began his public ministry, which would have

---

4. Just as this verse says that John "grew, and waxed strong in spirit," these exact words are found in Luke 2:40 referring to Jesus Christ. However in Luke 2:40 the words "in spirit" are added; they are not in any critical Greek text. Thus only John, not Jesus, waxed spiritually strong before the age of thirty, because only John was filled with the holy spirit before that age.

been at the age of thirty. His years of preparation for his God-ordained mission played an essential part in preparing the way for the savior. So great was this man John that Jesus Christ declared a great truth of him which is recorded in both Matthew and Luke.

> Matthew 11:11:
> Verily I [Jesus Christ] say unto you, Among them that are born of women there hath not risen a greater than John the Baptist....

> Luke 7:28:
> For I [Jesus Christ] say unto you, Among those that are born of women there is not a greater prophet than John the Baptist....

This does not mean that John was superior to God's Son, Jesus Christ. John was not perfect. John was greater only in the truth that he was born with holy spirit and Jesus was not. These verses show Jesus' utmost regard for John as a man of God who courageously declared God's Word, a man whom God had blessed and had given a dynamic ministry.

Further truths regarding the greatness of John's ministry are set forth in the first chapter of the Gospel of John.

> John 1:6-8:
> There was a man sent from God, whose name *was* John.

> The same came for a witness, to bear witness of the Light [God],[5] that all *men* through him [through John and his ministry] might believe.
> He was not that Light [God], but *was sent* to bear witness of that Light [God].

John bore witness of God who had sent him. He did this by declaring God's Word and calling people back to the great truths within it. John himself was not God, not the Light, but rather he testified of God. He baptized with a baptism of repentance for the forgiveness of sins. He warned the religious leaders of God's displeasure with their perversion of the truth. And, as all great prophets, he proclaimed the coming Messiah, who was God's Word in the flesh.[6]

> John 1:9 and 10:
> *That* was the true Light [God], which lighteth every man that cometh into the world.
> He [God] was in the world. . . .

How was God in the world? By His revealed, written and spoken Word. In context, God was in the world by the written and spoken Word declared through the life and ministry of John the Baptist.

---

5. I John 1:5: ". . . God is light, and in him is no darkness at all."
6. See Matthew 3:11; Mark 1:7 and 8; Luke 3:15 and 16; John 1:15, 26-36; 3:28-36; Acts 19:4.

John 1:10 and 11:
He [God] was in the world, and the world was made by him [God],[7] and the world knew him [God] not.
He [God] came unto his own [Israel], and his own received him not.

God came in that moment of time to the world, especially to Israel, through the life and ministry of John the Baptist. But John's ministry was not heeded by Israel as a nation. When Israel rejected John, they rejected the God whom John was declaring; that is why it says God's own "received him not."

Although John's ministry was not received by Israel as a nation, there was a remnant of believing Israelites. They believed John's message from God, and they believed what he proclaimed about the Messiah.

John 1:12:
But as many as received him [received God after hearing John the Baptist], to them gave he [God] power [the right, the authority] to become the sons of God, *even* to them that believe on [unto] his [God's] name [Greek: *onoma*, namesake].

Jesus Christ was God's namesake. It was Jesus who came in God's name. In John 5:43, Jesus Christ stated, "I am come in my Father's name."

---

7. Genesis 1:1: "In the beginning God created the heaven and the earth."

When John declared God's Word, he, of course, proclaimed God's Son, Jesus Christ, the promised seed. As it says in Acts 19:4, John preached of him, Christ, that came after him. In God's plan, as indicated in John 1:31, John was sent as God's prophet immediately prior to the coming of Christ, so that John's ministry would help to make the promised seed manifest to Israel.

When Jesus Christ began his ministry, John described himself as "the friend of the bridegroom" (John 3:29). Israel was the bride espoused to her bridegroom, the Messiah; and John was a "friend of the bridegroom," a best man to Jesus Christ. When hearing of the Messiah from the lips of John, those who believed became adopted as God's sons. That is the greatness of John 1:12 when studied in context.

Surely John the Baptist was as great a man of God as ever lived. His ministry as a prophet of God was brief, perhaps less than a year; yet it was of such a nature and had such impact that it set in proper order and sequence all things so that God could manifest Himself by bringing the Messiah, His Son, the promised seed to Israel. John's entire life and ministry meshed with Jesus Christ's in a marvelous way. So important and timely was the mission of John the Baptist.

CHAPTER FIFTEEN

MARY, JOSEPH, AND THE ANGEL

Mary left the house of Zacharias and Elisabeth when Elisabeth was in her ninth month of pregnancy, and returned to her hometown of Nazareth.[1] The Word of God does not state why Mary left Elisabeth's. However, we know the time of Mary's own wedding ceremony was approaching, and she needed to return to her home to make preparations. Besides, Elisabeth would soon have her baby. Knowing that Mary left shortly before John's birth is of utmost importance in studying the time factors of the events that followed.

---

1. Again, this can be determined from the following information: (1) The angel appeared to Mary when Elisabeth was in her sixth month of pregnancy (Luke 1:26 and 36). As we have seen, her sixth month ended in December. (2) During this time, Mary made the journey from Nazareth to Elisabeth's home in Judea and stayed with her "about three months" (Luke 1:39 and 56) until March. (3) Taking into account travel time, the about three-month stay, and possible time into the sixth month, one can safely calculate that Elisabeth was in her ninth month of pregnancy (March) when Mary left.

Sometime after leaving Zacharias and Elisabeth's house, Mary and her betrothed, Joseph, would have had a wedding ceremony. In the Eastern culture, the wedding could last as long as ten days. After the wedding, an elder, a holy man, or a priest would decide the best time for the newly wed couple to come together for sexual intercourse, thus consummating their marriage. The person who determined this first coming together would set a specific time, within a few days after the wedding, at the wife's fertile time of the month for conception.

With this background information, we need to go to the Gospel of Matthew to study the relationship of Mary and Joseph at the time of their wedding.

> Matthew 1:18:
> Now [But] the birth [Greek: *gennēsis*, origin, birth, begetting; Aramaic: *yalda*, birth, begetting] of Jesus Christ was on this wise: When as his mother Mary was espoused [betrothed] to Joseph, before they came together, she was found with child of the Holy Ghost [Holy Spirit].

In order to understand what this verse is saying in the original we must study each word. In verse 18, the first word "now" is the Greek word *de*, and it should be translated "but." In some Greek and Aramaic sources the word "Jesus" is omitted. The words "on this wise" can simply be rendered "in this manner." The expression, "when as his mother

Mary was espoused to Joseph,'' should be translated: ''his mother, Mary, having been betrothed to Joseph.'' ''Come together'' in this context refers to coming together for sexual intercourse.[2] The words ''was found'' are the Greek word *eurethē*, and mean ''was discovered.'' The words ''with child'' in Greek are *en gastri exousa* and mean ''having in the womb,'' implying she was carrying a child.

With this in mind, a more accurate translation of Matthew 1:18 according to usage would be: ''But the birth of the Christ was in this manner: his mother, Mary, having been betrothed to Joseph, before their living together and having sexual intercourse, was discovered to have a child in the womb by the Holy Spirit (God).''

This verse of Matthew 1:18 is filled with information. It pointedly contrasts the begetting of Jesus Christ with that of the others listed in the genealogy of Matthew 1:2-16. Whereas those men listed were all begotten of human fathers, this child in Mary's womb was God's Son, having been conceived by the Holy Spirit, who is God. That Jesus Christ was of divine conception is further authenticated by the fact

---

2. This same usage of ''come together'' regarding a husband and wife is found in I Corinthians 7:5: ''Defraud [deprive] ye not one the other, except *it be* with consent for a time, that ye [husband and wife] may give yourselves to fasting and prayer; and come together [have sexual intercourse] again, that Satan tempt you not for your incontinency [unrestrained sexual passions].'' Matthew 1:18 refers to the initial coming together for sexual intercourse, and beginning to live together.

that he was conceived before Mary and Joseph had any sexual contact. Thus, no confusion could arise as to his being God's, not Joseph's, child.

By the time of Matthew 1:18 Mary and Joseph had already gone through the wedding ceremony, for a betrothed couple did not have sexual relations before marriage. In Matthew 1:19 and 20 they are called husband and wife. The context is clearly the time of their coming together after the wedding, when they were to have sexual intercourse. At that time Mary was discovered to be with child. How Joseph found out is not stated. Perhaps Mary told him, for she was over three months pregnant. In any case, when Joseph discovered Mary's pregnancy, he had to consider what to do. Now Joseph was in a dilemma.

> Matthew 1:19:
> Then [''But'' or ''Moreover''] Joseph her husband, being a just *man*, and not willing to make her a publick example, was minded to put her away privily [privately].

Joseph was ''a just *man*,'' meaning he obeyed God's law as given in the Old Testament. According to that law, a man who found his betrothed wife to be pregnant by another was to have her taken to the elders of the city and stoned to death publicly at the gate of her father's house;[3] or else he could write her

---

3. See Deuteronomy 22:13-22.

a bill of divorcement and send her away.[4] Because of Joseph's love for Mary and his uncertainty regarding the situation, he preferred to do the latter as secretly as possible. However, God intervened at this point.

> Matthew 1:20 and 21:
> But while [after] he [Joseph] thought [had pondered] on these things, behold, the angel of the Lord appeared unto him in a dream [vision], saying, Joseph, thou son of David, fear not to take unto thee Mary thy wife: for that which is conceived [begotten] in her is of the Holy Ghost [Holy Spirit].
> And she shall bring forth a son, and thou [Joseph] shalt call his name JESUS: for he shall save his people [Israel] from their sins.

This vision appeared to Joseph, according to verse 18, "before they came together," referring to sexual intercourse; but now he is specifically instructed "take unto thee Mary thy wife," which means to have sexual intercourse with her.[5]

Joseph had discovered that Mary was pregnant

---

4. See Deuteronomy 24:1: "When a man hath taken a wife, and married her, and it come to pass that she find no favour in his eyes, because he hath found some uncleanness in her: then let him write her a bill of divorcement, and give *it* in her hand, and send her out of his house." According to Lightfoot, to put her away privately involved handing her a bill of divorcement in front of only two witnesses. See Lightfoot, *New Testament from the Talmud and Hebraica*, 2:19.

5. Similar usages of "to take" can be found in the following scriptures: Genesis 34:2; Exodus 2:1; Leviticus 18:17 and 18; 20:14,17,21; Deuteronomy 20:7; 22:13 and 30.

before they had their first sexual encounter together. Consequently, Joseph was unwilling to have sexual relations with Mary, for such an act would consummate their marriage. Instead, he had decided to give Mary a bill of divorcement and send her away quietly. But, then, in a vision an angel appeared to him saying, "Fear not to take unto thee Mary thy wife."

In essence, the angel's message in verses 20 and 21 was, "Joseph, don't be afraid to take Mary unto yourself and have sexual intercourse with her. Go ahead and consummate your marriage with her. Don't give her a bill of divorcement. Why? Because that which is conceived in her is by God, not by another man. Your wife shall bring forth a son, and you shall call his name Jesus, because he shall save his people Israel from their sins." This, when understood in context, is what the angel was revealing to Joseph. What an impact these words must have had on Joseph!

The angel told Mary, according to Luke 1:31, what the child should be named long before Joseph knew. But since the father was responsible for naming the child at the time of circumcision, the angel now revealed God's will to Joseph. As the man who would perform the role of a father in raising the child, Joseph was directed to call him Jesus. This revelation came from an angel sent by the child's actual Father, God. What a wonderful truth from God's Word.

As we noted before, "Jesus" is the Greek rendering of the Hebrew name "Joshua." "Joshua," in Hebrew, is made up of a combination of two words: (1) *yah*, which is a contracted form of *yehovah* and (2) *yeshu* which means "salvation," "saves," or "savior." Most scholars and theologians recognize the truth that "Jesus" is the same word as "Joshua" in the Old Testament, yet no one has ever claimed that the Joshua of Old Testament renown was God. Yet some theologians have deduced that the name "Jesus," meaning "Jehovah our savior," proves that Jesus was God. Handling the Word of God in this manner is certainly inconsistent for the same logic would cause one to conclude that the Joshua of the Old Testament was also God. The name "Jesus" simply signified that the child, as God's Son, would bring Jehovah's salvation to Israel.

> Matthew 1:22 and 23:
> Now all this was done, that it might be fulfilled which was spoken of the Lord by the prophet, saying,
> Behold, a virgin shall be with child, and shall bring forth a son, and they shall call his name Emmanuel, which being interpreted is, God with us.

To be called Emmanuel (also spelled Immanuel), again, does not make a person so named God. This prophecy was recorded in Isaiah 7:14 where the reference is twofold: (1) to a child born in Isaiah's day whose birth and early growth would be a sign to

Ahaz that the threat of two enemy kings would be gone, as a study of Isaiah 7:1-16 and 8:6-18 shows; and (2) to the Messiah, the Christ, as Matthew 1:21-25 declares.[6] The child born in the time of the Prophets Isaiah and Ahaz, although named Immanuel, was not God. Likewise, neither did being called Emmanuel indicate that Jesus was God. As the child born in Isaiah's time signified that God was with Israel to deliver them, the same can be said for Jesus in a far more comprehensive way.

The revelation in II Corinthians 5 states that "God was in Christ, reconciling the world unto himself...," not "God *was* Christ." In the same way that God was in Christ to reconcile the world to Himself, the name Emmanuel in relation to Jesus signified that God was in Christ to deliver Israel.

The name "Jesus" emphasized that this child would bring Jehovah's deliverance to Israel. *Yehovah* or *yah* is the divine name used when God deals with that which He has created on a horizontal level. It is used of God in His covenant relationship to Israel. Similarly, the name Emmanuel emphasizes the truth that the Creator (God as the Creator is called *Elohim*), the Mighty One, was present with Israel to deliver them. In Matthew 1:21-25 naming the child Emmanuel showed that God would be present with

---

6. See chapter 9, "Prophecies about the Promised Seed," pp. 91-111.

Israel through the life of His Son, Jesus Christ. This briefly capsulizes the great significance of the names "Jesus" and "Emmanuel."[7]

In Matthew 1:23, the word "virgin" is *parthenos* in Greek. In Isaiah 7:14, from which Matthew 1:23 is quoted, the Hebrew word for "virgin" is *almah* meaning "young woman." This further supports translating *parthenos* as "young woman," for the Greek Septuagint has the word *parthenos* in Isaiah 7:14.[8] We must carefully distinguish the Biblical usages of the word "virgin" from our modern usage. In Matthew 1:23, "virgin" would be better translated "young woman."

To return to the narrative in Matthew 1, the angel had just told Joseph in a vision not to be afraid to take his wife Mary unto him for sexual intercourse.

> Matthew 1:24:
> Then Joseph being raised from sleep did as the angel of the Lord had bidden him, and took unto him his wife.

---

7. In Hebrew, Isaiah 9:6 says, "...Wonderful in counsel is the mighty God, the everlasting Father, the Prince of peace."

8. As Isbell states, "It should be clear, first of all, that neither the Massoretic [Hebrew] Text nor the Septuagint translation of Isaiah 7:14 have anything to do with the idea of a virginal conception. And it is further clear that neither Matthew nor Luke interpreted Isaiah 7:14 incorrectly." Isbell goes on to show that it is the context in Matthew and Luke which shows Mary was a virgin when she conceived Jesus Christ, not the word *parthenos*. Isbell, "Does the Gospel of Matthew Proclaim Mary's Virginity?" p. 52. See also chapter 12, "Mary and the Angel," pp. 147-161.

Joseph took Mary unto him and had sexual intercourse with her, thus consummating their marriage. The sheets they slept on would show the "tokens of virginity." These tokens were the blood left on the sheets after a woman had her first intercourse with her husband. The blood, coming from the broken hymen, was evidence of her virginity, and proof that she had not previously had sexual relations.

The phrase "being raised from sleep" has caused misunderstanding, not only in this verse but in Matthew 1:20 and 2:13. First of all, the words "being raised" are an aorist participle, which does not indicate the time of the event, but rather the singleness of the action. If Joseph were sleeping, he was aroused from sleep so that God could give him revelation. Secondly, the phrase "roused from sleep" is used of arousing one's awareness spiritually to receive revelation, as in Zechariah 4:1, "And the angel that talked with me came again, and waked me, as a man that is wakened out of his sleep." He was not literally awakened, but he was aroused as one who is awakened. God had to get Joseph's attention before He could talk with him.

When studied in context, Matthew 1 makes it clear that Joseph had sexual intercourse with Mary before Jesus was born, but not before Jesus was conceived. This should have been very evident to us long ago. However, because tradition has taught that Mary was a perpetual virgin, our minds were led away from the simple accuracy of God's Word. Many people have considered the subject of sex as unclean, and so do not properly understand passages like this one which specifically deals with sex. God's Word covers all facets of life, from man's deepest physical and emotional desires to the great spiritual realities of man's redemption. God's Word never degrades such aspects of living, but elevates them, dealing with them honestly and openly.

Joseph, after receiving the revelation, took Mary unto him and had sexual intercourse with her. At that time, Mary was over three months pregnant. It has never been unusual for a husband to have sexual intercourse with a pregnant wife. Indeed it is quite normal. What Joseph did was natural and appropriate. However, misunderstandings of the next verse have caused confusion.

> Matthew 1:25:
> And knew her not till she had brought forth her firstborn son: and he [Joseph] called his name JESUS.

The words "knew her not" have been taken to mean Joseph had no sexual relations with Mary until after Jesus was born. We have already seen from the context that he did indeed have sexual relations with her. The problem has been the misunderstanding of the expression "to know" when it is in the context of a man's sexual intimacy with a woman. In such a context, "to know" does not mean simply "to have sexual intercourse with." It means "to impregnate." It means to have sexual intercourse resulting in conception. Since Mary was already pregnant through divine conception, Joseph could not "know," or impregnate, his wife at that time. This usage of "to know" is consistent and clearly documented in God's Word.

> Genesis 4:1:
> And Adam knew Eve his wife; and she conceived, and bare Cain....

> Genesis 4:17:
> And Cain knew his wife; and she conceived, and bare Enoch....

> Genesis 4:25:
> And Adam knew his wife again; and she bare a son, and called his name Seth....

Each time the word "knew" is used in this fashion, it refers to sexual intercourse which results in pregnancy, conception.

> Genesis 19:8 and 14:
> Behold now, I [Lot] have two daughters which have not known man....
> And Lot went out, and spake unto his sons in law, which married his daughters....

The sons-in-law were husbands to Lot's daughters. They had had sexual intercourse with them, but the daughters had not conceived by them. Therefore, the daughters had "not known man."

> I Samuel 1:19 and 20:
> And they rose up in the morning early, and worshipped before the Lord, and returned, and came to their house to Ramah: and Elkanah knew Hannah his wife; and the Lord remembered her.
> Wherefore it came to pass, when the time was come about after Hannah had conceived. . . .

Hannah had been barren. She had had sexual intercourse with Elkanah before, but they had produced no children. Therefore, Elkanah never "knew" her until the time recorded in the above verses. When he finally knew her, she conceived and gave birth to Samuel who became a great prophet. Obviously then, "to know" in this context means to have intercourse resulting in conception, to impregnate. That is also its usage in Matthew 1.[9]

> Matthew 1:25:
> And [Joseph] knew her not [did not impregnate her][10] till she had brought forth her firstborn son. . . .

---

9. See Pillai, *Orientalisms of the Bible*, pp. 60-61.

10. It is also interesting that an old Aramaic manuscript, the Sinaitic Palimpsest, omits the words "knew her not till." Instead, it simply reads, "and she brought forth." Thus, it is possible the words "knew her not till" were not in the original, but were later scribal additions. However, the King James Version reading is preferred because of its clear emphasis that Joseph was not the father of Jesus.

Joseph had sexual intercourse with Mary before Jesus was born. However, although she did not conceive by him until after Jesus Christ was born, she did conceive by Joseph later. That is the great revelation of Matthew 1:25. It simply and emphatically declares that Joseph was not responsible for the conception of Jesus, Mary's first son; but he was responsible for the conception of his and Mary's other children.[11]

Mary had other children, as is clear from the term "firstborn son." As we use the term "virgin" in modern times (meaning "a woman who has had no sexual relations"), Mary was a virgin when she conceived Jesus by divine conception. However, with this modern usage of "virgin," the belief in the "virgin birth" is erroneous, for by the time Jesus was born, Mary had had sexual intercourse with Joseph. Clearly, at Jesus' birth, she was not a "virgin" as the term is currently used, nor was she a "perpetual virgin" after Jesus was born, for she bore several children thereafter. Thus, when dealing with the subject of Jesus Christ's conception and birth, the word "virgin" must be used carefully, noting the

---

11. Besides Jesus, Mary had at least three daughters and four other sons. Except for Jesus, all were fathered by Joseph. Matthew 13:55 and 56: "Is not this the carpenter's son? is not his mother called Mary? and his brethren, James, and Joses, and Simon, and Judas? And his sisters, are they not all [not 'both'; there must have been at least three] with us?. . ."

difference between Biblical and modern usage, as well as accurately relating it to Mary's situation.

Notice in Matthew 1:25 that God's Word says, "And he called his name JESUS." This refers to Joseph's naming of the child at the time of circumcision. Joseph did this in obedience to the angel's command in Matthew 1:21: "Thou [Joseph] shalt call his name JESUS." Joseph thus accepted the responsibility of rearing the child.

Throughout this record in Matthew 1:18-25, we see the heart and believing of Mary's husband Joseph. We also see the things God had in store for His Son, the Christ, and for those to whom the Christ was sent. With the cloud of religious tradition removed, God's Word shines in brilliant simplicity regarding these matters.

CHAPTER SIXTEEN

THE BIRTH OF JESUS CHRIST

Jupiter-Regulus Conjunction Sept. 14

Feast of Trumpets
Birth of Jesus Sept. 11

Circumcision of Jesus Sept. 18

First Jupiter-Venus Conjunction
Aug. 12

Simeon and Anna at the Temple
Oct. 21

TAMMUZ	AB	ELUL	TISHRI	MAR-CHESHVAN	KISLEV	TEBETH
29	30	29	30	29	30	29

JULY	AUGUST	SEPT	OCT	NOV	DEC
31	31	30	31	30	31

3 B.C.*

Many of the details and events surrounding the subject of Jesus' birth are brought to light in the second chapter of the Gospel of Luke. As we take up the record in Luke 2:1, keep in mind that John the Baptist had been born approximately six months prior to this, in March of 3 B.C. Mary was now in

*This calendar gives significant Biblical events in the year 3 B.C. The Hebrew months are given alongside our modern months. Because the Hebrew months were determined by the moon, their dates according to our calendar would shift from year to year.

her ninth month of pregnancy, it being early September of 3 B.C.

> Luke 2:1:
> And it came to pass in those days, that there went out a decree from Caesar Augustus, that all the world should be taxed [registered].

The expression "all the world" is the figure of speech *synecdoche*, in which "all the world" is put for a part of it. The usage here of this figure emphasizes the immensity of the Roman Empire, the area over which Caesar asserted authority.[1] The word "taxed" is from the Greek word *apographō* meaning "to register." Rather than a taxation, this decree was for an enrollment or registration.

Historically, there is evidence that a registration was conducted throughout the Roman Empire and its subject states in 3 B.C. Although registrations were usually conducted in the Roman Empire for tax purposes, this registration was for an official declaration of political allegiance to Caesar Augustus.[2] The

---

1. The decree even affected areas beyond the provincial limits of the empire, showing that it was indeed a wide-ranging registration. According to Luke 2:4 the order was in effect even in Judea, which was not a province at this time but a client kingdom of Rome. Judea had its own king, Herod the Great.

2. In an inscription dated at 3 B.C. from Asia Minor there is a reference to the conducting of an official declaration of allegiance to Caesar by all in that area. See Nepthali Lewis and Meyer Reinhold, eds. *Roman Civilization*, 2 vols. (New York: Harper Torchbooks), 2:34-35. According to native sources, in 3 B.C. Roman authorities

purpose of this mandated registration was to record an official declaration of allegiance from all of his subjects to present to Caesar Augustus in celebration of his Silver Jubilee (twenty-fifth anniversary—27 B.C. to 2 B.C.) of supreme power, which coincided with the seven hundred fiftieth anniversary of the founding of Rome, and Caesar Augustus' sixtieth birthday. The oath of allegiance was a part of the preparations for this festive time and set the stage for the twenty-fifth anniversary celebration in 2 B.C. In honor of the occasion, the Senate of Rome bestowed upon Caesar Augustus the supreme title of *Pater Patriae*, "Father of the Country."

A logical time of the year for such a registration to take place was September because the weather was mild for travel, the crops were harvested, and one Judean civil year was closing and another beginning.[3]

Luke 2:2:
(*And* this taxing [enrollment, registration] was first made when Cyrenius was governor [Greek: *hēgemōn*, leader, chief, commander] of Syria.)

---

came to Armenia to set up images of Caesar Augustus in the temples of the area. Moreover, these same sources state it was the registration mentioned in Luke which brought them there (Armenian historian Moses of Khorene, *History of the Armenians*, 2:26). Finally, in Josephus it is recorded that "all the people of the Jews gave assurance of their good-will to Caesar, and to the king's government" (*Antiquities* 17.2.4) within two years before Herod's death, Herod probably dying early in 1 B.C. See Martin, *Birth of Christ Recalculated*, pp. 89-105.

3. William M. Ramsay, *Was Christ Born at Bethlehem?* (1898; reprint ed., Minneapolis: James Family Publishing Co., 1978), pp. 192-193.

The second verse of Luke 2 has long been a target of skeptics who criticize Luke's accuracy as a historian. Historically, the following outline of Quirinius' (which is the preferred and more common spelling of "Cyrenius") life is known: in 12 B.C. he was a consul in Rome; sometime between 12 B.C. and 1 A.D. he conducted the Homanadensian War in Asia Minor; in 2/3 A.D. he was an advisor to Gaius Caesar in Armenia; and in 6 A.D. he was sent by Caesar to be the governor of Syria.[4] The 6 A.D. date for Quirinius' governorship of Syria is historically very clear. He ruled both Syria and Judea after the year 6 A.D. when Archelaus was deposed as king of Judea. Both scripture and Josephus indicate this was well after Jesus' birth and Herod's death.[5] Yet Luke 2:2 seems to say that Quirinius governed Syria when Jesus was born. We must bear in mind that it is very probable that because this registration was a special part of the Silver Jubilee celebration, and for the express purpose of declaring Augustus *Pater Patriae*, that Quirinius was appointed as a special legate to oversee this enrollment.[6]

---

4. Finegan, *Handbook of Biblical Chronology*, p. 235-236.
5. Matthew 2:1,16,22; Josephus *Antiquities* 17.8.1-4,17.13.1-5;18.1.1-6.
6. With this historical point understood, an apparent difficulty in the writing of a second-century church father, Tertullian, becomes clear. The difficulty is that Tertullian states Saturninus was the governor of Syria at this time, which is corroborated by secular sources. Tertullian points out, "But there is historical proof that at this very time a *census* had been taken in Judaea by Sentius Saturninus." Alexander Roberts

The reason for including verse 2 in the narrative in Luke now becomes apparent. This verse serves to help pinpoint the exact year of Christ's birth; but more important, it precludes any possibility on the part of the reader to confuse this empire-wide Silver Jubilee registration of 3 B.C. with a later registration and taxing in 6/7 A.D. which is generally better known to historians, but was not empire-wide. Thus the word "first" in Luke 2:2 has a clear meaning. For the word "first" has been a problem to historians,[7] but now it can be seen that it is essential in order to distinguish between the two registrations both under Quirinius' supervision, differentiating the later and better known registration of 6/7 A.D. from the one occurring when Jesus Christ was born

---

and James Donaldson, eds. *The Ante-Nicene Fathers*, 10 vols. (reprint ed.; Grand Rapids: Wm. B. Eerdmans, 1978), "Tertullian Against Marcion," 3:4.19.

The Greek word *hēgemōn*, sometimes translated in English as "governor," is actually indefinite regarding the exact title of the office, so both Saturninus and Quirinius could loosely be referred to as *hēgemōn*, leaders, chiefs, or commanders, and yet fulfill different functions. Tertullian, a lawyer of the second century, had no trouble reconciling the statement of Luke 2:2 that Quirinius was *hēgemōn* of Syria with Saturninus' governorship of Syria, because he would have understood Quirinius' position in Syria as a special assignment. Because of the special assignment of Quirinius, Luke refers to him as the *hēgemōn* during the registration.

Schürer mentions other scholars who have accepted the position that Quirinius was a special legate to carry out this census. See Emil Schürer, *The History of the Jewish People in the Age of Jesus Christ*, 2 vols. Geza Vermes, Fergus Millar, and Matthew Black, eds. (1885; rev. ed., Edinburgh: T. & T. Clark, 1973), 1:424; and Martin, *Birth of Christ Recalculated*, p. 119-120.

7. Schürer, *History of the Jewish People*, 1:421-422.

in 3 B.C. Therefore Luke 2:2 would more clearly read: "This first registration took place when Quirinius was on special assignment in Syria."

> Luke 2:3 and 4:
> And all went to be taxed [enrolled, registered], every one into his own city.
> And Joseph also went up from Galilee, out of the city of Nazareth, into Judaea, unto the city of David, which is called Bethlehem; (because he was of the house and lineage of David).

The Old Testament records that David, the son of Jesse, was from the small town of Bethlehem (I Samuel 16:1-4). So, as a descendant of David (Luke 1:27; 2:4; 3:23-31), Joseph went to his ancestral town in order to register. Thus, a series of seemingly unrelated factors—Joseph's genealogy, Mary's pregnancy, Mary and Joseph's marriage, and the timing of the registration—worked together to fulfill the prophecy of Micah that the Messiah would be born in Bethlehem.[8]

> Luke 2:5:
> To be taxed [registered] with Mary his espoused [betrothed] wife, being great with child.

---

8. Micah 5:2: "But thou, Bethlehem Ephratah, *though* thou be little among the thousands of Judah, *yet* out of thee shall he come forth unto me *that is* to be ruler in Israel; whose goings forth *have been* from of old, from everlasting." The name "Bethlehem" means "house of bread."

When Joseph and Mary went to Bethlehem, Mary was in her ninth month of pregnancy, "great with child." The phrase "to be registered with Mary" indicates Mary also registered in Bethlehem, because she also was a descendant of David. This is expressly stated in two old Aramaic manuscripts, the Curetonian Syriac and the Sinaitic Palimpsest, which say: "That there they might be enrolled, because they were both of the house of David."

When Joseph went to Bethlehem, Mary accompanied him. Having already been through both the betrothal ceremony and the wedding ceremony, they were now living together as husband and wife. This is clear from our study of Matthew 1:18-25. Both Aramaic manuscripts just mentioned omit the word "espoused," which is more accurate since "espoused" would be redundant. Indeed, as Lewis says, "wife is more explicit" in that it clearly shows Mary was now "under the full legal protection of Joseph."[9]

Luke 2:6 and 7:
And so it was, that, while they were there [in Bethlehem of Judah], the days were accomplished that she should be delivered.
And she brought forth her firstborn son, and wrapped him in swaddling clothes, and laid him in a manger; because there was no room for them in the inn.

---

9. Agnes Smith Lewis, *Light on the Four Gospels from the Sinai Palimpsest* (London: Williams & Norgate, 1913), pp. 86-87.

When Mary was delivered of her firstborn child, the prophecy of Micah 5:2 was fulfilled, for the child was born in Bethlehem of Judah. In His foreknowledge God knew where His only begotten Son would be born, that is why He could reveal it to an earlier prophet.

A greater appreciation for this passage can be savored when one understands Eastern customs regarding childbirth. Whenever a son of a king, a prince, was born, that child was "salted" and "swaddled." To salt a child meant that soon after birth the newborn babe was gently washed with water having a small portion of salt in it. Salt symbolized the qualities of truth and honesty. Bathing a newborn in salt water indicated that the child would have these characteristics. His words would be "salted."[10]

After salting the newborn child, strips of fine linen cloth, about two inches wide, were then wrapped around his body. These were called "swaddling clothes." The child was wrapped from head to foot, with only a part of his face being left uncovered so he could breathe. The baby's body and limbs were held very straight when wrapped in this fashion. These

10. The significance of salt and childbirth customs in the Eastern culture are discussed by Pillai, *Light Through an Eastern Window*, pp. 24-48. Colossians 4:6 is then clearly saying a Christian's speech should be truthful and honest: "Let your speech *be* alway with grace, seasoned with salt, that ye may know how ye ought to answer every man."

linen strips were not rags and did not mean Joseph and Mary were poverty-stricken, but rather, this was a sign to God that these parents would raise the child to be upright before the Lord, and that he would be free from crookedness and waywardness. The babe would normally be left in the swaddling clothes for only a brief period of time, while the parents took time to meditate and make their commitment to God concerning the sacred trust which was given them in having the child.[11]

Salting and swaddling were recognizably significant to an Eastern person. In Biblical times, any child born to nobility or royalty would be salted and swaddled. If this were not done, there would be doubt regarding the person's integrity both in his youth and in his adulthood. Note the following insult in the Old Testament.

> Ezekiel 16:4:
> . . . thou wast not salted at all, nor swaddled at all.

To say to a noble-born person that he had not been salted or swaddled was to indicate he was unreliable, dishonest, without integrity—as though his parents had not gone through the proper ritual at his birth.

According to the customs of the time, Mary and Joseph washed Jesus in salt water before they

11. Pillai, *Light Through an Eastern Window*, pp. 42-43.

swaddled him, indicating that he was of royal lineage, as God's Son and as heir to the throne of David.

The inn of verse 7 was a lodging house or khan, a place where caravans stopped for lodging. Normally, the design of an inn consisted of an inner court surrounded on four sides by the building itself. Along the back wall on the outside of the inn would be stables for asses, camels, and other animals.[12] Within each stable would be a manger with straw in it. Normally the manger would be used as a feeding trough for the animals in the stable. Thus, by context, the manger in which the newborn Christ child was laid was located in a stable or stall connected to the back of the inn.[13] This is a more likely location of the manger than the traditional site of a cave in the Bethlehem area.[14] In Luke 2:7, we also learn the great truth, as we did in Matthew 1:25, that Jesus was Mary's firstborn son, not her only son.

---

12. Freeman, *Manners and Customs*, pp. 405-407.
13. See Freeman, *Manners and Customs*, pp. 406-407.
14. The inn of Luke 2:7 raises some interesting possibilities. King David's family originally lived in Bethlehem and so owned property there (I Samuel 16:1-4). Thus it may be that Jesus was born on that very property originally belonging to the family of David. Furthermore, when David was king, he rewarded a servant named Chimham at the request of an aged man named Barzillai (II Samuel 19:31-40; I Kings 2:7). Evidently this reward to Chimham included a habitation (or, at least, the property upon which the habitation was located) in the area of Bethlehem of Judah. The description of this habitation in Jeremiah 41:17 indicates it was a khan or inn that served as a stopover point for caravans traveling through Palestine to Egypt. Thus, it is distinctly possible that the inn of Luke 2:7 was the inn given to Chimham which originally belonged to the family of David. This would put Christ's birth literally "in the house of David."

Shepherds were watching their flock in the area outside Bethlehem. In this same vicinity centuries before, the Prophet Samuel anointed the shepherd David to be king.

> Luke 2:8:
> And there were in the same country [the same vicinity as Bethlehem] shepherds abiding in the field, keeping watch over their flock by night.

The Greek words for "keeping watch" are in the plural form, indicating that the shepherds watched by turns. The words "abiding in the field" are translated from the one Greek word *agraulountes*, which is made up of two words: *agros* and *aulē*. The word *agros* may refer to any field, but it is frequently a field cultivated for farming. The word *aulē* refers to an enclosed area in the open air—such as a courtyard, a sheepfold, or a cultivated field surrounded by a low wall of stones.

It is likely the shepherds were using a cultivated field as their fold for the sheep this particular night. This can be understood by a knowledge of Eastern customs. In the late summer or early fall of the year, a farmer in the Bible lands would often hire shepherds to keep their flocks in his field overnight. In this way, the sheep's manure would fertilize his field.

In December, the month in modern times when Jesus Christ's birth is celebrated, it is too cold for shepherds to watch their sheep at night in fields or pastures. The coldest temperatures, frost, heavy rains, and even snow occur from November to February. Shepherds would not be grazing sheep at night during those months; nor would a registration be conducted at that time of year because travel would be difficult. Since Mary would have been in her ninth month of pregnancy in September of 3 B.C., Luke 2:8 gives strong supporting evidence to that fall date as the time of Jesus Christ's birth.

> Luke 2:9:
> And, lo, the angel of the Lord came upon [stood by] them [the shepherds], and the glory of the Lord shone round about them: and they were sore afraid.

The words "came upon" are translated from the Greek word *epestē*, meaning "stood by." This sudden appearance was brilliant and unique. The shepherds were struck with fear by such surprising brilliance.

> Luke 2:10:
> And the angel said unto them, Fear not: for, behold, I bring you good tidings of great joy, which shall be to all people.

First, the angel exhorted the shepherds not to fear. Then the angel told them he brought them good news of great joy.

Luke 2:11:
For unto you is born this day in the city of David a Saviour, which [who] is Christ the Lord.

What a great announcement this message to these shepherds was! Of course, "the city of David" referred to Bethlehem. The angel promised the shepherds a sign confirming the truth of his message regarding the child: that this newborn babe was the lord, the promised seed, the long-awaited Messiah.

Luke 2:12:
And this *shall be* a sign unto you; Ye shall find the babe [Greek: *brephos*; Aramaic: *ula*, both meaning a newly delivered babe] wrapped in swaddling clothes, lying in a manger.

The sign to the shepherds that they had found the Christ was that they would find the infant still wrapped in swaddling clothes. Remember, a newborn remained in the swaddling clothes for only a brief period of time. Since the babe had already been born when the angel appeared to them, the shepherds needed to hurry to find him still swaddled.

Luke 2:13:
And suddenly there was with the angel a multitude of the heavenly host praising God, and saying.

The multitude of the heavenly host were other

angels. The Gospel of Luke does not describe the angels as having halos, hovering in the air, flapping their wings, playing musical instruments, or singing. Such characteristics of angels are a part of man-made traditions, not the truth of God's Word. The Word of God says the angels were "saying," not "singing." Nor is there any other scripture stating that angels sing.

It says in verse 13 that the multitude of the heavenly host was "with the angel" that stood by the shepherds. Therefore, these angels also must have been standing by the shepherds, not floating in the air above them. When the scene is viewed in accordance with God's Word, what a breathtaking experience this must have been for the shepherds!

> Luke 2:14:
> Glory to God in the highest, and on earth peace, good will toward men.

This was the message of the angels: that the birth of Jesus, the Christ, glorified God. With this birth, God's peace and good will were manifested on earth to mankind.[15]

---

15. The King James Version's translation of verse 14 is attested to by many Greek manuscripts and is in accordance with the Aramaic (although the Aramaic reads "hope" or "tidings" instead of "will"). The translation from other Greek manuscripts found in some English versions have God's peace coming only to men of goodwill. That is not an accurate translation of the passage.

Luke 2:15:
And it came to pass, as the angels were gone away from them into heaven, the shepherds said one to another, Let us now go even unto Bethlehem, and see this thing which is come to pass, which the Lord hath made known unto us.

Upon leaving, the angels went "into heaven." This again indicates that they had been on the earth standing near the shepherds.

The shepherds were responsive to the angel's message. When the angels left, they immediately began acting on the angel's declaration. These shepherds never doubted that the message had come from the Lord God.

Luke 2:16:
And they [the shepherds] came with haste, and found Mary, and Joseph, and the babe lying in a manger.

The shepherds "came with haste," and found Mary and Joseph with the baby Jesus, still swaddled, lying in the manger, as the angel had told them. The precise timing and greatness of God's dealings with them filled their hearts with awe.

Luke 2:17 and 18:
And when they had seen *it*, they made known abroad [made known everywhere] the saying which was told them concerning this child.

And all they that heard *it* wondered at those things which were told them by the shepherds.

The shepherds enthusiastically declared the Messiah's birth wherever they went, and their listeners' response was that of wonder.

God did not send the angel to declare Jesus Christ's birth to King Herod or to the high priest or to the religious leaders or to other wealthy, powerful men in Judea. Instead He sent His angel to humble, receptive shepherds—to those He knew would believe and obey. As any proud Father, God wanted the news of the birth of His Son heralded throughout the land. And so the shepherds spread the glorious news.

Luke 2:19 and 20:
But Mary kept all these things [these sayings], and pondered *them* in her heart.
And the shepherds returned, glorifying and praising God for all the things that they had heard and seen, as it was told unto them.

Mary, the wonderful new mother of the promised seed, the Christ, pondered all the things the shepherds had related to her. She put them in her "lock-box," deep in her heart, where she kept the most personal, meaningful treasures of her life.

The shepherds returned to the Bethlehem hills

glorifying and praising God. What believing men! What a unique experience they had. The Lord's Anointed, the promised seed, had been born.

* * *

Eight days after the birth of a male child, Hebrew parents were responsible to see that their son was circumcised in accordance with Old Testament law. Mary and Joseph carried out this legal requirement for Jesus. Indeed, in this case it was most important of all for Jesus needed to fulfill the law to perfection in order to redeem mankind.[16]

> Luke 2:21:
> And when eight days were accomplished for the circumcising of the child, his name was called JESUS, which was so named of the angel before he was conceived in the womb.

Before Mary had even conceived, the angel had declared to her the name God had selected for the child (Luke 1:31). Later, after she had conceived, the name had been revealed to Joseph by the angel (Matthew 1:21). As his earthly parent, Joseph was ultimately responsible for naming the child at the

16. Galatians 4:4 and 5: "But when the fulness of the time was come, God sent forth his Son, made of a woman, made under the law, To redeem them that were under the law, that we might receive the adoption of sons."

time of circumcision. And Joseph obediently gave the child the name God desired for him—Jesus (Matthew 1:21 and 25; Luke 2:21).

At the time of his naming, Jesus was circumcised. Circumcision is an operation in which the foreskin of the penis is removed. The methods and tools in ancient times were different from those available in modern hospitals today, yet, there is no indication of complications in Biblical times when this operation was performed on the eighth day according to God's command.[17]

Although circumcision was part of the law given to Moses, Moses was not the first one to practice it. Long before Moses, circumcision was ordained by God to Abraham and his seed. It was the token, the sign, of a blood covenant God had made with Abraham and his descendants.[18] Among other things this covenant with Abraham included God's

---

17. The reason that circumcision was done on the eighth day is that before that time, the blood-clotting factor is insufficient and circumcision could thus be dangerous to the infant. After that time, the blood's disease-fighting content begins to decrease and thus there is a heightened possibility of infection. Therefore, the safest time for circumcision is at that very point when both the blood-clotting factor and its disease-fighting elements are at their peak, on the eighth day of the infant's life. Also the number eight indicates a new beginning. With circumcision on the eighth day, a newborn male officially joins the covenant of Israel. Further details on circumcision from a medical perspective are found in M.R. DeHaan, *The Chemistry of the Blood* (Grand Rapids: Zondervan, 1971), pp. 84-87; S.I. McMillen, *None of These Diseases* (Old Tappan, N.J.: Fleming H. Revell, 1963), pp. 17-21.
18. See Genesis 17:1-27; 21:1-12.

promise of the promised seed, the redeemer, to come out of Abraham.

In light of this, the circumcision of Jesus had added significance. He was to be the ultimate fulfillment of the covenant of which circumcision was the token. As a descendant of Abraham and Isaac, that covenant would need to be carried out in Jesus Christ's life according to God's command to Abraham. It also further confirmed Jesus' fulfillment of the law of Moses. Therefore, when Luke 2:21 tells us Jesus was circumcised, it contains more significance than we glean from just a cursory reading.

Forty-one days after Jesus' birth, his parents again fulfilled another law of Moses in offering sacrifice for the new son.

> Luke 2:22-24:
> And when the days of her [Mary's] purification according to the law of Moses were accomplished, they [Mary and Joseph] brought him [Jesus] to Jerusalem, to present *him* to the Lord;
> (As it is written in the law of the Lord, Every male that openeth the womb shall be called holy to the Lord;)
> And to offer a sacrifice according to that which is said in the law of the Lord, A pair of turtledoves, or two young pigeons.

Mary and Joseph were obeying two Old Testament laws in these three verses. One of them was presenting Jesus to the Lord.

According to Old Testament law, every firstborn male belonged to the Lord. Sometime after the child was a month old, his parents were to bring five shekels to the priests and Levites at the sanctuary as redemption money. This redemption money served as a reminder of God's deliverance in Egypt, when the firstborn was allowed to live in those households protected by the blood of the Passover lamb on their doorposts. The payment of the redemption money signified that the child was rightfully God's and that the parents would raise him accordingly.[19]

The reason Mary and Joseph brought Jesus to present him to the Lord, according to Luke 2:23, was that it was required by Old Testament law, and Jesus Christ had to totally fulfill that law.[20]

---

19. Numbers 18:14-16: "Every thing devoted in Israel shall be thine. Every thing that openeth the matrix in all flesh, which they bring unto the Lord, *whether it be* of men or beasts, shall be thine: nevertheless the firstborn of man shalt thou surely redeem, and the firstling of unclean beasts shalt thou redeem. And those that are to be redeemed from a month old shalt thou redeem, according to thine estimation, for the money of five shekels, after the shekel of the sanctuary, which *is* twenty gerahs." See also Exodus 13:11-16; 22:29. The concept of payment of redemption money and of the firstborn belonging to God can be studied further in Exodus 34:19 and 20; Numbers 3:12 and 13, 39-51.

20. Luke 2:23 is a figure of speech called *gnome*. It is a compilation of several verses in the Old Testament dealing with offerings and the presentation of the firstborn (Exodus 13:2 and 12). The author, God, rather than dealing with every specific instance mentioned in the law regarding the offering of firstborn males simply gives the essence of what is written in the law as a whole, that "every male that openeth the womb shall be called holy to the Lord." See E.W. Bullinger, *Figures of Speech Used in the Bible* (1898; reprint ed., Grand Rapids: Baker Book House, 1968), pp. 778-803 for more information on this subject.

Luke 2:24 records the second Old Testament law being carried out by Mary in order for her purification to be accomplished according to what is written in Leviticus.

Leviticus 12:1-8:
And the Lord spake unto Moses, saying,
Speak unto the children of Israel, saying, If a woman have conceived seed, and born a man child: then she shall be unclean seven days; according to the days of the separation for her infirmity shall she be unclean.
And in the eighth day the flesh of his foreskin shall be circumcised.
And she shall then continue in the blood of her purifying three and thirty days; she shall touch no hallowed thing, nor come into the sanctuary, until the days of her purifying be fulfilled.
But if she bear a maid child, then she shall be unclean two weeks, as in her separation: and she shall continue in the blood of her purifying threescore and six days.
And when the days of her purifying are fulfilled, for a son, or for a daughter, she shall bring a lamb of the first year for a burnt offering, and a young pigeon, or a turtledove, for a sin offering, unto the door of the tabernacle of the congregation, unto the priest:
Who shall offer it before the Lord, and make an atonement for her; and she shall be cleansed from the issue of her blood. This *is* the law for her that hath born a male or a female.
And if she be not able to bring a lamb, then she shall bring two turtles, or two young pigeons; the one for the burnt offering, and the other for a sin offering: and the

priest shall make an atonement for her, and she shall be clean.

The "days of her purification" in Luke 2:22 refer to the forty days after the birth of a son required for purification by the law. The first seven days after giving birth were considered days of uncleanness, and legally the woman was treated the same as if she had had a menstrual period. Therefore anyone who touched her during this seven-day period also became unclean. The details of this type of uncleanness are recorded in Leviticus 15:19-28.

On the eighth day after his birth, the male child was circumcised. This eighth day also began the final thirty-three days of the woman's purifying according to Leviticus 12. A woman was not unclean to touch during this latter thirty-three days of her purification, but she could not go into the Temple or touch any holy thing. After forty days, the woman would be considered clean and could go into the Temple on the forty-first day. At this time she was to bring both a sin offering and a burnt offering to the Lord. The priest would offer them before the Lord and, with this, the new mother was considered cleansed.

The sin offering could be a turtledove or a young pigeon. The burnt offering was to be a lamb of the first year. However, if she could not bring a lamb of the first year, she could bring another turtledove or another young pigeon. Mary and Joseph did not bring a lamb of the first year. Therefore, they brought the same sacrifices for both the sin offering and burnt offering: two turtledoves or two young pigeons. Some theologians have conjectured that the reason Mary and Joseph did not bring a lamb for Mary's purification was that they could not afford one. This is totally untrue and inaccurate. Mary and Joseph were not poverty-stricken. God, in giving the law long before, made a provision that Mary and Joseph had to use for both the sin and burnt offerings. They presented in the Temple that historic day a pair of turtledoves or two young pigeons because the lamb of the first year, Jesus Christ, God's only begotten Son, was with them. His sacrifice as the burnt offering for all men would come years later on the cross for he, Jesus Christ, was the "lamb of God."

It is obvious from Luke 2:22-24 that Joseph and Mary brought Jesus to the Temple to present him to the Lord at the same time Mary came to offer her sacrifices, officially ending her purification. To take care of these two requirements at one time would have been perfectly acceptable according to Old Testament law, as well as being the reasonable thing to do since this would save them from making a second trip to Jerusalem.

When Mary and Joseph brought Jesus to the Temple, they encountered two wonderful people. The first was an aged man named Simeon.

Luke 2:25-28:

And, behold, there was a man in Jerusalem, whose name *was* Simeon; and the same man *was* just and devout, waiting for the consolation of Israel: and the Holy Ghost [holy spirit] was upon him.

And it was revealed unto him by the Holy Ghost [holy spirit], that he should not see death, before he had seen the Lord's Christ [God's Anointed].

And he came by the Spirit [Simeon came by the spirit, by revelation] into the temple: and when the parents [Mary and Joseph] brought in the child Jesus, to do for him after the custom of the law,

Then took he him up in his arms, and blessed God. . .

Simeon was an elderly man, dedicated to God, and "waiting for the consolation of Israel," waiting for the promised Messiah. His waiting was attended with special hope, for God had previously given him the revelation that he would not die before seeing "the Lord's Christ." Thus Simeon received revelation to go to the Temple at the same time that Mary and Joseph came there to present Jesus. What a wonderful believer Simeon must have been.

Simeon instantly recognized, again by revelation, the child that was the Christ. No man had to tell him. With amazement and thanksgiving, Simeon took the tiny Messiah in his arms and praised God.

Luke 2:28-32:

Then took he him up in his arms, and blessed [eulogized, praised] God, and said,

> Lord, now lettest thou thy servant depart in peace, according to thy word:
> For mine eyes have seen thy salvation,
> Which thou hast prepared before the face of all people;
> A light to lighten the Gentiles, and the glory of thy people Israel.

These are great words of prophecy. Jesus Christ was the salvation God had prepared "before the face of all people"; Jesus Christ was the "light to lighten the Gentiles"; Jesus Christ was the glory of God's people, Israel. Think of the impact these words must have had on Joseph and Mary.

> Luke 2:33-35:
> And Joseph and his [Jesus'] mother marvelled at those things which were spoken of him [Jesus].
> And Simeon blessed them, and said unto Mary his mother, Behold, this *child* is set for the fall and rising again of many ["the falling and rising up of many" is the text] in Israel; and for a sign which shall be spoken against;
> (Yea, a sword shall pierce through thy [Mary's] own soul also,) that the thoughts of many hearts may be revealed.

The child was set for "the falling and rising up of many in Israel." For many he would be a stumbling block, he was set for their falling; they would reject him and reap the results of their unbelief. But others would believe, for these he would be the cause of their rising up. This is the first record in which it is intimated to Mary that she herself would endure suffering on account of her son. She would need courage to raise a son whom so many would speak against.

The phrase "a sword shall pierce through thy own soul also" is not literal.[21] Mary would be confronted with the responsibility of rearing Jesus, watching his unprecedented and controversial ministry, and then experiencing the agony and sorrow of seeing her perfect son suffer and die the most horrible of deaths. The truth he embodied would reach the depths of her heart, as a sword piercing her soul.

Jesus Christ is the magnet, the cornerstone, the way, the truth, the light, and life of the ages. He draws those that believe, those that have eyes to see and ears to hear. Because of unbelief, others are repelled from him. As the truth, Jesus Christ separates the two groups of people, believers from unbelievers, the wheat from the chaff.

Such were the dimensions of the words Simeon uttered by divine revelation. His words further informed Mary and Joseph of the greatness of the child

---

21. Matthew Black makes the interesting observation that this may be a Semitic idiom in which "thy own soul" is a sudden change of person, in which case it would refer to Israel rather than Mary. The word "also" is omitted in the Aramaic, as well as several Greek sources. Black suggests, "Through thee thyself, (O Israel), will the sword pass. . . ." See Matthew Black, *An Aramaic Approach to the Gospels and Acts*, 3d ed. (Oxford: Clarendon Press, 1967), pp. 153-155.

and the vast challenge he would present to them, his parents, and to all of mankind.

As Simeon finished his prophecy, another great believer encountered this small gathering of Simeon with Joseph, Mary, and Jesus, and that was the Prophetess Anna.

> Luke 2:36-38:
> And there was one Anna, a prophetess, the daughter of Phanuel, of the tribe of Aser: she was of a great age, and had lived with an husband seven years from her virginity;
> And she *was* a widow of about fourscore and four years, which departed not from the temple, but served *God* with fastings and prayers night and day.
> And she coming in that instant [as soon as Simeon was through prophesying] gave thanks likewise unto the Lord, and spake of him to all them that looked for redemption in Jerusalem.

Notice that God's Word gives many details of Anna's background, whereas very little personal background was given for Simeon. This account in Luke 2 reflects Eastern culture. To an Eastern mind a woman's words were not regarded with as much credibility as a man's. Therefore, her words would be more readily received if her personal credentials were given.

Anna's faithfulness in service to God was tremendous. She was a prophetess; she had served God in the Temple for decades; she was faithful in prayers and fastings; she was of the tribe of Asher (or Aser) and the daughter of Phanuel; and she was elderly, having the wisdom that comes with age and experience in God's service.

Anna had been married as a young woman. She lived with her husband seven years before he died. By the time of the record in Luke 2, she had been a widow for eighty-four years. Then, in Luke 2:36-38, when she was probably over one hundred years old, God worked in her heart so that she would come into the Temple at the proper time to see the promised seed, the Christ child. Upon seeing Jesus, she gave thanks to the Lord and then proceeded to declare the good news to those in Jerusalem who had been waiting for God's redemption, the Messiah.

With verse 38 of Luke 2 the scriptural record of Christ's birth and the events immediately surrounding it are concluded. The next verse in Luke, Luke 2:39, relates the return of Mary and Joseph with Jesus to Nazareth in Galilee. However, many events and many months elapse between the record of Anna in Jerusalem and the return of Joseph and Mary with Jesus to Nazareth. These events are not recorded in the Gospel of Luke, but are found in Matthew.

Conclusion

The noted events surrounding Christ's birth according to Luke's record begins with the census decreed by Rome which prompted Mary and Joseph to leave Nazareth during their honeymoon year and go to the hometown of their common ancestor David. In September of 3 B.C., in Bethlehem of Judah, as the prophecy had foretold long before, Jesus was born. Upon his birth, Jesus was salted and swaddled as Mary and Joseph dedicated themselves to raising him in the truth and integrity of God's Word, upright before the Lord.

While the child was still in swaddling clothes, shepherds came to see him, having heeded the message of an angel and rejoiced upon finding Jesus in a stable. Having seen him, they went out enthusiastically sharing the wonderful news throughout the area.

On his eighth day, Jesus was circumcised and named. On the forty-first day, Mary and Joseph took Jesus to the Temple in Jerusalem and there they offered two turtledoves or two young pigeons according to the law, one as a burnt offering and the other as a sin offering for Mary's purification. At that time they also presented Jesus to the Lord. With this, Joseph formally assumed the responsibility of rearing the child, acting as his father.

While at the Temple to present Jesus to God, Mary and Joseph encountered two wonderful people. The first was Simeon who experienced God's personal promise of not dying before seeing the Christ. By prophecy, Simeon declared the greatness of the child as well as the challenge and controversy that would surround him. Then came faithful Anna, the prophetess. She also expressed her great thanks for having lived to see the Christ. She declared this good news of God's having sent the redeemer to all those who were seeking such a hope in Jerusalem.

For centuries prophets had spoken of the Messiah, and people had clung to the promise of his appearance. At long last, the Messiah, the promised seed, the Christ, had come. The promised seed of the woman was now beginning his life's purpose, even as an infant, of fulfilling every segment of the law in order to redeem mankind.

CHAPTER SEVENTEEN

THE MAGI

Jupiter-Regulus Conjunction Feb. 17
Passover April 18-24
Jupiter-Regulus Conjunction May 8
Last Jupiter-Venus Conjunction June 17
Massing of Planets in Leo August 27
Jupiter on Meridian Dec. 4
Hanukkah Dec. 22-29
Arrival of Magi in Bethlehem
Joseph, Mary, Jesus Flee to Egypt

SHEBAT	ADAR	ADAR II	NISAN	IYYAR	SIVAN	TAMMUZ	AB	ELUL	TISHRI	MAR-CHESHVAN	KISLEV
30	29	30	29	30	29	30	29	30	30	30	29

JAN	FEB	MARCH	APRIL	MAY	JUNE	JULY	AUGUST	SEPT	OCT	NOV	DEC
31	28	31	30	31	30	31	31	30	31	30	31

2 B.C.

Lunar Eclipse Before Herod's Death Jan. 9
Archelaus Disrupts Passover April 8
Joseph, Mary, Jesus Return to Nazareth

TEBETH	SHEBAT	ADAR	NISAN	IYYAR	SIVAN	TAMMUZ	AB	ELUL	TISHRI	MAR-CHESHVAN	KISLEV
30	30	29	30	29	30	29	30	29	30	30	30

JAN	FEB	MARCH	APRIL	MAY	JUNE	JULY	AUGUST	SEPT	OCT	NOV	DEC
31	29	31	30	31	30	31	31	30	31	30	31

1 B.C.*

Of the many aspects surrounding the birth of the Christ, one topic which has attracted attention and stirred interest is that of the "wise men," spoken of in Matthew 2:1-13. In Part I of this book, we

*This calendar gives significant Biblical events in the years 2 and 1 B.C. The Hebrew months are given alongside our modern months. Because the Hebrew months were determined by the moon, their dates according to our calendar would shift from year to year.

studied these men, the Magi: who they were, where they came from, why they alone observed in the heavens the coming of the Messiah, and what the astronomical displays were which they perceived as indicating this birth.

In this chapter we will dwell on other aspects of Matthew 2 to see the effects of their visit to Jerusalem and Bethlehem. The first verse of Matthew 2 gives the context of the Magi's arrival in Jerusalem.

> Matthew 2:1-3:
> Now when Jesus was born in Bethlehem of Judaea in the days of Herod the king, behold, there came wise men from the east to Jerusalem,
> Saying, Where is he that is born King of the Jews [Judeans]? for we have seen his star in the east [in the rising], and are come to worship him.
> When Herod the king had heard *these things*, he was troubled, and all Jerusalem with him.

The political and religious leaders in the city of Jerusalem had not been aware that a king of the Judeans had been born, let alone that a star announced his birth before the Magi arrived. Since the present king, Herod, was intensely disliked, to some people the arrival of a new king—especially their expected Messiah—would have been most welcome news. To others, including Herod, the news was disturbing and troubling. The city churned with anxiety as the

Magi's assertion began to be more widely broadcast.

Herod was not pleased at the thought that anyone would be a threat to his throne. Had such a child truly been born? And was this child really destined to take over the throne of Judea? Why had he not been informed of the child's birth before this? Why had these Magi known of it when those of his own court and kingdom and the Temple had not? Was this indeed the Messiah? Wrestling with these questions, Herod was deeply troubled.

> Matthew 2:4:
> And when he [Herod] had gathered all the chief priests and scribes of the people together, he demanded of them where [the] Christ should be born.

This verse clearly demonstrates that the Magi were not inquiring about a child who would be just an ordinary king. This child they sought was the Christ, God's long-promised Messiah, the one clearly foretold in the Old Testament Scriptures. Herod vehemently demanded that the religious leaders tell him where the Messiah was to be born. These Judean leaders were totally oblivious of the Christ's birth, while the Magi, religious Gentiles of Persia, were acutely aware and certain of the arrival of the king to Israel. Herod, distraught with anger at the religious leaders who had not informed him, called the chief priests and scribes into account. He ordered them to tell him where the promised king was supposed to be born.

> Matthew 2:5 and 6:
> And they [the chief priests and scribes] said unto him, In Bethlehem of Judaea: for thus it is written by the prophet,
> And thou Bethlehem, *in* the land of Juda, art not the least among the princes of Juda: for out of thee shall come a Governor [a leader], that shall rule [or shepherd] my people Israel.

The prophecy of Micah 5:2 clearly set the place of birth as Bethlehem of Judah.

> Matthew 2:7:
> Then Herod, when he had privily [secretly] called the wise men [Magi], inquired of them diligently what time the star appeared.

The words "inquired of them diligently" are the Greek words *ēkribōsen par autōn*, meaning, "inquired accurately from them." Herod wanted to know with exactness, with precision, when the Magi had seen this star "in the rising." His intention was to use this information in estimating the age of "he that is born King of the Jews [Judeans]." After making this inquiry about the timing of the star, Herod sent the Magi to Bethlehem.

Matthew 2:8:
And he sent them to Bethlehem, and said, Go and search diligently for the young child;[1] and when ye have found *him*, bring me word again, that I may come and worship [pay homage to] him also.

Herod spoke deceitfully to the Magi. In reality, Herod wanted to find the child and slay him so this young king would not be a threat to his throne. Acting out of desperation and fear, Herod demanded accurate information about the promised king of the Judeans. Having concluded his private conference and inquiry with the Magi, Herod sent the Magi to Bethlehem of Judea, his strategy being to use the information the Magi would bring back to him, rather than send his own men who would be treated in Bethlehem with reserve and anxiety.

Matthew 2:9 and 10:
When they [the Magi] had heard the king [Herod], they departed; and, lo, the star, which they saw in the

1. Notice that, after learning when the star appeared, Herod referred to Jesus as a "young child." The words "young child" are in Aramaic *talya* and in Greek *paidion*. A child can be referred to as a *talya* or *paidion* at least as early as his circumcision, as in Luke 2:21, and up to twelve years of age, as in Luke 2:40 and Mark 5:39-43. Therefore, the words *talya* and *paidion* alone are too general to precisely set Jesus' age. Nevertheless, the Word of God distinguishes the age of the newborn infant that the shepherds saw, from the young child that the Magi came to see, by referring to Jesus as an *ula* or *brephos* in Luke 2:12 and 16 on the night of his birth, and as a *talya* or *paidion* in Matthew 2:8, 9, and 11 when the Magi arrived more than a year and three months later.

east [which they saw "in the rising," as noted in verse 2], went before [Greek: *proēgen*, went or guided in front of] them, till it came and stood [until having come, it stood] over where the young child was.
When they saw the star, they rejoiced with exceeding great joy.

The phrase "came and stood over" in Matthew 2:9 is notable. Astronomically, stars and planets are similar to the sun in that they rise in the east and set in the west. Furthermore, a star or planet is like the sun in that it will reach a high point in the sky in relation to the observer. At this point it is on the meridian (longitude) of the observer. During the day, the sun reaches this point at noon.

Consider stars and planets in their nightly courses. They rise in the east. At some time during the night each will reach its highest point in relation to the observer, the meridian. If this occurs in the southern sky when one is traveling south, as with the Magi traveling from Jerusalem to Bethlehem, the star would appear to come and stand over one's destination. This does not mean it stands still; it simply reaches its apex and from that point on it appears to the observer to descend in the western sky.

The word "stood" in Matthew 2:9 is from the Greek word *histēmi*, which means "to stand as opposed to either rising or falling." That highest point of a planet or star in its trajectory is described by the phrase "came and stood over."

Previously, it was stated that Jesus was born in September of 3 B.C. and that Jupiter was "his star" of Matthew 2. This aids us in setting the time frame of Matthew 2:9, for the Magi would have observed Jupiter at the time it was visibly reaching its meridian, or "high point," over Bethlehem.

The Magi's journey from Jerusalem to Bethlehem had to occur between Jesus' birth in September of 3 B.C., and Herod's death some time prior to Passover in April of 1 B.C. Furthermore, according to Matthew 2:16, Herod chose to execute the children two years and under based on the time of the star's rising, the time of which he had learned from the Magi when he privately conferred with them. Since the star's initial appearance was on August 12, 3 B.C., what is recorded in Matthew 2:9 occurred between September of 2 B.C. and April of 1 B.C., a seven-month period.

According to astronomical calculations, Jupiter was not visible crossing the meridian, the "high point," over Bethlehem from September through November of 2 B.C. During this time Jupiter was too close to the sun to be visible when it reached that meridian. However, by December 4 of 2 B.C., Jupiter became visible at the meridian shortly before dawn. From December 4 until Herod's death before the Passover on April 8, Jupiter continued to visibly cross this meridian each night at a progressively earlier time. However, the eclipse that shortly preceded Herod's death occurred on January 9, 1 B.C. Thus, it was sometime during this five-week period, from December 4, 2 B.C., to January 9, 1 B.C., that the Magi journeyed from Jerusalem to Bethlehem and saw the star of Matthew 2:9. Interestingly, their journey brought them to Jerusalem in December, at which time a joyous festival called the Feast of Dedication, Hanukkah, took place. The significance of this time is apparent when one considers that the Feast of Dedication marked the restoration of worship in the Temple after a period of foreign occupation. Now, the Magi were coming to pay respect to, or worship, the young king of the Judeans, who was the true Temple.[2] In 2 B.C. this Feast of Dedication was celebrated from December 22 to 29.[3]

If the Magi had been advised in Jerusalem to travel in any direction other than south, they could not have followed as the star "went before them."

---

2. John 2:19: "Jesus answered and said unto them, Destroy this temple, and in three days I will raise it up."

3. The Feast of Dedication, which is mentioned in John 10:22, commemorated the cleansing of the Temple which had been defiled during the reign of Antiochus Epiphanes in 164 B.C. during the time of the Maccabees. Because the feast was not derived from the Old Testament law, it was not observed in the same fashion as other feasts, such as Passover. There was no holy convocation at the beginning of the Feast of Dedication, and work was allowed on that first day. Since there was no prohibition against work for the Judeans, or a holy convocation, the Magi, though being Gentiles, were able to secure all the aid they required from the Judeans to find the child. The first day of the feast was on Kislev 25 of the Hebrew calendar, and continued for eight days. In the year 2 B.C., this was from December 22 to 29 (Akavia, *Calendar for 6000 Years*).

When they traveled south towards Bethlehem, they saw the same star which they had observed previously in their homeland. It was rising in its nightly course towards the meridian over their destination, confirming for them that they were going in the right direction to find the child born a king. The star finally reached and stood at its highest point on the meridian directly over Bethlehem in the southern sky.[4] The Magi "rejoiced with exceeding great joy" for they recognized this as verification of the child's whereabouts. They realized they were about to find the child who was the king of the Judeans.

Herod had directed them to Bethlehem because of a scriptural prophecy. Now the star confirmed this location by appearing directly before them as they approached the city of David. Both Scripture and the heavens were directing them.

The star did not indicate a specific house, as this is astronomically impossible. The star simply confirmed that Bethlehem was the village in which they would find the "king of the Judeans" whom they sought. The Magi only required a couple of hours to travel to Bethlehem from Jerusalem. Upon arriving in Bethlehem, it would not have been difficult for the Magi to find the child, for local inhabitants would be

---

4. The planet Jupiter began to be seen crossing the meridian by December 4, at 6:09 A.M. Jupiter continued to rise four minutes earlier each day. By December 24, Jupiter crossed the meridian at 4:44 A.M. Calculated from Paul V. Neugebauer, *Sterntafeln* (Leipzig: J.C. Hinrichs'sche Buchhandlung, 1912).

aware of this special child born in the area previously, since the shepherds had spread the news of Christ's birth throughout the region. Thus the Magi were able to locate the young king.

> Matthew 2:11:
> And when they were come into the house, they saw the young child with Mary his mother, and fell down, and worshipped [paid homage to] him: and when they had opened their treasures, they presented unto him gifts; gold, and frankincense, and myrrh.

The Magi found the young child in a house, not in a stable or in a manger. There were no shepherds present. This was not the night Jesus was born, but more than one year and three months later.

Upon finding the child, the Magi fell down before him as a sign of utmost reverence to a king, the king of Israel born in Judea. The Magi themselves opened the gifts they had brought before presenting them to the king, which was the custom whenever an Easterner presented gifts to royalty. The Magi's gifts of gold, frankincense, and myrrh were very precious and costly indeed, suitable for giving to royalty. Also, that there were three gifts given is no indication whatsoever that there were three Magi. Although modern tradition consistently depicts three Magi, this is guesswork and has no scriptural verification.

There were many more Magi than three because this was a great moment in history and in the lives of these religious men. Also, when traveling long distances, Easterners normally moved in a large group or caravan for security purposes. The company of Magi was not mistaken for a band of charlatan magicians or astrologers, but their ambassadorial retinue, representing the astronomical elite and the courts of the East, was so impressive that King Herod and the people of Jerusalem were astonished and amazed.

The Magi's stay in Bethlehem was brief. Herod was waiting impatiently just a few miles away for their return to him with the desired information so he could act swiftly with regards to the perceived threat. But God immediately gave new instructions to the Magi via a vision.

> Matthew 2:12:
> And [the Magi] being warned of God in a dream [vision] that they should not return to Herod, they departed into their own country another way.

The word for "dream" in Matthew 2:12 and 13 is the Greek *onar*. It is used six times in the New Testament, all in Matthew (1:20; 2:12, 13, 19, 22; 27:19). In these passages *onar* is used of visions to Joseph, the wise men, and Pilate's wife. Another word, *enupnion*, suggests a mere dream as opposed to a dream with divine guidance.[5] The usage of *onar* in the New Testament also suggests it to be more than a dream in sleep. It is more like a daydream with God's divine instruction inspiring the vision. "Dream" would be better translated as "vision" since a dream suggests an occurrence during sleep.

In a vision the Magi received God's revelation not to return to Herod. These men of astronomical learning were given this revelation and then obediently carried it out. They obeyed God rather than Herod, and yet they were not Judean or of Israel, but Gentiles.

> Matthew 2:13:
> And when they were departed, behold, the angel of the Lord appeareth to Joseph in a dream [vision], saying, Arise, and take the young child and his mother, and flee into Egypt, and be thou there until I bring thee word: for Herod will seek the young child to destroy him.

God will help His children to stay ahead of the Adversary if they will hear and then obey. Joseph received this revelation from God even before Herod had given the command to find and slay the child.

> Matthew 2:14:
> When he [Joseph] arose, he took the young child and his mother by night, and departed into Egypt.

---

5. Second-century usage distinguishes *enupnion*, a mere dream, from *oneiros* (a form of *onar*), a significant, prophetic one. Liddell and Scott's *Greek-English Lexicon*, p. 579.

As soon as Joseph received God's Word, the revelation from God, he acted on it immediately as implied by the Biblical sense of "arose." He rose up, taking Mary and the child with their belongings and departed for Egypt under cover of darkness, before the massacre descended on Bethlehem the following morning.

> Matthew 2:15:
> And was there until the death of Herod: that it might be fulfilled [with the result that it was fulfilled[6]] which was spoken of the Lord by the prophet, saying, Out of Egypt have I called my son.

Joseph, Mary, and Jesus remained in Egypt for about three months, until Herod's death, which occurred before Passover on April 8, 1 B.C. This sojourn in Egypt and their subsequent return to Palestine fulfilled the prophecy found in Hosea 11:1 and repeated in Matthew 2:15: "Out of Egypt have I called my son." Hosea's declaration referred specifically and immediately to God's calling of Israel, His adopted sons, out of Egypt during the time of Moses.[7] However, Hosea's revelation had its ultimate fulfillment in the Messiah, for the Christ would return to his homeland from Egypt as a young child.

---

6. For further insight into this phrase see Wierwille, "That It Might Be Fulfilled," *Jesus Christ Our Passover*, Appendix 7, pp. 463-467.
7. See Exodus chapters 12—15.

> Matthew 2:16:
> Then Herod, when he saw [perceived] that he was mocked of the wise men [Magi], was exceeding wroth, and sent forth, and slew all the children [male children] that were in Bethlehem, and in all the coasts thereof [its borders, its surrounding areas], from two years old and under, according to the time which he had diligently [accurately] inquired of the wise men [Magi].

That very day Herod knew of the Magi's departure for their homeland. He was furious that they did not return to him according to his request. Consequently, enraged and acting with utmost secrecy and speed, Herod marshaled his army under the cover of night and surrounded Bethlehem and "all the coasts thereof"[8] to execute all the male children aged two years and under early the following morning.

Why did Herod choose two years as the upper age limit? He chose it according to the time of the star's first appearance on August 12, 3 B.C., which had been related to him by the Magi. Matthew 2:16 indicates that Herod's knowledge of the star's first appearance convinced him that the child was certainly no more than two years old by the time the mass

8. The cities and villages of Palestine during the Old and New Testament times were quite small, being only acres in size. Hazor, the largest city in Palestine during the Old Testament was only about two hundred acres, with the average town being less than fifteen acres. These cities and villages were surrounded by farmland. Bethlehem and the land around it was where Herod sent his men.

slaying was ordered. Herod's execution of these children occurred the day after the Magi left Bethlehem.

This vicious execution of the innocent children by Herod had to occur after December 4 of 2 B.C. and before Passover, April 8 of 1 B.C., for Herod died before the Passover. Since Jesus Christ was born on September 11, 3 B.C., Jesus Christ would be one year and three months of age by December, 2 B.C. In killing the male children two years and under, Herod was giving himself a margin for error in the calculation of Christ's birthdate.

Herod's cruel, maniacal execution of young children fulfilled a prophecy that had been spoken by the Prophet Jeremiah.

> Matthew 2:17 and 18:
> Then was fulfilled that which was spoken by Jeremy the prophet, saying,
> In Rama was there a voice heard, lamentation, and weeping, and great mourning, Rachel weeping *for* her children, and would not be comforted, because they are not.

This prophecy of Jeremiah was spoken as well as written. Verse 18 of Matthew 2 is taken from Jeremiah 31:15 where it is set in a different context. Matthew 2:18 shows that the prophecy had a second intended sense, its total fulfillment being when Herod slaughtered the children in Bethlehem and its outlying area.[9]

This fulfillment is the figure of speech *gnome*, a quotation where the sense is adapted by analogy to a different event or circumstance.[10] By using the figure *gnome*, God related the prophecy of "Rahel [Rachel] weeping for her children" in Jeremiah 31:15 to the slaying of infants in the area of Bethlehem in the last days of Herod's reign.

From this it is evident that there was no need for Herod to execute the children in Jerusalem and the town of Rama five miles north of Jerusalem as some have suggested.[11] Herod, as is plainly stated,

---

9. In Jeremiah 31:15 the prophecy concerns the desolation of Palestine, when Israel (and soon Judah) was dispersed and taken into captivity. That is why Jeremiah said that Rachel's (or, Rahel's) children "*were* not." Rachel was the grandmother of Ephraim, which was the major tribe of the northern kingdom of Israel. Ephraim is referred to several times in Jeremiah 31 for the kingdom of Israel as a whole. Rachel was also the mother of Benjamin, one of the tribes of the southern kingdom of Judah. Thus, this could also be a reference to Judah's impending removal from the land and Judah's captivity. Rachel died long before the time of Jeremiah, so that the phrase "Rahel weeping" is the figure of speech *prosopopoeia*, attributing a human trait to something not human, since a dead person cannot weep. The figure and the use of Rachel's name emphasizes sorrow over the removal of God's people, both kingdoms, from the land. However, in Jeremiah 31:16-40, God makes the promise that Israel and Judah will one day return to the land and have God's blessing. That is the immediate meaning of Jeremiah 31:15 in its context.

10. See *The Companion Bible*, p. 1311 and Appendix 107, p. 151-152; also, see Bullinger, *Figures of Speech Used in the Bible*, p. 786.

11. There are a number of places in the Bible lands that were called Rama (sometimes spelled "Ramah") in antiquity. The word "Rama" in Aramaic and Hebrew means "height" or "high place." Although it is transliterated as a proper place name, it is also used in a literal sense

ordered the execution of the children in Bethlehem and all of its outlying area ("coasts"). This expression would not by any means include Jerusalem. Furthermore, the child had been born in Bethlehem according to Herod's information.

Despite Herod's violent reaction, he failed in his attempt to slay the king of the Judeans because Joseph and Mary were already taking him to Egypt.[12]

> Matthew 2:19 and 20:
> But when Herod was dead, behold, an angel of the Lord appeareth in a dream [vision] to Joseph in Egypt, Saying, Arise, and take the young child and his mother, and go into the land of Israel: for they are dead which sought the young child's life.

How wonderfully God watched over His Son. After the family had been in Egypt for a three-month period, as soon as the danger was gone, God sent an angel to bring this news to Joseph and to direct him to bring Jesus and Mary back to their homeland, Israel. Joseph's response, again, was one of prompt obedience, with no hesitancy or delay.

---

at times—such as in Ezekiel 16:24,25,31,39; and Luke 3:5. A note in *The Companion Bible*, p. 1060, on Jeremiah 31:15 suggests there was a "high place" near Bethlehem. It cites the Targum and Vulgate reading of Jeremiah 31:15 as "in a high place."

12. Herod's search was the first attempt on Jesus Christ's life. There are at least twelve other attempts on his life recorded in the Gospels. They are: Matthew 8:24; 26:3 and 4; Luke 4:3-11; 4:28-30; 8:22-25; John 5:16-18; 7:1; 7:30; 7:32-48; 8:59; 10:31 and 39; 11:53-57.

> Matthew 2:21 and 22:
> And he arose, and took the young child and his mother, and came into the land of Israel.
> But when he heard that Archelaus did reign in Judaea in the room of his father Herod, he [Joseph] was afraid to go thither: notwithstanding, being warned of God in a dream [vision], he turned aside into the parts of Galilee.

At Herod's death, his son Archelaus became the new governor of Judea. Verse 22 of Matthew 2 indicates that Joseph wanted to return with Mary and Jesus to Judea, probably to settle in Bethlehem again from where they had departed to go to Egypt. But the danger of being in the territory ruled by the new king Archelaus gave Joseph pause. His concern for settling in Judea was not unfounded, as corroborated by another vision. Therefore, Joseph took his family to the northern part of Israel, going into the region of Galilee to the city of Nazareth.

> Matthew 2:23:
> And he [Joseph] came and dwelt in a city called Nazareth: that it might be fulfilled which was spoken by the prophets, He shall be called a Nazarene.

This prophecy about the Messiah's being a Nazarene was spoken but not necessarily written. It cannot be found in the Old Testament. However, it had to have been a prophecy spoken by a prophet referring to the Messiah.

So Joseph and Mary took Jesus to Nazareth, the city that had been their home before Jesus' birth in Bethlehem and their flight into Egypt. This return to Nazareth is further recorded in the Gospel of Luke.

> Luke 2:39:
> And when they had performed all things according to the law of the Lord, they returned into Galilee, to their own city Nazareth.

The phrase "performed all things according to the law of the Lord" refers to the legal requirements fulfilled in Luke 2, with the circumcision of Jesus and his presentation in the Temple, as well as his trip to Egypt. The word "law" can at times refer to other passages of scripture beside the five books of Moses. Jesus Christ divided the Old Testament into three categories: the law, the prophets, and the psalms (Luke 24:44). There are instances however when writings from the prophets or psalms are referred to in a general sense as part of the law. In I Corinthians 14:21 a passage from Isaiah is called part of the law, plus John 10:34 and 15:25, both quotations from Psalms, are said also to be from the law. Here in Luke 2:39, the general term "law" is used to refer to Mary and Joseph's taking Jesus with them to Egypt in order to completely fulfill all that which was required of the Messiah, a part of which was Hosea 11:1: "I [God]...called my son out of Egypt." Luke quite accurately states that they returned to Nazareth when these requirements were completed.

Thus concludes the record of the visit of the Magi, the reaction of Herod, the sojourning of Joseph, Mary, and Jesus in Egypt, and their return to Nazareth in Galilee. How beautifully we see God's working in the hearts of people to herald His Son's birth and to protect him in infancy. This wonderful child named Jesus, this long-awaited Messiah, this king of the Judeans, the promised seed, had a mission to accomplish and Satan could not and would not take his life. Jesus the Christ would fulfill God's plan of redemption, he was the designated one, the one who would fulfill the law and thereby make possible the Age of Grace.

CHAPTER EIGHTEEN

JESUS AS A YOUTH

After Herod's death and their return to the land of Israel from Egypt, Joseph and Mary brought Jesus to Nazareth, where they had lived before Jesus' birth. Here in this city in the hills of Galilee, the Son of God was raised from childhood to adulthood. What little is known of this period of Jesus Christ's life is recorded in the Gospel of Luke.

> Luke 2:40:
> And the child grew, and waxed strong in spirit [all critical Greek texts omit "in spirit"], filled with wisdom: and the grace of God was upon him.

Jesus Christ grew up like any other child. Genetically he had many advantages, but he was still a person, a human individual, who had to develop and utilize his learning processes like any other human being. He was not God. God is unchangeable, God is omniscient, omnipresent, and omnipotent. God would not have needed to grow and learn, but Jesus Christ did.

People have failed to consider the self-taught discipline and effort exerted by Jesus as he grew, because they have so often pictured him as a "pre-packaged god" who was born knowing all things and being all-powerful. That is a degradation of both Jesus Christ and his heavenly Father, for it veils the truth of who Jesus was, what he accomplished, and why God sent him. Jesus Christ was a human who grew and learned.

Luke 2:40 states that Jesus "waxed strong," grew strong. As a child he did not grow strong in spirit because he did not receive holy spirit until he was thirty. Jesus also was being "filled with wisdom."

Joseph and Mary diligently taught him God's Word from the Old Testament Scriptures, and Jesus fervently studied that written Word, maturing more and more in the realization of who he was and of the mission he was to accomplish.

> Luke 2:41:
> Now his parents went to Jerusalem every year at the feast of the passover.

The Passover and the Feast of Unleavened Bread occurred in the spring of the year, during the month called Nisan. This feast was one of the three important Judean feasts which the head of each household was required to attend each year in Jerusalem. God's

Word records that Mary and Joseph went annually to Jerusalem for this occasion.[1]

> Luke 2:42:
> And when he [Jesus] was twelve years old, they went up to Jerusalem after the custom of the feast.

When Jesus was twelve years of age, he accompanied Joseph and Mary to Jerusalem for the Passover. In Biblical culture, a male at twelve was considered mature and responsible, being on the threshold of manhood. On this visit, a notable incident occurred.

> Luke 2:43 and 44:
> And when they [Joseph and Mary] had fulfilled the days, as they returned, the child Jesus tarried behind in Jerusalem; and Joseph and his mother knew not *of it*. But they, supposing him to have been in the company, went a day's journey; and they sought him among *their* kinsfolk and acquaintance.

---

1. If Joseph and Mary went "every year" to the feast in Jerusalem, then they would have returned from Egypt in time for the Passover that followed Herod's death. However, Matthew 2:22 states that Joseph "was afraid to go thither" because of Archelaus' reign in Jerusalem. The angel would not have called Joseph and his family back from Egypt if Archelaus was as great a threat as Herod had been. However, Josephus records that the Passover following Herod's death was marred with insurrections against Archelaus, the new king. He was finally forced to send in his army and disperse the crowds in Jerusalem just as the Passover began, thus abruptly ending the feast. Therefore, the angel warned Joseph to turn aside into Galilee to avoid the turmoil Archelaus' army was causing in Jerusalem.

The words "fulfilled the days" refer to the completion of the seven-day feast, the Feast of Unleavened Bread. One Aramaic source, the Curetonian Syriac manuscript, reads, "And when the days of the feast were completed. . . ."

Joseph and Mary traveled from Jerusalem in a caravan. It is quite understandable that Joseph and Mary could travel for an entire day before noticing Jesus' absence. Jesus was a responsible young man. In a large caravan, the youth traveled together, separate from the adults. As parents, Joseph and Mary simply assumed Jesus was "in the company." The Peshitta Version of the Aramaic reads, "They supposed he was with the sons of their company."

When the caravan stopped at the end of the first day, Joseph and Mary looked for Jesus; they became concerned when they could not find him. The other children had returned to their parents for the night, but Jesus had not. They sought him among relatives and friends in the caravan, but he was not to be found. They spent the second day traveling back to Jerusalem.

> Luke 2:45 and 46:
> And when they [Joseph and Mary] found him not, they turned back again to Jerusalem, seeking him.
> And it came to pass, that after three days they found him in the temple, sitting in the midst of the doctors, both hearing them, and asking them questions.

Upon arriving in Jerusalem on the third day, Joseph and Mary searched diligently for Jesus, as great concern grew in their hearts. Finally, they found him in the Temple.

Jesus, at the age of twelve, sat "in the midst of the doctors," the most learned theologians of all Judaism. In Eastern culture, twelve was the age at which a youth would be allowed to begin asking questions of his teachers. Jesus did not teach in the normal sense of the word. He was simply listening and asking questions; but to those watching, his knowledge and acute perception were apparent.

> Luke 2:47:
> And all that heard him were astonished at his understanding and answers.

Jesus had studied the Scriptures intensely before the age of twelve! His questions exhibited unusual insight; indeed his listeners gained answers by listening to his questions. They were astonished at this knowledgeable young person so boldly conversing with the learned leaders in the Temple. Joseph and Mary were struck with amazement when they came upon their lost son.

> Luke 2:48:
> And when they saw him, they were amazed: and his mother said unto him, Son, why hast thou thus dealt with us? behold, thy father and I have sought thee sorrowing.

With natural maternal concern, Mary asked Jesus to explain why he had remained behind, frightening his father and her. Jesus' response consisted of two simple questions.

> Luke 2:49 and 50:
> And he [Jesus] said unto them, How is it that ye sought me? wist [knew] ye not that I must be about my Father's business?
> And they understood not the saying which he spake unto them.

On the third day of searching they finally found him in the Temple. They should have known he would have been in the Temple[2] involved in the affairs of his true Father, God.

Here, in his first recorded words, Jesus explicitly stated that he was to be about his Father's business in his Father's house. Years later, while dying on the cross, he knowledgeably uttered the words, "It is finished." What was finished? His Father's business, which he started in the Father's house, the work which God had allowed him to accomplish.

Joseph and Mary did not understand what Jesus was saying to them at that time in the Temple. They

---

2. According to the Aramaic manuscripts, "about my Father's business" is literally "in my Father's house." This fits well with the context. The Greek rendering of "about my Father's business" is understandable, as that is the purpose Jesus Christ had in being at the Temple. Black suggests this as an example of a Greek translation from Aramaic. See Black, *Aramaic Approach to the Gospels and Acts*, p. 3.

knew that Jesus was the Messiah, the promised seed. Yet when Jesus told his parents that he must be about his Father's business, they did not understand the meaning and impact of his words. Jesus, at the age of twelve, was already diligently preparing for his mission as mankind's redeemer, even beyond his full comprehension.

> Luke 2:51:
> And he went down with them, and came to Nazareth, and was subject unto them: but [and] his mother kept all these sayings in her heart.

After finding him, Joseph, Mary, and Jesus returned to their home in Nazareth. Although Jesus' words had not been completely understood by his mother, Mary did not forget them. She recorded them in the depths of her being.

A number of questions arise regarding this incident. Why did he leave his parents? Where did he sleep and eat during those three days? Why did he appear to "talk back" to his parents?

Jesus would have had no trouble in securing a place to stay and food to eat. It was customary for people to invite strangers to stay with them and to provide both food and shelter. This custom can be seen throughout the Bible: "Be not forgetful to entertain strangers: for thereby some have entertained angels unawares" (Hebrews 13:2). Even if no person would have invited Jesus to stay, there were always places to stay with food available to travelers.[3]

When his parents returned and questioned his actions, Jesus answered, not from insubordination, but with earnestness concerning his spiritual responsibility, "Didn't you realize I have to start my work?" Such was the heart of a maturing youth determined to walk with God, one who was zealous to find favor with God and man.

Verse 51 of Luke 2 clearly states that Jesus "was subject" to Joseph and Mary. He had been subject to them since his birth and he was only twelve by this time. Like every child, he was expected to obey his parents. Jesus was fully a human being, he was not God. God would not be subject to Joseph, Mary, or anyone else. But Jesus was not God, and therefore he was subject to his earthly parents, and in need of their parental care and guidance.

Jesus was raised and taught by Mary and Joseph as well as religious leaders in the synagogue at Nazareth. He studied the Old Testament scrolls and

---

3. This is why the angels told Lot in Genesis 19:2 that they would abide in the street all night, and also explains a traveling Levite saying the same thing to a man living in Gibeah in Judges 19:15-19. Regarding these places for travelers it is known that: "In every village there is a public room, or more than one, called a *menzil* or *medâfeh*, devoted to the entertainment of strangers. The guest lodges in the menzil and his food is supplied by the families to whose circle it belongs. He takes nothing when he leaves. To offer money would be taken as an insult; and to receive it would be a great disgrace." E.P. Barrows, *The Manners and Customs of the Jews* (London: Religious Tract Society, n.d.), p. 108.

knew the Word of God, as well as the traditions and customs of the times. His parents observed the practices of the law which he learned by their example. They knew he was God's Son, not Joseph's, and certainly told him so as he grew. Jesus also learned about himself and his ministry from the Old Testament.

As Jesus Christ grew he was greatly inspired and influenced by various examples in the Old Testament. One such example was Samuel. According to I Samuel 1:24-28 when Hannah had weaned Samuel she brought him to the tabernacle where she gave him to the Lord. Samuel ministered before the Lord there and grew up being "in favour both with the Lord, and also with men" (I Samuel 2:18 and 26), just as Jesus grew "in favour with God and man" (Luke 2:52).

The Talmud says, "Let a man deal gently with his son until he come to be twelve years old, but from that time let him descend with him into the way of living."[4] So Jesus, at the age of twelve, and knowing who his Father was, determined his readiness to "be about my Father's business."

Jesus, in coming to the Temple, followed the example of Samuel. While he remained in the Temple, hearing the teachers and asking them questions, his understanding of God's Word astounded them. After

4. Quoted by Lightfoot, *New Testament from the Talmud and Hebraica*, 3:43.

Jesus returned to Nazareth, he grew into manhood, all the while continuing to grow and develop.

> Luke 2:52:
> And Jesus increased in wisdom and stature, and in favour with God and man.

Jesus increased in wisdom and stature. He grew and learned as any other human being. However, since he was the only begotten Son of God, the effect of the perfect genetic contribution of the sperm God created in Mary must have produced in Jesus Christ the keenest mind since the first Adam. God cannot increase in wisdom and stature, but Jesus Christ worked hard, both physically and mentally, as he matured to manhood.

While developing as a youth, Jesus also increased in favor with God and man. As he pleased God with his individual growth and walk, God's divine grace was with him. Jesus' life as a youth was an example, and thus he gained the favor of man, as well as God. Had he been God he would not have needed to gain God's favor.

What a youth Jesus of Nazareth was. As the son of a carpenter, Jesus also took up that trade. Having four half brothers and at least three half sisters, all born of Joseph and Mary, Jesus' youth included a meaningful family life as well as hard work. However, nothing took priority over his closest family tie, that bond he had with God his Father.

CHAPTER NINETEEN

OUR PROMISED SEED

Jesus Christ is the fulcrum of all history. To bring about our redemption, he had to be wholly a man with all the credentials of the Messiah, the second Adam. By conception Jesus was the Son of God and a son of Mary, therefore, a descendant of Adam, Abraham, and David according to the flesh. By the circumstances he became the son of Joseph, gaining full earthly legal standing in the House of David. His credentials through his mother genetically gave him legal ascendency to inherit the throne of David. Thus Jesus came with flawless credentials as the king to and of Israel, the promised Messiah, God's Anointed.

Jesus Christ's conception and birth meshed remarkably with that of John the Baptist's six months before. The birth of John came to pass in a context of dramatic events. The angel Gabriel appeared to Zacharias while he was performing one of the greatest privileges of his life, that of burning incense to the Lord in the Holy Place of the Temple, as he served in the course of Abia in late May of 4 B.C. The angel's revelation was beyond Zacharias' belief—that he would be the father of a son borne by Elisabeth, even though she had long been barren. The angel declared to Zacharias that his son was to be named John and that he would be a great prophet of God.

Following the angel's declaration, Zacharias became dumb, unable to speak. However, Elisabeth still did conceive by Zacharias in June of 4 B.C. and gratefully nurtured the child promised of the Lord as it developed within her womb.

While Elisabeth was in her sixth month of pregnancy, in December of 4 B.C., an astounding revelation was delivered to a young woman in Nazareth of Galilee. This woman, Mary, learned from the angel that by the Holy Spirit, God, she would conceive a child, the Messiah, who would inherit David's throne. Mary, who considered herself the handmaid of the Lord, literally believed Gabriel's words, conceived, and with haste went to Judea to stay with her older kinswoman, Elisabeth. There Mary remained with Elisabeth for about three months.

The miracle wrought by God in Mary's womb brought with it a personal dilemma. Being pregnant could not only cost her the loss of a future relationship with Joseph, the man to whom she was betrothed, and make her an outcast of society, but it could even cost her her life. In visiting Elisabeth, Mary found great consolation and encouragement. Surely the God who had wrought such a great work in her would also take care of her relationship with Joseph, and He did.

When Elisabeth was in her ninth month of pregnancy, in March of 3 B.C., Mary returned to Nazareth. Shortly thereafter, John was born to Zacharias and Elisabeth. When he was eight days old, his parents, relatives, and neighbors gathered for the circumcision and naming of the child. To everyone's dismay, Elisabeth named him John, a name that had never been in Zacharias' family. When the people involved, ignoring Elisabeth's wishes for the child's name, sought Zacharias' decision, Zacharias firmly asserted that the child's name was to be John, as the angel had told him. At that very moment Zacharias' tongue was loosed. And with the loosing of his tongue, Zacharias delivered a powerful prophecy praising God for His great blessings to Israel.

Shortly after John's birth, Mary and Joseph were married in Nazareth. They had already been betrothed as husband and wife, but were not yet living together. By the time they were to first come together in a sexual relationship, Joseph discovered that Mary was already pregnant. Understandably perplexed, he had to decide what course of action to pursue. Should he make Mary a public example by having her openly renounced and stoned or should he simply give her a bill of divorcement and send her quietly away? As a just man, he had only these two courses of action available to him according to Old Testament law.

Out of concern for Mary, Joseph decided that he would give Mary a bill of divorcement and send her away. However, an angel appeared in a vision to Joseph declaring that the child in Mary's womb was conceived by God, and not by a man. Thus, understanding Mary's pregnancy and following the angel's encouragement, Joseph took Mary unto him and consummated their marriage. From that time on they lived together as husband and wife.

In Mary's ninth month of pregnancy, September of 3 B.C., the time came for Joseph and Mary to appear for an official registration in Bethlehem of Judea, the hometown of both Joseph's and Mary's forefathers. When Mary and Joseph arrived in Bethlehem, they had to stay in a stable or stall because no other place was available. While they were residing there, Mary gave birth to Jesus. The child was salted, wrapped in swaddling clothes for a few moments, and laid in a manger. Such was the simplicity and humbleness of the Messiah's beginning.

That same night an angel, later joined by a host of angels, appeared to shepherds watching their flock in the fields near Bethlehem. Heeding the angel's exhortation, the shepherds sought out the babe while the newborn was yet in swaddling clothes lying in the manger. With great excitement, the shepherds left the stable rejoicing and spreading the good news throughout the area.

When Jesus was eight days old, Joseph and Mary had him circumcised and named, according to God's Word. When he was forty-one days old, they took him to the Temple for the presentation of the child to the Lord and for fulfilling the legal requirements of Mary's purification. All of these actions demonstrated that Joseph was accepting the responsibility of being the child's earthly guardian. In effect, Joseph took Jesus and raised him as his son.

When Jesus was being presented in the Temple, an aged prophet named Simeon was inspired to come into the Temple. Upon seeing Jesus, Simeon picked him up in his arms with praise to God for the blessing of seeing the promised Christ. Then Simeon uttered a marvelous prophecy of the blessing Christ would bring to God's people. Simeon also blessed Mary and Joseph, and straightforwardly told Mary of the controversy that would surround her child, a controversy that would tear at the heartstrings of Mary herself.

After Simeon's prophecy, an aged prophetess named Anna came in, saw the child, and also praised God for him; Anna spoke of this child to the faithful in Jerusalem. After these joyous encounters, Joseph and Mary returned with Jesus to Bethlehem.

While Joseph and Mary were residing in Bethlehem, Eastern Magi arrived in Jerusalem seeking the king of the Judeans. This occurred in December of 2 B.C. In their homeland the Magi had seen a planet rise in the eastern sky, a planet they continued to watch as it majestically heralded the birth of a king in Judea, whom we know as the Messiah. Their arrival and questions caused no small stir in Jerusalem, especially disturbing Herod the Great.

Herod demanded that the Temple leaders tell him where the Christ was supposed to be born. They told him in Bethlehem of Judea. Thus Herod sent the Magi to Bethlehem, instructing them to bring him word when they found the child.

As the Magi traveled to Bethlehem, the king planet Jupiter which they had originally seen in the east was again visible. This time the planet "went before them," reaching its highest point in the southern sky directly in front of them as they traveled. There the planet stood over Bethlehem, confirming their destination.

In Bethlehem the Magi found the child who by then was more than a year and three months old. They presented gifts to him and paid him homage. Before they returned to Jerusalem, an angel appeared to the Magi in a vision, instructing them not to return to Herod to inform him of the whereabouts of the child. So the Magi obediently headed back to their homeland by a different route.

When the Magi did not return to Jerusalem, Herod was exceedingly angry. In order to insure the elimination of this child who was prophesied to be a king, Herod ordered an execution of all male children two years old and under throughout the region of Bethlehem. However, by that time Jesus was en route to Egypt with his family, because Joseph had been instructed by an angel to take Mary and Jesus and go to Egypt to avoid Herod's destruction.

After Herod died, sometime before the Passover on April 8, 1 B.C., an angel revealed to Joseph that it was safe to return to Israel from Egypt. Joseph's initial plan upon returning was to settle again in Bethlehem. However, because of an uprising against Archelaus, Herod's son who ascended his father's throne in Jerusalem, Joseph took his family to Galilee and settled in his own hometown of Nazareth.

There in Nazareth Jesus was reared. He was instructed in the Scriptures, and more and more he came to realize who he was and the mission he was sent to accomplish.

When Jesus was twelve years old, his mother and father took him with them to Jerusalem for the Feast of Unleavened Bread. But he did not rejoin the caravan on its return to Nazareth after the feast ended. Unaware of this, Mary and Joseph began their journey home without him. Upon finding him missing, they hurried back to Jerusalem. Their three-day search ended with their discovery of Jesus in the Temple listening to and questioning the learned religious leaders before an awed audience. When Mary questioned Jesus, Jesus replied by asking, "How is it that ye sought me? Know ye not that I must be about my Father's business?" The parents should have realized that Jesus would be in the Temple preparing himself for the mission for which God had sent him.

With no further account of Jesus' youth, God's Word simply summarizes the quality of his youth by saying that Jesus Christ grew and increased in wisdom and stature and in favor with God and man. By the age of thirty he was completely prepared to publicly and officially begin his ministry to Israel.[1]

Jesus Christ accepted the challenge God had set before him of accomplishing man's redemption. As the long-awaited seed of the woman, as the Messiah foretold throughout the ages by the prophets, Jesus Christ prepared himself for the mission given to him. In his brief life and ministry, he would do more for mankind than any other person in all history: he would fulfill the law and bring salvation to all who would believe.

Jesus Christ gives to those who believe the victory of all of God's promises. Yet he, as the king of the Judeans, was born in a lowly stable and laid in a manger in Bethlehem. Although in outward appear-

---

1. Thirty was the age that the priests and Levites were originally numbered by Moses and Aaron according to Numbers 4:3, 23, and 30.

ances he had a humble beginning, Jesus Christ was God's only begotten Son, God's anointed king, the world's redeemer. The coming of our savior, the promised seed, which was surrounded by so many magnificent, miraculous, and significant events, was the fulfillment of God's promise made long before, as recorded in Genesis 3:15. Jesus Christ was the promised seed who would crush the very head of the Adversary and once more give mankind ready access to God Himself.

This promised seed was God's seed, His only begotten Son, the Christ. As God's Son, Jesus Christ was God's seed bearer and thus His namesake. Because Jesus Christ lived without sin and then gave his life as the ultimate sacrifice, it became possible for God to give His incorruptible, spiritual seed to all who would believe on the name of Jesus Christ and be God's namesake. Thus, all of us who are born again of God's Spirit carry God's gift of seed in us. It is God in Christ in us. This seed gives us eternal life and access to the very power of God, and all of this has come about because, just as He had promised in the stars and in His written Word, God sent His Son, Jesus Christ our promised seed.

APPENDICES

APPENDIX 1

THE TRIPLE PLANETARY CONJUNCTION OF 7 B.C.

One proposal submitted as "his star" of Matthew 2 has been the three conjunctions of Jupiter and Saturn in Pisces in 7 B.C. Although the dates of these conjunctions are too early to fit the rest of the historical context of Jesus' life, this celestial display is worth observing for other reasons. These planets came into conjunction three times in one year—May 27, October 5, and December 1 of 7 B.C.—a great rarity, made possible by what is known in astronomy as "retrograde motion."

If this proposal were valid, then the conjunction on May 27, 7 B.C., would have been the star appearance of Matthew 2:2. This conjunction occurred near dawn in the eastern sky; it would therefore have been described as "in the rising." The conjunction on December 1, 7 B.C., would then have been the star appearance which "went before" the Magi as they traveled from Jerusalem to Bethlehem in

Matthew 2:9. On December 1, 7 B.C., both Jupiter and Saturn were visibly close together high in the eastern sky at sunset, approximately one and one-half hours east of the meridian of Jerusalem and Bethlehem. By 8 P.M. that night they would have been visible from Jerusalem in the southern sky on the meridian of Jerusalem and Bethlehem, thus appearing over Bethlehem when viewed from Jerusalem. The actual point of conjunction was then reached later in the evening, high in the western sky. Finally, there was a massing of planets involving Jupiter, Saturn, and Mars in Pisces on February 25, 6 B.C. At that time the three planets appeared in the same part of the sky forming an isosceles triangle in which the long side was seven degrees long and the other sides were four degrees each.

Aspects of this proposal are interesting. In medieval Judean tradition, conjunctions of Jupiter and Saturn were believed to have Messianic significance. Pisces, the sign of the fishes, was thought to designate the House of Jacob. Pisces is regarded by many as the ruling constellation of Near Eastern lands, especially Palestine. Conjunctions of Jupiter and Saturn were believed by some medieval Judean philosophers to portend an important birth or event that would affect Israel.[1] Thus, a Jupiter-Saturn conjunction in the constellation of Pisces could well

1. A.H. Silver, *A History of Messianic Speculation in Israel* (Boston: Beacon Press, 1927), p. 125.

have been recognized as a sign of the Messiah's birth. Finally, the appearances of this conjunction on the dates of May 27 and December 1 fit well with the details given in Matthew 2:2 and 9 in that the conjunction appeared "in the rising" in May and in the southern sky over Bethlehem in December.

The reason this proposal is too early is that if Jesus had been born in 7 B.C., then he would have been less than a year old when the Magi arrived that December. Indeed, if he were born in the fall, the Magi would have found a child only two or three months old. Less than eight months would have elapsed since the conjunction was first seen. In light of these facts, it would be difficult to explain why Herod slew children two years and under.

Also, if Jesus were born in 7 B.C., his thirtieth birthday could not possibly occur after 23 A.D. Jesus was baptized at "about thirty" and began his ministry soon thereafter. Historical and chronological details become nearly irreconcilable if Jesus' thirtieth birthday is placed before 26 A.D. It is simply too early.[2]

2. The fifteenth year of Tiberius in which John the Baptist began his ministry, according to Luke 3:1, has been reckoned to be one of the years from 26 A.D. to 29 A.D. Pontius Pilate was sent as procurator of Judea in 26 A.D. The date of 23 A.D. for Jesus' thirtieth year is thus clearly too early by at least three years.

APPENDIX 2

THE HISTORICAL ROOTS OF THE MODERN CHRISTMAS CELEBRATION

On the modern calendar, December 25 is the day set aside by most of Christendom to celebrate Jesus Christ's birth. Although Biblical scholars have long recognized that Jesus was not born on this date,[1] Christians continue to celebrate his birth at that time. The origin of this tradition is interesting to research.

There is no historical evidence of a holiday designated in observance of Jesus Christ's birth before the fourth century A.D. The observance of December 25 as the date of Jesus Christ's birth can be traced back to 336 A.D. in Rome; in Antioch, to

---

1. Major outside sources used in this study have been: J.D. Douglas, ed., *The New International Dictionary of the Christian Church* (Grand Rapids: Zondervan, 1974), s.v. "Christmas," by James Taylor; Alexander Hislop, *The Two Babylons*, 2d American ed. (1916; Neptune, N.J.: Loizeaux Brothers, 1959), pp. 91-103; and Finegan, *Handbook of Biblical Chronology*, p. 132.

375 A.D.; in Constantinople, to 380 A.D.; and in Alexandria, to 430 A.D. The celebration of Christ's birth on December 25 was unknown in Jerusalem until the sixth century A.D.

So how did it come about that December 25 is observed as Jesus Christ's birthday? December 25 is near the time of the winter solstice, when the sun reaches its lowest point in the southern sky and from there would rise daily higher in the sky. In ancient times, long before Christ, many cultures had a festival in late December at the time of the winter solstice in celebration of the birth of the sun god. In ancient Babylon, the winter solstice celebrated the birth of the sun god, Tammuz. The sun was not worshipped as simply a symbol, but actually as the god incarnate. In India, the sun, known as Surya, was represented as being incarnate and born for the purpose of subduing the enemies of the gods. In Egypt, the sun god's name was Osiris. Other gods supposed to have been born at this time are Horus, Bacchus, Adonis, and Mithra. These are a few of the many gods the ancients believed had been born during the time of the winter solstice.

When this midwinter festival was adopted in Rome, it was known as the Saturnalia or the Feast of Saturn, characterized by Devil worship, excessive drunkenness, orgies, and other licentious activity. The celebration also included the exchanging of gifts, the decorating of fir trees, the yule log, and other customs which remain in the modern

Christmas celebration. Saturnalia was usually celebrated over a period of several days, December 17-24.

In 274 A.D., the Romans designated December 25 as the birthday of the unconquered sun, being the time when the sun begins noticeably to show an increase in light, resulting in longer daylight hours. By 336 A.D., the church in Rome was adapting this festival, spiritualizing its significance as a reference to Jesus Christ, and calling it the "Feast of the Nativity of the Sun of Righteousness." Attempting to Christianize and incorporate the pagan traditions of antiquity, the church in Rome adopted this midwinter holiday celebrating the birth of the sun god as one of its own observances, somewhat changing its significance, but retaining many customs of the pagan festival. As the Roman church spread its influence religiously and militarily, this holiday of December 25 became the most popular date in Christendom to celebrate the birth of Jesus Christ. A special mass was established for Christ, hence, the name "Christ-mass," abbreviated "Christmas."

Later, in the ninth century, Nicholas, a fourth-century bishop of Myra (southwest Turkey) was canonized, and eventually St. Nicholas Day (December 6) became a popular pre-Christmas holiday, especially in northern Europe. The name St. Nicholas was corrupted to Santa Claus and he became associated with the Christmas tradition in Protestant countries. In the Roman church, the adoration of the Magi is celebrated twelve days after December 25 on January 6 and called "Three Kings' Day" or "Epiphany." Traditionally in Roman Catholic countries the children await the "three kings," rather than Santa Claus, bearing gifts on January 6. This celebration dates to the fourth century. January 6 is when some of the Eastern orthodox churches celebrate the birth of Christ.

In 525 A.D., a Roman Catholic monk, named Dionysius Exiguus, erroneously calculated the year of Jesus Christ's birth to be the 754th year after the founding of Rome.[2] Designating that year as the start of a new era, Dionysius renumbered subsequent years from that time and labeled them as years *ab incarnatione Domini*, "from the incarnation of the Lord." This term was later simplified to *anno Domini*, "in the year of the Lord," and is now simply abbreviated "A.D." Thus, modern time reckoning came to place the birth of Christ in the year 1 A.D. Historians have long since proved Dionysius' calculations regarding the year of Christ's birth to be wrong, though we must credit him for centering on Jesus Christ as the pivotal point of all history. Dionysius' system of reckoning time has remained in use as a matter of tradition and convenience.

---

2. Dionysius' calculations made 1 A.D. the equivalent of the 754th year of Rome by Varronian reckoning. This would place the founding of Rome in 753 B.C. However, there is evidence that 752 B.C. was the recognized date of the founding in the time of Caesar Augustus.

BIBLIOGRAPHY

For a complete bibliography of works relating to "his star" until 1978 see Ruth S. Freitag, comp. "The Star of Bethlehem—Part II." *Library of Congress Information Bulletin* 22 (December 1978): 778-784.

Akavia, A.A. *Calendar for 6000 Years: Comparative Calendar of All Chronological Tables from the Creation until the End of the Sixth Millennium*. Jerusalem: Mossad Harav Kook, 1975.

Allen, Richard Hinckley. *Star Names: Their Lore and Meaning*. 1899. New ed. New York: Dover Publications, 1963.

Allen, Willoughby C. *The International Critical Commentary: A Critical and Exegetical Commentary on the Gospel According to S. Matthew*. 3d ed. Edinburgh: T. & T. Clark, n.d.

Anstey, Martin. *The Romance of Bible Chronology*. London: Marshall Brothers, 1913.

Asimov, Isaac. *The Planet that Wasn't*. New York: Doubleday, 1976.

Barnes, T.D. "The Date of Herod's Death." *Journal of Theological Studies* 19 (1968): 204-209.

Barrows, E.P. *The Manners and Customs of the Jews*. London: Religious Tract Society, n.d.

Bengel, John Albert. *Gnomon of the New Testament*. Translated by C.T. Lewis and M.R. Vincent. 3 vols. Philadelphia: Perkinpine & Higgins, 1860.

Bernegger, Peter M. "The Star of Bethlehem." Master's thesis, Colgate University, 1977.

______. "The Star of Bethlehem—Part 1: The Biblical Record." *The Way Magazine*, November/December 1978, pp. 6-10.

______. "The Star of Bethlehem—Part 2: The Evidence." *The Way Magazine*, January/February 1979, pp. 6-9.

Black, Matthew. *An Aramaic Approach to the Gospels and Acts*. 3d ed. Oxford: Clarendon Press, 1967.

Bloch, Abraham P. *The Biblical and Historical Background of the Jewish Holy Days*. New York: KTAV, 1978.

Brockelmann, Carolo. *Lexicon Syriacum*. Edinburgh: T. & T. Clark, 1895.

Brown, Francis; Driver, S.R.; and Briggs, Charles A., eds. *The New Hebrew and English Lexicon*. 1907. Reprint. Lafayette, Ind.: Associated Publishers and Authors, Inc., 1978.

Bruce, F.F. [''Review of *The Birth of Christ Recalculated!*'']. *The Evangelical Quarterly* 12 (1980): 64.

Bullinger, E.W. *A Critical Lexicon and Concordance to the English and Greek New Testament*. 1877. Reprint. Grand Rapids: Zondervan, 1975.

______. *Figures of Speech Used in the Bible*. 1898. Reprint. Grand Rapids: Baker Book House, 1968.

______. *The Witness of the Stars*. 1893. Reprint. Grand Rapids: Kregel, 1967.

Burder, Samuel. *Oriental Customs*. Philadelphia: William W. Woodward, 1804.

Burke-Gaffney, W. ''Kepler and the Star of Bethlehem.'' *The Journal of the Royal Astronomical Society of Canada* 31 (1937): 417-425.

Burkitt, F. Crawford, trans. and ed. *Evangelion Da-Mepharreshe: The Curetonian Version of the Four Gospels*. 4 vols. Cambridge: Cambridge University Press, 1904.

Carter, G.W. *Zoroastrianism and Judaism*. New York: AMS Press, 1970.

Ciotti, Joseph. ''The Magi's Star: Misconceptions and New Suggestions.'' *Griffith Observer*, December 1978, pp. 2-14.

Companion Bible, The. Reprint. Grand Rapids: Zondervan, 1974.

Culican, W. *The Medes and Persians*. New York: Frederick A. Praeger, 1965.

Cummins, Walter J. "The Righteous Offspring." *The Way Magazine*, January/February 1974, pp. 6-9.

Cumont, Franz. *The Mysteries of Mithra*. Chicago: Open Court Publishing Co., 1910.

Custance, Arthur C. *The Seed of the Woman*. Brockville, Ontario: Doorway Publications, 1980.

______. *The Virgin Birth and the Incarnation*. Grand Rapids: Zondervan, 1976.

DeHaan, M.R. *The Chemistry of the Blood*. Grand Rapids: Zondervan, 1971.

Dhalla, M.N. *Zoroastrian Theology*. New York: AMS Press, 1972.

Dobin, Joel C. *To Rule Both Day and Night: Astrology in the Bible, Midrash, and Talmud*. New York: Inner Traditions International, 1977.

Douglas, J.D., ed. *The New Bible Dictionary*. Grand Rapids: Wm. B. Eerdmans, 1962.

______., ed. *The New International Dictionary of the Christian Church*. Grand Rapids: Zondervan, 1974.

Edersheim, Alfred. *The Life and Times of Jesus the Messiah*. Rev. ed. (2 vols. in 1). Grand Rapids: Wm. B. Eerdmans, 1971.

______. *The Temple: Its Ministry and Services*. Reprint. Grand Rapids: Wm. B. Eerdmans, 1958.

Encyclopaedia Britannica, 1954 ed.

Ezra, Abraham Ibn. *Le Livre des fondements astrologiques précède de le commencement de la sapience des signes*. Paris, 1977.

Fenton, Ferrar, trans. *The Holy Bible in Modern English*. 1903. Merrimac, Mass.: Destiny, 1966.

Ferguson, Clyde L. *The Stars and the Bible*. Hicksville, N.Y.: Exposition Press, 1978.

Filmer, W.E. "The Chronology of the Reign of Herod the Great." *Journal of Theological Studies* 17 (1966): 283-298.

Finegan, Jack. *Handbook of Biblical Chronology*. Princeton: Princeton University Press, 1964.

______. *Light from the Ancient Past*. 2 vols. 2d ed. Princeton: Princeton University Press, 1959.

Freeman, James M. *Manners and Customs of the Bible*. Reprint. Plainfield, N.J.: Logos International, 1972.

Geldenhuys, Norval. *Commentary on the Gospel of Luke*. Grand Rapids: Wm. B. Eerdmans, 1951.

Godley, A.D., trans. *Herodotus*. 6 vols. New York: G.M. Putnam's Sons, 1920.

Goldstine, Herman H. "New and Full Moons One Thousand and One B.C. to A.D. Sixteen Fifty One." *American Philosophical Society: Memoirs* 94 (1973).

Hastings, James, ed. *A Dictionary of Christ and the Gospels.* 2 vols. 1906-1908. Reprint. New York: Charles Scribner's Sons, 1921.

Hertz, J.H. *The Pentateuch and Haftorahs.* 2d ed. London: Soncino Press, 1966.

Hislop, Alexander. *The Two Babylons.* 1916. 2d American ed. Neptune, N.J.: Loizeaux Brothers, 1959.

Hodson, F.R., ed. *The Place of Astronomy in the Ancient World.* Organized by D.G. Kendall, S. Piggott, D.G. King-Hele, and I.E.S. Edwards. London: Oxford University Press, 1974.

Huart, C. *Ancient Persia and Iranian Civilization.* London: Kegan, Paul, Trench, Trubner & Co., 1927.

Hughes, D.W. "The Star of Bethlehem." *Nature,* December 1976, pp. 513-517.

Interpreter's Dictionary of the Bible, The. 4 vols. and supplementary vol. Nashville: Abingdon Press, 1962-1976.

Isbell, Charles D. "Does the Gospel of Matthew Proclaim Mary's Virginity?" *Biblical Archaeology Review* 3 (June 1977): 18-19.

Jewish Encyclopedia, The. 12 vols. New York: Funk and Wagnalls, 1901-1906.

Jung, C.G. *Aion*. 2d ed. Translated by R.F.C. Hull. Princeton: Princeton University Press, 1968.

Kastner, Sidney O. "Calculation of the Twilight Visibility Function of Near-Sun Objects." *The Journal of the Royal Astronomical Society of Canada* 70 (1976): 153-168.

Kennedy, E.S., and Pingree, D. *The Astrological History of Māshā'allāh*. Cambridge, Mass.: Harvard University Press, 1971.

______. "The Sassanian Astronomical Handbook Zīj-i Shāh and the Astrological Doctrine of the 'Transit' (MAMARR)." *Journal of the American Oriental Society* 78 (1958): 246-262.

Kent, Charles Foster, trans. and ed. *The Shorter Bible*. 3d ed., rev. New York: Charles Scribner's Sons, 1925.

Kittel, Gerhard, and Friedrich, Gerhard, eds. *Theological Dictionary of the New Testament*. 10 vols. Translated and edited by G.W. Bromiley. Volume 10 compiled by R.E. Pitkin. Grand Rapids: Wm. B. Eerdmans, 1964-1976.

Kudlek, Manfred, and Mickler, Erich H. *Solar and Lunar Eclipses of the Ancient East from 3000 B.C. to 0 with Maps*. Neukirchener Verlag des Erziehungsvereins Neukirchen-Vluyn: Verlag Butzon & Bercker Kevelaer, 1971.

Lamsa, George M. *Gospel Light*. Rev. ed. Philadelphia: A.J. Holman, 1936.

———. *The Holy Bible from Ancient Eastern Manuscripts*. Nashville: A.J. Holman, 1957.

Lewis, Agnes Smith. *Light on the Four Gospels from the Sinai Palimpsest*. London: Williams & Norgate, 1913.

———., ed. *The Old Syriac Gospels*. London: Williams & Norgate, 1910.

———., trans. *A Translation of the Four Gospels from the Syriac of the Sinaitic Palimpsest*. London: Macmillan and Co., 1894.

Lewis, Nepthali, and Reinhold, Meyer, eds. *Roman Civilization*. 2 vols. New York: Harper Torchbooks.

Liddell, Henry George, and Scott, Robert, comps. *A Greek-English Lexicon*. 1843. Revised by Henry Stuart Jones. 9th ed. Oxford: Clarendon Press, 1940.

Lightfoot, John. *A Commentary on the New Testament from the Talmud and Hebraica: Matthew — I Corinthians*. 4 vols. 1859. Reprint. Grand Rapids: Baker Book House, 1979.

Lundmark, K. "The Messianic Ideas and Their Astronomical Background." *Actes du vii congrès international d'histoire des sciences, Jerusalem* 4 (1953): 436-439.

———. "Suspected New Stars Recorded in Old Chronicles and Among Recent Meridian Observations." *Publications of the Astronomical Society of the Pacific* 33 (October 1931): 225-238.

Mackie, G.M. *Bible Manners and Customs*. London: A. & C. Black, 1903.

Marshall, Roy K. *The Star of Bethlehem*. Chapel Hill, N.C.: Morehead Planetarium, 1949.

______. "The Star of Bethlehem." *Planetarium Director's Handbook*, March 1972, pp. 1-4.

______. "Star of Bethlehem?" *Sky and Telescope*, December 1943, p. 15.

Martin, Ernest L. *(Additional) Supplement to the Book Birth of Christ Recalculated*. Pasadena: Foundation for Biblical Research, n.d.

______. *The Birth of Christ Recalculated*. 2d ed. Pasadena: Foundation for Biblical Research, 1980.

______. "The Birth of Christ Recalculated!—Revised" *The Foundation Commentator*, June 1980, pp. 7-12.

______. "The Celestial Pageantry Dating Christ's Birth." *Christianity Today*, 3 December 1976, pp. 16-18.

M'Clintock, John, and Strong, James. *Cyclopaedia of Biblical, Theological, and Ecclesiastical Literature*. New York: Harper & Brothers, 1874.

McMillen, S.I. *None of These Diseases*. Old Tappan, N.J.: Fleming H. Revell, 1963.

Moffatt, James, trans. *The Bible: A New Translation*. Rev. ed. New York: Harper & Row, 1935.

Moses of Khorene. *History of the Armenians*. 2 vols. Translated by R.W. Thomson. Armenian Texts and Studies, No. 4. Cambridge: Harvard University Press, 1978.

Mosley, John, and Martin, Ernest L. "The Star of Bethlehem Reconsidered: An Historical Approach." *Planetarium*, Summer 1980, pp. 6-9.

Moulton, Harold K., ed. *The Analytical Greek Lexicon*. 1860. Rev. ed. Reprint. Grand Rapids: Zondervan, 1977.

Moulton, James Hope. *Early Zoroastrianism*. 1913. Reprint. Amsterdam: Philo Press, 1972.

______. *The Treasure of the Magi*. London: Oxford University Press, 1917.

Murdock, James, trans. *The Syriac New Testament Translated into English from the Peshitto Version*. 1851. 9th ed. Boston: H.L. Hastings & Sons, 1896.

Neil, James. *Everyday Life in the Holy Land*. 4th ed. 1913. Reprint. London: Church Missions to Jews, 1930.

Neugebauer, Paul V. *Sterntafeln*. Leipzig: J.C. Hinrichs'sche Buchhandlung, 1912.

New English Bible, The. Cambridge: Cambridge University Press, 1961.

Norton, Arthur P. *Norton's Star Atlas and Reference Handbook*. 16th ed. Revised and edited. Cambridge, Mass.: Sky Publishing Co., 1973.

Nweeya, Samuel K. *Persia: The Land of the Magi*. 5th ed. rev. Philadelphia: John C. Winston, 1913.

Olmstead, A.T. *History of the Persian Empire*. Chicago: University of Chicago Press, 1948.

Parker, Richard A., and Dubberstein, Waldo H. *Babylonian Chronology 626 B.C.—A.D. 45*. 2d ed. Chicago: University of Chicago, 1946.

Phillips, J.B., trans. *The New Testament in Modern English*. New York: Macmillan Co., 1958.

Pillai, K.C. *Light Through an Eastern Window*. New York: Robert Speller & Sons, 1963.

______. *The Orientalisms of the Bible*. Fairborn, Ohio: Munkus Publishing Co., 1969.

Plummer, Alfred. *The International Critical Commentary: A Critical and Exegetical Commentary on the Gospel according to S. Luke*. 1896. 5th ed. Edinburgh: T. & T. Clark, n.d.

Prat, Ferdinand. *Jesus Christ: His Life, His Teaching, and His Work*. Vol. 1. Translated from the 16th French ed. by J.J. Heenan. Milwaukee: Bruce Publishing Co., [1950].

Pritchard, Charles. "On the Conjunctions of the Planets Jupiter and Saturn in the Years B.C. 7, B.C. 66, and A.D. 54." *Royal Astronomical Society: Memoirs* 25 (1857): 119-123.

Ramsay, William M. *Was Christ Born at Bethlehem?* 1898. Reprint. Minneapolis: James Family Publishing Co., 1978.

Rand, Howard B. *The Stars Declare God's Handiwork*. Merrimac, Mass.: Destiny, 1944.

Rawlinson, George. *The Sixth Great Oriental Monarchy*. New York: Dodd, Mead & Co., 1872.

Reahard, Bo. "The Espousal of Mary and Joseph." *The Way Magazine*, January/February 1976, pp. 9-11.

Roberts, Alexander, and Donaldson, James, eds. *The Ante-Nicene Fathers*. 10 vols. Reprint. Grand Rapids: Wm. B. Eerdmans, 1978.

Robertson, A.T. *A Grammar of the Greek New Testament in Light of Historical Research*. Nashville: Broadman Press, 1934.

———. *Word Pictures in the New Testament*. 6 vols. Nashville: Broadman Press, 1930-1933.

Rodman, Robert. "A Linguistic Note on the Christmas Star." *Griffith Observer*, December 1976, pp. 8-9.

Rolleston, Frances. *Mazzaroth; or, the Constellations*. 1863. New ed. London: Rivingtons, 1882.

Rosenberg, Roy A. "The 'Star of the Messiah' Reconsidered." *Biblica* 53 (1972): 105-109.

Sands, Percy C. *The Client Princes of the Roman Empire Under the Republic*. 1908. Reprint. New York: Arno Press, 1975.

Schaff, Philip, and Wace, Henry, eds. *A Select Library of Nicene and Post-Nicene Fathers of the Christian Church*. 2d series. Vol. 13. New York: Christian Literature Co., 1898.

Scherer, George H. *The Eastern Colour of the Bible*. London: National Sunday School Union, n.d.

Schoch, Karl. *Planaten—Tafeln für Jedermann*. Berlin: Pankow, Linser-Verlag G.M.B.H., 1927.

Schürer, Emil. *The History of the Jewish People in the Age of Jesus Christ*. 2 vols. Revised and edited by Geza Vermes, Fergus Millar, and Matthew Black. Edinburgh: T. & T. Clark, 1973-1979.

Seiss, Joseph A. *The Gospel in the Stars*. 1882. Illus. ed. Grand Rapids: Kregel, 1972.

Sepharial. *The World Horoscope: Hebrew Astrology*. London: W. Foulsham & Co., 1965.

Septuagint Version of the Old Testament and Apocrypha, The. English translation by Lancelot C.L. Brenton. 1851. Reprint. Grand Rapids: Zondervan, 1978.

Silver, A.H. *A History of Messianic Speculation in Israel.* Boston: Beacon Press, 1927.

Sherwin-White, A.N. *Roman Society and Roman Law in the New Testament.* Oxford: Oxford University Press, 1963.

Sinnott, Roger W. "Thoughts on the Star of Bethlehem." *Sky and Telescope*, December 1968, pp. 384-386.

Smith, J.M. Powis, and Goodspeed, Edgar J., trans. *The Bible: An American Translation.* Chicago: University of Chicago Press, 1931.

Smith, J. Payne, ed. *A Compendious Syriac Dictionary.* 1903. Reprint. Oxford: Clarendon Press, 1957.

Smith, William, ed. *Smith's Dictionary of the Bible.* Revised and edited by H.B. Hackett. Vol. 4. Boston: Houghton Mifflin, 1888.

Stahlman, William D., and Gingerich, Owen. *Solar and Planetary Longitudes for Years -2500 to +2000 by 10-Day Intervals.* Madison: University of Wisconsin Press, 1963.

Steinmetzer, Franz X. *Der Stern von Bethlehem.* 1st and 2d ed. Munster: Aschendorffsche Verlagsbuchhandlung, 1913.

Thiele, Edwin R. *The Mysterious Numbers of the Hebrew Kings.* Rev. ed. Grand Rapids: Wm. B. Eerdmans, 1965.

Thorley, John. ["Review of *The Birth of Christ Recalculated!*"]. *Joint Association of Classical Teachers: Bulletin*, November 1979.

Torrey, Charles Cutler, trans. *The Four Gospels: A New Translation*. London: Hodder and Stoughton, 1934.

Trumbull, H. Clay. *Studies in Oriental Social Life*. Philadelphia: John D. Wattles & Co., 1894.

Tsē-tsung, Hsi. "A New Catalog of Ancient Novae." *Smithsonian Contributions to Astrophysics* 2 (1958): 109-130.

Tuckerman, Bryant. *Planetary, Lunar, and Solar Positions: 601 B.C. to A.D. 1969 at Five-Day and Ten-Day Intervals*. 2 vols. Philadelphia: American Philosophical Society, 1962.

Turner, Nigel. *A Grammar of New Testament Greek*. Vol. 3. Edited by J.H. Moulton. Edinburgh: T. &. T. Clark, 1963.

Van Goudoever, J. *Biblical Calendars*. Leiden: E.J. Brill, 1959.

Vincent, M.R. *Word Studies in the New Testament*. Reprint. Wilmington, Del.: Associated Publishers and Authors, 1972.

Webster's New Twentieth Century Dictionary. 2d ed. 1978.

Wenning, Carl J. "The Star of Bethlehem Reconsidered: A Theological Approach." *Planetarium*, Summer 1980, p. 2.

Weymouth, Richard Francis. *The New Testament in Modern Speech*. 1903. 5th ed. Revised by James Alexander Robertson. Boston: Pilgrim Press, 1943.

Whiston, William, trans. *Josephus: Complete Works*. Reprint. Grand Rapids: Kregel, 1960.

Wierwille, Victor Paul. "The Announcement of John the Baptist." *The Way Magazine*, November/December 1980, pp. 4-7.

———. *Are the Dead Alive Now?* 2d ed. New Knoxville, Ohio: American Christian Press, 1982.

———. *The Bible Tells Me So*. New Knoxville, Ohio: American Christian Press, 1971.

———. "The Coming of John the Baptist." *The Way Magazine*, November/December 1973, pp. 2-8.

———. *God's Magnified Word*. New Knoxville, Ohio: American Christian Press, 1977.

———. *Jesus Christ Is Not God*. 2d ed. New Knoxville, Ohio: American Christian Press, 1981.

———. *Jesus Christ Our Passover*. New Knoxville, Ohio: American Christian Press, 1980.

———. *The New, Dynamic Church*. New Knoxville, Ohio: American Christian Press, 1971.

———. *Power for Abundant Living*. New Knoxville, Ohio: American Christian Press, 1971.

______. *Receiving the Holy Spirit Today*. 7th ed. New Knoxville, Ohio: American Christian Press, 1982.

______. "The Star of Bethlehem." *The Way Magazine*, December 1967, pp. 4-6.

______. *The Word's Way*. New Knoxville, Ohio: American Christian Press, 1971.

Wieseler, Karl G. *A Chronological Synopsis of the Four Gospels*. Translated by Edmund Venables. 2d ed., rev. London: G. Bell, 1877.

Wight, Fred H. *Manners and Customs of Bible Lands*. Chicago: Moody Press, 1953.

Williams, J. *Observations of Comets from B.C. 611 to A.D. 1640*. London: Strangeways and Walden, 1871.

Womack, David A. *12 Signs, 12 Sons: Astrology in the Bible*. New York: Harper & Row, 1978.

Wuest, Kenneth S. *Wuest's Word Studies from the Greek New Testament*. 3 vols. Grand Rapids: Wm. B. Eerdmans, 1973.

SCRIPTURE INDEX

ABOUT THE AUTHOR

Victor Paul Wierwille has spent a lifetime, over forty years, searching out the truths of God's Word. As part of his search he consulted and worked with many outstanding individuals in Christian studies for keys to power-filled, victorious living. Such men as Karl Barth, Joseph Bauer, Glenn Clark, Karl J. Ernst, Josiah Friedli, Louis C. Hessert, Elmer G. Homrighausen, E. Stanley Jones, George M. Lamsa, Richard and Reinhold Niebuhr, K.C. Pillai, Paul Tillich, Ernst Traeger, and many others, aided Dr. Wierwille in his quest to find the truths of the Word of God.

Dr. Wierwille's academic career includes Bachelor of Arts and Bachelor of Theology degrees from Mission House (Lakeland) College and Seminary, graduate studies at the University of Chicago and at Princeton Theological Seminary, where he earned the Master of Theology degree in Practical Theology.

Later he completed his work for the Doctor of Theology degree.

For over forty years, Dr. Wierwille has devoted his major energies to intensive research and teaching of the accuracy of God's Word. Since 1953 he has taught Biblical research and teaching classes on Power for Abundant Living. He is the founder and first president of The Way International, a nonsectarian, nondenominational Biblical research, teaching, and fellowship ministry. He is noted as founder and first president of several colleges and learning centers, including The Way College of Biblical Research, Indiana Campus; Camp Gunnison, The Way Family Ranch; and LEAD Outdoor Academy International. He is also past president of The Way College of Emporia.

As Dr. Wierwille perseveres in his research of the Word of God, he continues to write more research works and to develop further classes in Biblical studies, including The University of Life outreach courses, an international Biblical studies correspondence school. As a dynamic teacher and lecturer, he travels worldwide to hold forth the greatness of God's Word.

The Way International reaches out with the accuracy of God's Word to all parts of the United States and the world—helping people to receive power for abundant living.